Brief Person-Centred Therapies

Brief Therapies Series

Series Editor: Stephen Palmer
Associate Editor: Gladeana McMahon

Focusing on brief and time-limited therapies, this series of books is aimed at students, beginning and experienced counsellors, therapists and other members of the helping professions who need to know more about working with the specific skills, theories and practices involved in this demanding but vital area of their work.

Books in the series:

Brief Person-Centred Therapies

Edited by Keith Tudor

Los Angeles • London • New Delhi • Singapore

SAGE Publications Ltd
1 Oliver's Yard
55 City Road
London EC1Y 1SP

SAGE Publications Inc.
2455 Teller Road
Thousand Oaks, California 91320

SAGE Publications India Pvt Ltd
B 1/I 1 Mohan Cooperative Industrial Area
Mathura Road
New Delhi 110 044

SAGE Publications Asia-Pacific Pte Ltd
33 Pekin Street #02-01
Far East Square
Singapore 048763

Library of Congress Control Number: 2008920464

British Library Cataloguing in Publication data

A catalogue record for this book is available from
the British Library

ISBN 978-1-84787-346-0
ISBN 978-1-84787-347-7 (pbk)

Typeset by CEPHA Imaging Pvt. Ltd., Bangalore, India
Printed in Great Britain by The Cromwell Press Ltd, Trowbridge, Wiltshire
Printed on paper from sustainable resources

Praise for the book

'This is a book that the person-centered psychotherapy community has been waiting for. An accomplished and wide-ranging group of theoreticians, practitioners and researchers convincingly demonstrates how an approach that puts the client's process at its center may be enriched by techniques from many more instrumental orientations without losing its integrity. Resembling nothing so much as a therapeutic Goldberg Variations on a basic Rogerian theme, the authors included in this volume reveal the enduring power of Rogers' original emancipatory theory even in a time-strapped world that demands swift results.

'The inclusion of case material – including a historical case of Lewis, Rogers and Shlien, enlivens the book and provides a glimpse of a variety of brief person-centered therapies in action. Particularly useful are chapters that operationalize person-centered practices within settings such as trauma centers, prisons and in the workplace where access to therapeutic contact is severely limited. By sharing their own challenges and solutions to dilemmas such as instrumentalism vs. emergent humanism, or reliance on expert systems vs. trust in the self-healing capacities of the client, this book opens a creative space in which the ongoing conversation about therapeutic efficacy in times of shrinking resources can be successfully engaged'.

Professor Maureen O'Hara, PhD, Chair, Department of Psychology,
National University, La Jolla, California

'Critics of person-centred therapy have at various times accused the approach of being ill-equipped to engage in brief therapy, inadequate to respond to the seriously disturbed and the marginalised, or trapped in a fossilised theoretical framework. This wide-ranging and scholarly book convincingly refutes all such accusations. It demonstrates the theoretical and clinical vibrancy of an approach which is fully alive to the challenges of the twenty-first century and whose practitioners demonstrate a creativeness which, while drawing on the rich inheritance of the past, breaks new ground and offers fresh hope to a wide range of clientele.

'A wide-ranging and scholarly book which shows that person-centred therapy is fully alive to the challenges of the 21st century and is breaking new ground both clinically and theoretically. It demolishes convincingly and authoritatively the common criticisms that the approach can only serve an articulate middle-class and is ill-suited to brief and focused work'.

Professor Brian Thorne, Emeritus Professor of Counselling, University of East Anglia, and Co-founder, The Norwich Centre.

Contents

Introduction

Keith Tudor

'Time', they say, 'is a great healer'. This is usually taken to mean that, given time, we get over things, such as trauma, loss or bereavement, and, in effect, heal ourselves. This also implies that we need to give things time: that we heal in our own, appropriate or *kairos* time, and not necessarily at or within a particular chronological or *chronos* time. At the same time, many of us, especially in Western cultures, live in a context which is time-conscious and even oppressive, as a result of which we can often feel driven by chronological time to meet deadlines and outcomes, usually set by external forces: other people, organisations, and authorities. In the therapeutic sphere, speed and solution reflect the *zeitgeist*, and these social, cultural and political pressures and 'realities' are reflected in debates in the field of therapy (psychotherapy and counselling) between time-limited and open-ended therapy, and between outcome and process. Brief therapy has become a contested area, and a highly political issue. In her article on person-centred brief therapy, Toal (2001) puts it succinctly: 'brief therapy has developed due to market forces, not therapeutic need'. Driven by its economic and social policy to reduce the number of people in receipt of invalidity benefit, influenced by Layard (2005) and his work on depression and happiness, and completely uncritical of the National Institute for Health and Clinical Excellence and its obsession with the medical model of 'evidence-based practice' and manualised interventions, the UK government has adopted Layard's (2006) proposal to train mental health professionals to deliver brief cognitive behavioural therapy. In this context, there is even more pressure on therapies and therapists to prove themselves, according to certain criteria, and thus, all too often, therapeutic discourse focuses on what is brief, limited, quick, efficient, and cheap. Whilst some therapists, clients and politicians, may think that this description of therapy is a consummation devoutly to be wished, others do not. From a person-centred perspective which values client choice, promotes mutuality, and generally echews any external locus of control and evaluation, the imposed limitation of brief or time-limited therapy is problematic. Rogers (1942) himself recommended time limits only with regard to the length of the session, and not the duration of the therapy. Mearns and Thorne (2007, pp. 216–17) address this point:

> For the counsellor to impose boundaries without a consultative process with the client would be a denial of the essential equality of the relationship which

it is hoped to establish ... Boundaries, like so much else in the person-centred tradition, are not simply imposed but explored and agreed. As a result, the practice of person-centred counselling is in its very essence a deeply ethical activity and is utterly at variance with a rule-bound or manual dictated practice which places inflexible regulations or procedures above the emerging needs of the person in the relationship.

As human beings we need to learn to deal with the inflexible, the arbitrary, and the imposition of external 'realities' in life such as time-limits and time-limited therapy, an argument I discuss in Chapter 1. Acceptance of such realities, however, does not – and should not – detract us from critiquing the trend to short-termism and to therapies which appear to promise, as Totton (2004, p. 6) puts it, the 'maximum amelioration of distress in minimum time'. Too often, brief therapies, approaches and 'treatments' which focus on symptom relief and 'cure' do not value psychological exploration, including the meaning of illness or ill-health, self-knowledge, or human encounter. Too much brief therapy operates, in Rowan's (2004) taxonomy, at the instrumental level as distinct from the authentic or transpersonal levels.

In editing this book, I have been mindful of this social context, as well as the debates about brief therapy, therapeutic approaches to brief therapy and, specifically, person-centred approaches to brief therapy. The plural is deliberate as there are a number of approaches to person-centred therapy, approaches which are sometimes referred to as 'tribes' in 'the nation' of person-centred and experiential therapies (see Warner, 2000; Sanders, 2004). The chapters in the book reflect a range of views from within this nation.

Time and form

Therapists have always been interested in time and time-limits. Holmes (1994) argues that Freud's original conception of the length of psycho-analytic treatment was relatively short by modern standards: then, six months was considered long. Freud himself experimented with setting a definite end date for therapy and wrote about this (Freud, 1937). Other early analysts, notably Ferenczi and Rank, also saw a need for time-limited treatment, and discussed the impact on and adaptation of psychoanalytic method. Over the years, therapists have experimented with different lengths and forms of treatment or therapy. As a result, there are a number of different terms in this field: short-term therapy, focal therapy, brief therapy, time-limited therapy, and time-conscious therapy (see Box I.1).

In addition, there are therapies which define and are defined by the particular time frame to which they work such as 'single session therapy' (Talmon, 1990); other variations include 'two plus one sessions' therapy, and 'four plus two sessions' therapy (see Aveline, 1995), and, what must be the briefest, 'five minute psychotherapy' which Zirkle (1961) advocates in the context of working with hospitalised schizophrenic patients, for whom, he argues, that scheduled, daily contacts of five minutes are more therapeutic than weekly therapy. In my own practice, I have experimented with brief, more frequent (three times weekly) contact with some clients for whom, for a period, it was necessary and successful.

Box I.1   Definitions of terms

Short-term therapy – a term which defines therapy as 'short-term', although there is no agreed definition of what constitutes short-term. Some forms of therapy use the term to describe the short form of the particular theoretical approach, such as eclectic short-term psychotherapy (Wolberg, 1965), and intensive short-term dynamic psychotherapy (Sifneos, 1979; Davanloo, 1990).

Focal therapy – a term which takes its name from medical treatments that have a particular focus, and refers to a form of therapy that has a focus, which Holmes (1994, p. 10) describes as 'a crystallization of the patient's core or nuclear problems, based in the past, but permeating present difficulties and conflicts'. Balint and Balint (1961) use the term to describe a focus in dynamic therapy; Holmes (1994) suggests that it can be used interchangeably with the term 'brief dynamic psychotherapy', and that, equally, it could be used to describe cognitive therapies; Aveline (2002) describes it as a 16–25 session interpersonal psychotherapy.

Brief therapy – a term which (1) is used synonymously with short-term therapy; and (2) is used as focal therapy, to describe a particular form of therapy such as Malan's (1963, 1976) brief psychotherapy. As with 'short-term therapy' some forms of therapy use the term to describe the brief form of the particular theoretical approach and argue that it is particularly suited to the brief form such as brief solution-focused therapy (O'Hanlon, 1990; O'Connell, 1998).

Time-limited therapy – a term which acknowledges that a particular therapy is time-limited rather than being necessarily limited in its scope. Mann (1973) uses the term to describe a therapy which makes time the issue and a variable which, if fixed to a particular number of sessions, e.g. 12, gives the opportunity to study the meaning of time in therapeutic treatment.

Time-conscious therapy – a term which 1. was coined by Elton Wilson (1996) to describe a therapy which adjusts to the developmental life-pattern of the client, and works with structured agreements related to the duration and focus of the particular therapeutic relationship; and 2. is more broadly used to refer to an *attitude* to therapy which is mindful of time.

It is obvious that some of these terms overlap, and that there is a confusion at the heart of brief therapy and much of the literature on the subject between *definition* and *form*; furthermore, there is some conflation of form with theoretical *orientation*. The *definition* 'short-term therapy' describes simply the term of the therapy, usually by the number of sessions. What is viewed as 'short-term' has changed over time, and varies according to different theoretical orientations. What psychodynamic therapists regard as 'short-term' will generally be longer than, say, a brief cognitive behavioural therapy. Moreover, this gives the lie to the notion that there is a specific *form* of or approach to therapy that is 'short-term'. Samuels, a transactional analyst (quoted in Samuels *et al.*, 1968, p. 83), asserts that 'there is no such thing as short-term psychotherapy – there is short-term intervention with salutory results'. In other words, brief therapy is not *an approach* to therapy as is transactional analysis, person-centred therapy, psychodynamic therapy, and so on. Thus, 'short-term dynamic psychotherapy' is not a particular *orientation* to therapy, but the application of psychodynamic principles to short-term therapy. Therapy may be brief or specifically limited in time, usually due to financial constraints which are external to both client and therapist, but this should not be confused with definitions of therapy, its purpose or scope.

This clarification is important for two reasons. Many practitioners outside the approach view person-centred therapy as not effective in a brief or short-term form. As a generalisation this is countered by many people's experience of person-centred therapy facilitating change in a moment (see Rogers, 1958/1967; O'Hara, 1999; Timulák and Lietaer, 2001). Other research also supports the efficacy of time-limited person-centred therapy. As early as 1957, Shlien conducted research comparing different experiences of person-centred therapy in brief, limited therapy (up to 20 sessions), longer, limited therapy, and longer, unlimited therapy. The results showed that brief, time-limited therapy compared favourably and, across a number of measures – the Butler-Haigh Q-sort, the Thematic Apperception Test, and counsellor outcome ratings – often exceeded the results from the longer, unlimited therapy. Some research suggests that there is a negative 'dose-effect' curve in psychotherapy (Howard *et al.*, 1986) which suggests that the most significant amount of change occurs early on in therapy i.e. 62% of clients are helped with 13 sessions, and more than two-thirds of the total therapeutic benefit is achieved within the first 25 sessions. More recently, Cornelius-White (2003) reports a study of brief person-centred therapy of clients in a college counselling centre who were seen for a maximum of 12 or 16 sessions, with an average of 7.72 sessions. The results of his research, using four global indices – the Derogatis Psychiatric Rating Scale and, specifically, the Global Pathology Index, the Quality of Life Inventory, and the Global

Assessment Scale – show consistent improvement throughout the weeks of therapy, with the most dramatic gains in the first four weeks of therapy. He concludes (p. 32) that: 'The study provides a refutation to the popular perceived need of [sic] specificity and directiveness in brief therapy'. Other research in person-centred therapy is reported in Chapters 1 and 7. In terms of research across theoretical orientation, some early research based on self-ideal correlations show that these rose in time-limited person-centred therapy at least as much as in time-limited Adlerian therapy and open-ended therapy (see Shlien *et al.*, 1962) – an equivalence which, again, has been replicated in recent comparative studies. Such research poses important questions for therapists and organisations whose 'default setting' is long-term therapy. Shlien (1957, p. 321) also reports, however, that 'in a blind analysis … the brief time-limited cases show sharp decline in a theoretically desirable score (affective complexity) during the follow-up period six months *after* therapy ends' – a finding which is not unusual in other follow-up studies of brief therapies across the theoretical board, and which, equally, poses questions about the long-term benefit of short-term therapy.

Secondly, given the Layard agenda, there is increasing pressure, especially in the UK National Health Service, on person-centred and, more broadly, humanistic therapists to undertake additional training in cognitive behavioural therapy which, it is claimed, is a more effective 'form' of brief therapy. This claim is not substantiated by comparative research. For example, a study of the effectiveness of cognitive-behavioural, person-centred and psychodynamic therapies as practised in UK National Health Service settings (Stiles *et al.*, 2006, p. 555) produced results consistent with previous findings which demonstrated 'that theoretically different approaches tend to have equivalent outcomes'. This particular study includes results which showed that person-centred therapy worked as well as the other approaches, in an average number of sessions of 6.5.

Mearns and Thorne (1999, p. 124) draw a distinction between 'time-limited' and 'short-term', arguing of the former, that:

> This kind of policy pays no regard to individual difference among clients and is a crude and inefficient way of structuring a counselling provision … stipulating the limit of, say eight sessions, at the beginning of counselling can set that as a *target* in the mind of the client, where three or four sessions might otherwise have sufficed. Also, it can be uneconomic to end prematurely with a client when he is at the point of particular readiness.

They suggest an alternative to time-limited therapy which is to acknowledge the 'short-term' context (and budgets), but not to limit sessions. Wakefield (2005) gives an example of this in a primary health care setting in which she reports that, with no limits on the number of sessions, between 60% and 70% of clients chose to use fewer than 12.

Approaches and interventiveness

Clearly, some situations, demand for therapy outstrips supply. In response, some services decide to impose a limit on the number of sessions for each client in order to maximise the number of clients having access to therapy, and, arguably, to make the most effective use of the available resources. Indeed, this was the motivation for Shlien's original research in 1957. In response to such limitations some therapists work in a more directive and/or focused way, but this is a choice of preference and should not be confused with any necessity for direction. Thorne (1994), for instance, reports on his own experiment with 'brief companionship' as a response to an escalating waiting-list in the counselling service in which he worked. He describes a 'focused counselling' of three sessions with (p. 62) 'high levels of empathic responsiveness from the outset'. Whilst this appears somewhat partial – I assume that Thorne would advocate high levels of therapist responsiveness for all clients – the experiment helps to clarify a common misconception: that brief or time-limited therapy connotes that the therapist should help the *client* to be more focused on what he or she wants to achieve. Thorne's work suggests that the 'more' focus, if there is any, is for the *therapist*, not the client. However, again, different therapists within the broad range of the person-centred and experiential tradition think differently. It is no coincidence that experiential therapists, who draw on Gendlin's (1981) original work on focusing, tend to advocate a more focused approach, and have led the field in applying their various forms of focusing to the context of time-limited, brief therapy. In the current context in which 'the articles of faith' include short-term effectiveness, experiential approaches are favoured – and, in acknowledgement of their influence, are well represented in this volume, specifically through three chapters in Part II.

Just as it's important to understand and evaluate the foundations of a particular approach to therapy, such as certain principles (see Sanders, 2000; Tudor and Worrall, 2007), it's also important to understand differences both within and between approaches or theoretical orientations. In terms of understanding some of the differences between person-centred and experiential therapies, and specifically those represented in this volume, I find Warner's (2000) meta-theoretical perspective useful. She has developed a framework by which she characterises different therapist responses and styles or 'levels of interventiveness', thus:

Level 1 – describes the therapist's pure intuitive contact (and is largely a hypothetical level).
Level 2 – is when the therapists conveys their understanding of the client's internal frame of reference.

Level 3 – describes the situation in which the therapist brings material into the therapeutic relationship in ways which foster client choice.

Level 4 – is when the therapist brings material into the therapeutic relationship from their own frame of reference, from a position of authority or expertise.

Level 5 – describes the situation when the therapist brings material into the therapeutic relationship that is outside the client's frame of reference, and in such a way that the client is unaware of both the intervention/s and the therapist's purpose or motivation.

Warner suggests that there is a fundamental dividing line between Levels 3 and 4: between the more client-directed therapies which focus on the nature of the client's process (Levels 1 to 3), and more authoritative therapies (Levels 4 and 5). Warner also suggests (p. 34) that 'there are very real dangers in trying to mix interventions and theories at different levels of intervention, since these therapies are grounded in quite different types of therapeutic relationship'. I think this is a useful framework for a number of reasons:

1   It is person-centred in that it draws on the concept of the client's internal frame of reference as the criterion for its distinctions.
2   It is an integrative framework in that it can be used to understand and compare different therapies, as well as different therapeutic 'interventions', transactions and responses.
3   It is also practical in that, although Warner herself uses this framework to generalise about 'therapies', it may also be used in a descriptive way to analyse how a therapist responds or intervenes from moment to moment.

When reading the different contributions, the reader may care to reflect on them with reference to these levels. So to the book itself.

The structure of the book

The book is divided into two parts, with introductory and concluding chapters. Chapter 1 introduces the subject and the themes of the book, beginning with discussions about time, limits and limitations, discussions and debates which draw on both the person-centred literature and the generic literature on brief and time-limited therapy. In this, I clarify what I see as some confusion between concepts and ideas about limits, structure, and direction. I also refer to what has been in recent years a lively debate within the person-centred community about time-limited counselling. In the final part of the chapter, I discuss two points about the practice of person-centred brief therapies: being conscious of time limits, and the question of 'suitability' and assessment. There is no agreement on what constitutes 'short-term' or 'brief' therapy either within the person-centred approach or beyond it in the generic literature. The case studies and vignettes represented in this volume range from one, to six, to 25 sessions.

In Part I, three chapters develop the dialogue between person-centred and experiential therapies. In Chapter 2 Mia Leijssen and Robert Elliott, both of whom are involved in and committed to research, discuss integrative experiential psychotherapy in brief. They draw on several of what they refer to as 'sub-orientations' within the person-centred nation, and identify four domains of human functioning which they use to guide their therapeutic work. Following a brief review of research on brief experiential therapies, they present a case study of a brief integrative experiential therapy for complex post-trauma difficulties. In Chapter 3 Bala Jaison, a focusing-oriented therapist, takes up the challenge of offering therapy which is both deep and brief. She traces the contribution of both Rogers and Gendlin to the literature and her own work and, drawing specifically on Gendlin's work, offers an integration or partnership of focused-oriented therapy (FOT) and solution-oriented therapy (SOT). In the last of these three integrative chapters, Henry Whitfield, who works with the traumatised victims of crime, discusses his integration of person-centred principles with a metapsychology approach to traumatic incident reduction (TIR). He views TIR, in effect, as a way of operationalising Rogerian theory, and illustrates this with reference to Rogers' (1958/1967) process conception of psychotherapy.

In Part II, eight chapters describe the practice of person-centred and experiential therapy in different contexts. The first four chapters discuss brief therapy in the context of independant practice (within a Counselling Centre), a university counselling service, a counselling service in primary health care, and an Employee Assistance Programme (EAP), respectively. These chapters appear in the historical order in which services in these contexts were established. Reflecting on the *zeitgeist*, it is interesting to note here that the definition of what constitutes 'brief', in terms of the number of sessions, has decreased over time. Chapter 5 reproduces, in part, one of the early papers on time-limited, client-centred psychotherapy, co-authored by Madge Lewis, Carl Rogers and John Shlien (1956). Here, for reasons of space, I have included only the one case of 'Mrs Teral' reported by John Shlien. This was part of a research project which compared different lengths of contact, time-limited and unlimited (see Shlien, 1957). The chapter includes some research findings regarding the comparative forms of therapy, and Shlien's responses to a questionnaire about the therapy. I am grateful to Pearson Education Inc. of Upper Saddle River, New Jersey, for permission to reproduce part of a chapter (pp. 309–26 and 348–51) which first appeared in a book edited by Burton (1956). In Chapter 6 Paul McGahey discusses his work in a University Counselling Service in which the counsellors can balance their workload between short- and longer-term work, 'short' in this context being about six sessions. Paul presents two case vignettes of his brief work with students, and follows this with his own reflections on the pros and cons of brief therapy. Given the political climate in the UK, the health service is one of the most challenging contexts in which person-centred therapists work. In Chapter 7 Isabel Gibbard reports on the work of a service providing person-centred counselling in primary care. She discusses the medical context and setting of her work, and argues that person-centred practitioners need to engage with the medical world and the medical model, including time limits, if we are to survive within the health service. Isabel draws on experiential and integrative perspectives in her work, and is clearly committed to public sector service and to research. In the last of these four chapters, Pam Winter offers a therapist's view of EAPs. She describes the complexities and tensions involved in holding a four-handed contract which involves the client, his or her employer, the EAP and the therapist. She describes a number of dilemmas in the clinical, professional/ethical, and organisational domains, and concludes with some thoughts about the social and political nature of the work and the role.

The next two chapters describe two particular contexts in which brief therapy takes place: a project working with traumatised victims of crime, and a young offenders' institution. In Chapter 9 Henry Whitfield offers a detailed application of TIR work with a client in six sessions, a model he describes in Chapter 4. One of the notable features of this work is a certain flexibility about time in terms of the length of sessions, the frequency of sessions, and the ending. Barkham (1993) distinguishes between therapy which is 'planned' to be brief, and therapy which is 'naturally' brief, by agreement. In my view, there is a third category of ending which is 'enforced' (see Tudor, 1995), whether by the client, for instance, not turning up; by the therapist, for example, giving notice; or by external circumstances. In Chapter 10 Barrie Hopwood describes his work in a young offenders' institution with clients who, by the nature of the context, are not in control of whether they can attend counselling, which means that the ending is often enforced. In a very personal account of his work and approach, Barrie captures this sense of the unknown, and the importance of immediacy, treating every session as if it's the last one.

The last two chapters focus on specific forms of therapy: couples and groups. In Chapter 11, viewing the couple as a system, I discuss brief therapeutic work with couples, and the benefits with regard to their relationship of this work being brief. In Chapter 12 Très Roche presents her work with women survivors of childhood sexual abuse in short-term groups. She draws on a model of traumagenic dynamics and integrates this with concepts of therapeutic or curative factors in groups, and describes how she and a co-worker facilitate a 10-week group in which women are able to work through the impact of their trauma. She illustrates this with reference to a particular individual in the group.

Acknowledgements

I have had the good fortune to be invited to edit two volumes in this series (see Tudor, 2002), and I am grateful to Stephen Palmer and Gladeana McMahon, the series editors, and to Alison Poyner at Sage for both opportunities. For me, the two volumes represent not only my two theoretical homes, but also the expression of my interest in time, culture, limits and limitations, and the psychological and existential challenges of living and ending. I also want to take this opportunity to thank: the contributors for their positive response to tight – even brief – deadlines; the clients who appear in these pages and who have given their permission for their stories to appear in order that we may learn from them; to my friend and colleague, Mike Worrall who, as ever, has been my best editor; and my family, Louise, Saul and Esther, for their support, encouragement and patience.

References

Aveline, M. (1995) 'Assessing the value of brief intervention at the time of assessment for dynamic psychotherapy', in M. Aveline and D. Shapiro (eds), *Research Foundations for Psychotherapy Practice*. Chichester: Wiley.

Aveline, M. (2002) Focal therapy, a brief interpersonally-focussed psychotherapy, *Psychiatry*, 1(4): 2–9.

Balint, M. and Balint, E. (1961) *Psychotherapeutic Techniques in Medicine*. London: Tavistock.

Barkham, M. (1993) 'Counselling for a brief period', in W. Dryden (ed.) *Questions and Answers in Counselling in Action*. Sage: London.

Burton, A. (ed.) (1956) *Case Studies in Counseling and Psychotherapy*. Englewood Cliffs, NJ: Prentice-Hall.

Cornelius-White, J.H.D. (2003) 'The effectiveness of a brief, non-directive person-centered practice', *The Person-Centered Journal*, 10: 31–8.

Davanloo, H. (ed.) (1990) *Short-Term Dynamic Psychotherapy*. New York: Jason Aaronson.

Freud, S. (1937) 'Analysis terminable and interminable', in J. Strachey (ed. and trans.) *The Standard Edition of The Complete Psychological Works of Sigmund Freud. Vol. 23*. London: Hogarth Press.

Gendlin, E.T. (1981) *Focusing* (rev. edn). New York: Bantam.

Holmes, J. (1994) 'Brief dynamic psychotherapy', *Advances in Psychiatric Treatment*, 1: 9–15.

Howard, K.I., Kopta, S.M., Krause, M.S. and Orlinsky, D.E. (1986) 'The dose-response relationship in psychotherapy', *American Psychologist*, 41: 159–64.

Layard, R. (2005) *Happiness: Lessons from a New Science*. London: Penguin.

Layard, R. (2006) *The Depression Report: A New Deal For Depression and Anxiety Disorders*. London School of Economics: Centre for Economic Performance.

Lewis, M.K., Rogers, C.R. and Shlien, J.M. (1956) 'Time-limited, client-centered psychotherapy: Two cases', in A. Burton (ed.) *Case Studies in Counseling and Psychotherapy* (pp. 309–52). Englewood Cliffs, NJ: Prentice-Hall.

Malan, D.H. (1963) *A Study of Brief Psychotherapy*. London: Tavistock Publications.

Malan, D.H. (1976) *Frontier of Brief Psychotherapy*. New York: Plenum.

Mann, J. (1973) *Time-Limited Psychotherapy*. Cambridge, MA: Harvard University Press.

Mearns, D. and Thorne, B. (1999) *Person-Centred Counselling in Action* (2nd edn). London: Sage.

Mearns, D. and Thorne, B. (2007) *Person-Centred Counselling in Action* (3rd edn). London: Sage.

O'Connell, B. (1998) *Solution-Focused Therapy*. London: Sage.

O'Hanlon, W.H. (1990) 'A grand unified theory for brief therapy: Putting problems in context', in J.K. Zeig and S.G. Gilligan (eds), *Brief Therapy: Myths, Methods and Metaphors*. New York: Brunner/Mazel.

O'Hara, M. (1999) 'Moments of eternity: Carl Rogers and the contemporary demand for brief therapy', in I. Fairhurst (ed.) *Women Writing in the Person-Centred Approach* (pp. 63–77). Llangarron: PCCS Books.

Rogers, C.R. (1942) *Counseling and Psychotherapy: Newer Concepts in Practice*. Boston, MA: Houghton Mifflin.

Rogers, C.R. (1959) 'The essence of psychotherapy: A client-centered view', *Annals of Psychotherapy*, 1: 51–7.

Rogers, C.R. (1967) 'A process conception of psychotherapy', in *On Becoming a Person* (pp. 125–59). London: Constable. (Original work published in 1958).

Rowan, J. (2004) 'Three levels of therapy', *Counselling & Psychotherapy Journal*, 15(9): 20–2.

Samuels, S.D., Teutsch, C.K. and Everts, K. (1968) 'Short-term psychotherapy', *Transactional Analysis Bulletin*, 7(28).

Sanders, P. (2000) 'Mapping person-centred approaches to counselling and psychotherapy', *Person-Centred Practice*, 8(2): 62–74.

Sanders, P. (ed.) (2004) *The Tribes of the Person-Centred Nation*. Ross-on-Wye: PCCS Books.

Shlien, J.M. (1957) 'Time-limited psychotherapy: An experimental investigation of practical values and theoretical implications', *Journal of Consulting Psychology*, 4(4): 318–22.

Shlien, J., Mosak, H.H. and Dreikurs, R. (1962) 'Effects of time limits: A comparison of client-centered and Adlerian psychology', *Journal of Counseling Psychology*, 9(318): 15–22.

Sifneos, P.E. (1979) *Short-Term Dynamic Psychotherapy: Evaluation and Technique*. New York: Plenum Press.

Stiles, W. B., Barkham, M., Twigg, E., Mellor-Clark, J. and Cooper, M. (2006) 'Effectiveness of cognitive-behavioural, person-centred, and psychodynamic therapies as practiced in UK National Health Service settings', *Psychological Medicine*, 36: 555–66.

Talmon, M. (1990) *Single Session Therapy*. San Francisco, CA: Jossey-Bass.

Thorne, B. (1994) 'Brief companionship', in D. Mearns, *Developing Person-Centred Counselling* (pp. 60–4). London: Sage.

Thorne, B. (1999) 'The move towards brief therapy: Its dangers and challenges', *Counselling*, 10(1): 7–11.

Timulák, L. and Lietaer, G. (2001) 'Moments of empowerment: A qualitative analysis of positively experienced episodes in brief person-centred counselling', *Counselling and Psychotherapy Research*, 1(1): 62–73.

Toal, K. (2001) 'An exploration of person-centred brief therapy', *Person-Centred Practice*, 9(1): 31–6.

Totton, N. (2004) 'Two ways of being helpful', *Counselling & Psychotherapy Journal*, 15(10): 5–8.

Tudor, K. (1995) 'What do you say about saying good-bye?: Ending psychotherapy', *Transactional Analysis Journal*, 25: 228–34.

Tudor, K. (ed.) (2002) *Transactional Approaches to Brief Therapy or What do you Say between Saying Hello and Goodbye?* London: Sage.

Tudor, K. and Worrall, M. (eds) (2007) *Freedom to Practise II: Developing Person-Centred Approaches to Supervision.* Ross-on-Wye: PCCS Books.

Wakefield, M. (2005, August) 'Person-centred practice in primary care: Evidence that without time limits the majority of clients opt for short-term therapy', *Person-Centred Quarterly*: 1–5.

Warner, M.S. (2000) 'Person-centered psychotherapy: One nation, many tribes', *The Person-Centered Journal*, 7(1): 28–39.

Wolberg, L.R. (1965) *Short-Term Psychotherapy.* New York: Grune & Stratton.

Zirkle, G.A. (1961) 'Five minute psychotherapy', *American Journal of Psychotherapy*, 2(118): 544–6.

1

Time, Limits, and Person-Centred Therapies

Keith Tudor

Brief, short-term or time-limited therapy inevitably raises issues of brevity, time and limits. I say 'inevitably' as, even if these issues remain implicit – perhaps especially if they remain implicit – practitioners' views and assumptions about therapy, time, change, and the context in which they work, influence their work and the therapeutic encounter. So, this introductory chapter begins with two discussions: one about time, and one about limits and limitations. Each discussion draws on person-centred literature and specifically on the literature on brief and time-limited therapy. Following this, I summarise a recent debate on time-limited person-centred counselling; and, in the fourth part of the chapter, I draw out a number of points about the practice of person-centred brief therapies.

Time

The concept of time, eternity and transience has preoccupied human beings, and especially philosophers, scientists and, more recently, psychologists and psychotherapists (see Hawking, 1988/1998; Davies, 1995) since time began. As Griffiths (2000) puts it: '"time" has, throughout history, been used like a mirror for human nature. It is a blank screen onto which societies have always projected images of themselves' (p. 32). Elsewhere (Tudor, 2002), I explore the meaning of time, limits, and limitations, including the philosophy, culture and politics of time.

In the person-centred context, Thorne (1999) writes eloquently about time. As he puts it (p. 8): 'certainly the Zeitgeist exerts its own pervasive influence. We live in an era of management values where the articles of faith are short-term effectiveness, value for money, performance indicators, return on investment, accountability'. Thorne, however, goes on to remind us: 'It is good to remember that this is a modern and upstart faith with few moral roots, with no power to nourish souls and every capacity to destroy them'. In response to the speed, rush and hurry of modern life and the common experience of the pressure of limited time, there is now more talk and public debate about the pace of life or, as Gleick (1999) puts it in the subtitle of his book *Faster*: *The Acceleration of Just About Everything*. Moreover, there are some signs of a move and a cultural shift to slow things down, so that we are more in charge or 'at cause' of our own time, rather than 'in effect' or the victims of time. In 1986, this movement found a particular voice in a protest against the opening of an outlet of McDonald's in the Piazza di Spagna in Rome, a protest which gave rise to a 'slow food' movement (see www.slowfood.com). The concept of 'slow' is well-articulated in a book *In Praise of Slow* by Honoré (2004), and has been extended to ideas about slow cities or *'città slow'* (see www.cittaslow.org.uk), and slow art (see, for instance, www.robertjarvis.co.uk/other/CFSA.htm).

Of course, as human beings we are time-limited. When we talk about time, in effect we are reminded of and resonate with the inevitable limits and limitations of life. As Taft (1933, p. 12) points out:

> Time represents more vividly than any other category the necessity of accepting limitation as well as the inability to do so, and symbolizes therefore the whole problem of living. The reaction of each individual to limited or unlimited time betrays his deepest and fundamental life pattern, his relation to the growth process itself, to beginnings and endings, to being born and to dying.

Also, the limit of our time on this earth is highly contextual, and directly related to where we are born and where we live. Thus, there is a huge variation in whether we can expect to live our allotted 'three score year and ten'. In Andorra we may, as the average life expectancy is 83.5 years; at the other end of the scale, however, we may not: in Swaziland, for instance, the average life expectancy is 32.6 years (Pearson Education, 2007).

We should not underestimate the impact of time, or our reactions to it. I have worked with a number of practitioners who work in particular time-limited contexts and who spend a lot of time complaining about the imposition of limits. Sometimes, they may even say to a client: 'We *only* have six session'. In my experience, this emphasis and the accompanying tone often 'betrays' the therapist's resentment of any limits or limitations on his or her work. At worst, this sets up both therapist and client to fail by not dealing with the limits and limitations of therapy and, ultimately, of life. I am not advocating an uncritical acceptance of time-limits and of short-term thinking and practice. Indeed, I agree with Thorne's (1999, p. 10) criticism of what he refers to as 'short-termism' in the therapeutic field:

> ... could it be ... that short-term therapy is the inevitable dysfunctional response to a sick society and that it seems to work for that very reason? We no longer have time to put down roots, to consolidate our beings, to reflect upon our place in the eternal order of things.

I am arguing that therapists – and clients – should engage actively with the context of therapy and of therapeutic services with regard to limits and limitations, both in terms of the particular therapeutic relationship and on the wider social/political level.

Rogers and others write about 'moments of movement'. This strand of person-centred literature is conscious of time but not overly concerned with time limits. In 1959, Rogers wrote a paper on such moments in which he writes about a 'molecule' of therapy or personality change which he describes (p. 53) as having four psychological qualities:

1   It is something 'which occurs in this existential moment. It is not a *thinking* about something, it is *experiencing* of something at this instant, in the relationship'.
2   It is an experiencing without barriers or inhibitions: a visceral, organismic, 'united integrated experience', and one marked by some define physiological changes which, Rogers goes on to suggest, may constitute the irreversible element of these moments.
3   It is a complete experience; whereas it may have been partially experienced before and repeated, 'This is the first time that organismic thema, which has hitherto been denied to awareness, is freely present in awareness'.
4   It is real and acceptable.

Personal integration is the goal of therapy and, as Rogers (p. 54) puts it: 'This is a molecular unit, a momentary experience, of what integration is' – and, by definition, this takes place in a moment.

Drawing on Rogers' (1942) work, O'Hara (1999) writes about the way in which the values and attitudes of person-centred therapists open sacred time and space or 'moments of eternity' (p. 67), 'within which the self-organizing formative tendency in nature can become manifest and effective in the world'. She describes her work with one client who had a transformative experience in four sessions but, as O'Hara (p. 73) points out:

> ... it wouldn't matter whether it had taken ten sessions or even thirty, it was the quality of the change that marks it as significant. It would miss her achievement altogether to think of what occurred in terms of 'numbers of sessions', 'symptom reduction', [or] 'problem-solving' ... this change permeated her whole existence. She had not only changed what she thought about the situation she was facing, she had changed how she was thinking. She had made an epistemological leap.

O'Hara's work perhaps most clearly articulates the experience and view that person-centred therapists can and do facilitate clients' movement in a moment and, therefore, that we needn't be concerned about time limits as clients will 'move' or have moments of movement in whatever timeframe. O'Hara argues that therapists, too, are faced with an epistemological choice: that between an instrumentalist approach which aligns with what she refers to (p. 75) as 'the rampant medicalization which is overtaking the psychotherapy world'; and that which aligns with the intrinsic self-healing forces in all persons.

Research on brief person-centred therapy supports these views about client movement and change. Timulák and Lietaer (2001) report their study of positively experienced episodes in brief person-centred counselling, based on three or four sessions, and identify what they refer to as 'moments of empowerment'. The most frequently reported positive client experiences were associated with empowerment, safety, and insight. They found (p. 66) that: 'The quality feeling of empowerment was present in every client and in 50 of the episodes'.

Cornelius-White (2003) also reports a study of brief therapy in a college counselling centre of clients who were seen for a maximum of 12 or 16 sessions, with an average of 7.72 sessions. The results of his research, using four global indexes – the Derogatis Psychiatric Rating Scale and, specifically, the Global Pathology Index, the Quality of Life Inventory, and the Global Assessment Scale – show consistent improvement throughout the weeks of therapy, with the most dramatic gains in the first four weeks of therapy. He concludes (p. 32) that: 'The study provides a refutation to the popular perceived need of [sic] specificity and directiveness in brief therapy', points which I discuss below.

Along with the pressure to be brief and briefer comes a pressure to be 'more' effective. These ideas about moments of movement, together with these research findings, may help practitioners to hold the therapeutic space, however, circumscribed by time-limits; and to work in *kairos* or appropriate time, and to resist the external pressures of *chronos* or chronological time (see Tudor, 2001). In my view, human existential reality suggests that, as practitioners, we cannot – and should not attempt to – hasten the client or the process. Indeed, Rogers (1942, p. 233) comments that:

> ... the desire to find short cuts, to hasten the client, nearly always increases the number of interviews necessary for improvement. The shortest successful series of therapeutic counselling interviews is the one which is handled with the greatest skill, the one which is the most completely client-centered.

The challenge of brief therapy is simply to be the best we can be in a shorter time; no more, no less: any less and we are not being authentic or doing our job; any more and we are in danger of treating brief therapy and clients with whom we work in this context in a particular, 'extra' special way. As ever, Taft (1933, p.11), talking about a single interview, puts it well:

> ... if I am willing to take that one hour in and for itself, there is no time to hide behind material, no time to explore the past or future. I myself am the remedy at this moment if there is any and I can no longer escape my responsibility, not for the client but for myself and my role in the situation. Here is just one hour to

be lived through as it goes, one hour of present immediate relationship, however limited, with another human being who has brought himself to the point of asking for help.

Limits and limitations

I consider that in the person-centred literature there are essentially two perspectives on the limits and limitations of therapy with regard to time: one, stemming from Taft (1933) and Rogers (1942), which acknowledges the existence of limits and argues their benefit; the other, represented variously by Mearns and Thorne (1999), Mearns (2002), Wakefield (2005), and MacDonald (2006), which argues that a person-centred approach to therapy is not compatible with externally imposed time-limits. Indeed, Mearns (2002) has refused to operate a time-limited service. These arguments and debates centre principally on issues of experience and perception; power and locus of evaluation; and structure and directiveness – which I now address.

In his book *Counseling and Psychotherapy* Rogers, (1942) echoes what Taft says about time (see above) when he says (p. 101):

> The time limits of the therapeutic situation, like any of the other limits, are of assistance in furnishing the counseling situation with all the aspects of the life situation. The time limit sets up an arbitrary human limit, to which the client must make adjustment. While it may be a microscopic issue compared to the issues in real life, yet it allows opportunity for all the feelings and patterns with which he responds to the larger issues.

In other words, time limits are a human existential reality to which we all have different responses and reactions, and it is the therapist's task to help the client clarify the feelings and perceptions behind his or her reactions. Indeed, elsewhere in the same book, Rogers positively advocates understanding and adhering to time limits as an example of necessary therapeutic limits which he views, along with warmth and responsiveness, permissiveness as regards the expression of feeling, and the freedom from pressure or coercion, as basic aspects of a therapeutic relationship. The same logic may be applied to the limits of a limited number of sessions. The client – and, for that matter, the therapist – may rail against the imposition of limits, and may spend some, most or even all of the time in therapy not 'adjusting' to the 'reality' of such limits; however, for Rogers (and the present author), it is both more interesting and more therapeutic to attend to all of the client's experiences and perceptions of, and responses and reactions to, any and all limits and limitations.

Other practitioners and writers, within the approach, take a different view. On the basis of her experience and research in primary health care, Wakefield (2005) argues (p. 1) that 'time-limited therapy as a fixed way of working in any setting is unwise and unnecessary'. One element of her argument, which she simply asserts, is that the imposition on the client of a time limit from an external authority, mediated through the counsellor's assessment of the client's suitability, thereby renders the client inactive or passive. Similarly, MacDonald (2006) links her objection to imposed time limits to the person-centred concept of the 'external locus of control' or evaluation, and argues that such limits disempower or disenfranchise the client (p. 41):

> Those who work within the limits of time usually justify the time-limiting practice in terms of 'fairness', i.e. being able to see more clients, or even offering concentrated beneficial work. Others see it as part of counselling boundaries, imposed by others (service managers, for example) and not by the counsellor, and by informing clients of the limits of sessions, they absolve themselves of any complicity. Since counselling concerns itself with the location of the locus of control, we have to ask where, in fact, that resides in the session involving a disenfranchised client and a disenfranchised counsellor.

From this perspective, any external limits are anti-therapeutic and, conversely, what is most therapeutic is for clients to be able to control all aspects of their therapy themselves, including its duration. Arguably, this is also a political point, as a person's ability to develop an internal locus of control and evaluation is a sign of emancipation and is one aspect of what Rogers variously refers to as the emerging person, the political person (1978), or the person of tomorrow (1980). From this perspective, any attempts to limit therapy could be seen as a method of disenfranchising people from truly liberating psychological change.

Whilst these arguments have merit in advocating an absolute freedom from constraint, they also appear unrealistic, especially in the context of the provision of therapy in the public sector. Also, while Wakefield appears to be a strong advocate of trusting the client, she doesn't appear to appreciate the irony that her own argument conceptualises the client as unable to be active in response to any time limits. Neither of these authors refers either to Taft (1933) or to Rogers (1942) and, thus, they do not directly address their original argument which recognises both the inevitability of time limits and the benefits of therapy which is conscious of such limits.

The third strand of argument on the limits and limitations of time concern structure and directiveness. For some, the imposition of a limit, say a limited number of sessions, gives a certain structure and that, in turn, creates a sense of or need for direction and directiveness. Commenting on the convention of time-limited counselling in primary care, Mearns and Thorne (1999, p. 124) argue that:

> This kind of policy pays no regard to individual difference among clients and is a crude and inefficient way of structuring a counselling provision ... stipulating the limit of, say eight sessions, at the beginning of counselling can set that as a *target* in the mind of the client, where three or four sessions might otherwise

have sufficed. Also, it can be uneconomic to end prematurely with a client when he is at the point of particular readiness.

I think that Mearns and Thorne make too much of the point that a limit becomes a target; and that, more broadly, they and others, such as Wakefield (2005), conflate three related arguments which are better separated and clarifed:

1   That a limit equals or implies a structure.
    This is not necessarily the case and, in my view, depends a lot on the attitude of the therapist. The fact of having, say, six sessions only does not mean that either client or therapist *has* to adopt a particular structure. Many brief therapies do, either in terms of specifying a specific number of sessions such as 'two-plus-one sessions' therapy (Barkham and Hobson, 1989), or even single session therapy (Talmon, 1990; McCann, 1992), the latter by means of the technique of eye movement desensitisation; or in terms applying a particular structure to the session or sessions as does the focal psychotherapy of Malan (1963) and Balint *et al.* (1972), and the solution-focused therapy of de Shazer (1985) and O'Connell (1998). However, for a therapy which is based on principles of and hypotheses about the human organism and its inherent direction, the non-directive attitude of the therapist, and certain co-created environmental conditions of therapy (see Tudor and Worrall, 2006), there is no need to adopt a specific or particular structure. In response to the question whether counselling can be carried on if only a brief contact is possible, Rogers (1942, p. 247) clearly states that 'a counseling relation of the sort described in this book is *particularly essential* if the contact is to be a short one' (my emphasis). He continues: 'The seeming advantages of the directive approach in a short contact are completely spurious', and justifies this with a certain humility in the face of complexity: 'If we have any reasonable regard for the complexity of human life, we should be able to recognise that in an hour or less, it is highly unlikely that we can reorganise the life structure of the individual'.

2   That a limit encourages a focus.
    Mearns and Thorne (1999) are explicit about this (as above). They stipulate that a limited number of sessions is a structure and that this can become a target for the client. I think this confuses something external to the client, that is, a target, with something internal to the client, i.e. his or her own direction. Other writers within the person-centred tradition, notably Coghlan and McIlduff (1990), draw a distinction between structure and directiveness. Their argument is that the inevitability – and even the imposition – of limits and structure is just that: it does not imply that the therapist, the system or the structure directs the client's experience. Of course, a person *may* take a set structure, such as a fixed

number of sessions, as a reason to set a target of resolving or achieving something, but equally, he or she may not. Again, I think this depends a lot on the attitude of the therapist and the extent to which he or she is willing to support the client's organismic direction and internal valuing process, sometimes in the face of an external context and external authorities which may impose or want to impose structure, direction, method, outcome, measurement and evaluation on both therapist and client. One way of clarifying the limit and of discouraging the client from viewing this as a target is for the therapist to say simply that: 'We have *up to* eight sessions'.

3   That the client has direction implies that the therapist should be directive or focused.

For some, there's nothing like a limit or an ending to focus the mind. As Johnson observes: 'Depend upon it, Sir, when a man knows he is to be hanged in a fortnight, it concentrates his mind wonderfully'. (Boswell, (1749/1887, p. 167)). In life, our response to notice of any ending such as a death, illness, or a relocation, is often marked by a concentration or focus. Some years ago, I ran with a colleague an open-ended therapy group. After three years, we gave the group nine months' notice of closing the group. Initially, there was disbelief, some bargaining, and then anger – processes which, in many ways, echoed Kübler-Ross's (1970) stages of responses to death and dying (see Tudor, 1995). Following this, there was a great sense of purpose in the group as a whole and an increased desire on the part of individuals to do their therapeutic work. This focus – even, I would suggest, a greater focus – however, came from the clients, not from us, the therapists. Rogers (1942, p.172) is clear that, when time is short or limited, the therapist does not need to be any more directive:

> The counselor is often faced with situations in which he knows that he will be limited to but one interview, or in which he is sure that he cannot carry on extended treatment. In such instances, the common practice is to be completely directive. Since time is short, the counselor quickly grasps the problem as he sees it, giving advice, persuading, directing.

'The results', he concludes, 'are almost inevitably and thoroughly bad'. Indeed, Rogers takes this argument further and suggests that non-directive 'relationship therapy' is, in effect, the therapy of choice when time is limited (p. 172): 'Even if counselling goes no further than this phase of free expression, it is helpful and constructive. It is this fact which makes the type of counselling described here most satisfactory for short-contact counselling'.

The same argument is true for goals. Just because time is limited doesn't mean that the person-centred therapist should suddenly set goals. It's uncalled for in terms of the approach and, more importantly, it's unnecessary as, in any case, the client behaves in a needs-driven and goal-directed way (Rogers, 1951). As Toal (2001, p. 33) puts it: 'I believe that conditionality is introduced into the relationship when a therapist assumes a client's goal ... When I offer empathic understanding of a client's desired goal I do not also assume that goal'.

In this chapter, I represent what one colleague has referred to as a 'classical/relational' perspective within the person-centred approach. Whatever the name or label, there is, as I see it, a difference between this approach (from Taft and Rogers) and that of others who, influenced by Gendlin's (1981) work on focusing and drawing on the experiential tradition or tribe of the person-centred nation, advocate more focus in time-limited settings and work. Gibbard (2004, p. 42), for instance, believes 'that the person-centred approach does have to be adapted to working to a time limit'. She describes her attempt, within the context of a primary care counselling service, to maximise the opportunity for the client's therapeutic movement by creating a safe relationship; by helping to identify 'what hurts'; and by helping to create the opportunity for insight. Gibbard proposes various ways of focusing the client on what she refers to as 'content identification' and, citing Rennie (1998), 'process identification' and 'process direction'. Gibbard is unapologetic about the time constraint on counselling which, she asserts (p. 47), 'is an unashamed response to the lack of resources and the demand for the service'. In another article (Gibbard, 2006) she expands this point with reference to the context of waiting lists; the necessity of maintaining a balance of clients with a range of severity of problems; the reality that many (nearly half of) counsellors working within primary care in the UK consider themselves to be person-centred; and the importance of counsellors learning from and adapting to the context of their work. However, whilst wanting to remain true to person-centred principles, and especially to the non-directive attitude, Gibbard advocates that the therapist needs to focus and, consequently, she adopts a directive strategy. For example, when she refers to clients avoiding what hurts them, she says (p. 45): 'in time limited work there is not the time to wait for this and the counsellor may have to draw the client's attention to what they are not talking about'. This appears to contradict the implications of Rogers' (1959, p. 222) view that people behave 'with adience toward positively valued *experiences* and with avoidance toward those negatively valued'.

In response, Wakefield (2005) argues that economic arguments in support of time-limited therapy are fallacious, and that a service without time limits is self-regulating. In support of this, she cites the audit of the practice in which she works, involving over 500 clients over 10 years, as revealing that between 60% and 70% of clients chose to use fewer than 12 sessions, with the average number of sessions as between six and 10. She comments (p. 4) 'that by trusting the clients there is actually no need to time limit the service since it is self-regulating. The fear that clients will hang on indefinitely if given an open-ended contract is shown to be completely unfounded'. In another article, based on her experience in a service which does limit the number of sessions, Gibbard (2006) reports her audit of the service, involving 452 clients over five years, which reveals that 98% of respondents were satisfied or very satisfied with the service they received, and that less than 7% of clients (p. 1) 'commented that the least helpful aspect of the service they received was the time limit'. Gibbard is clearly mindful of the impact on the service, which has the equivalent of two full-time counsellors, of the number of referrals, from 13 GP surgeries, and the need to reduce waiting lists. Her concern is client-centred, and her audit reflects this, as 5% of clients said that the least helpful aspect of their experience was the length of time they had to wait.

   This debate, I think, reflects and represents genuine differences about how to work on the basis of person-centred principles in a context or setting which isn't necessarily client- or person-centred, and in which therapists may subtlely (or not so subtlely) undermine the organisation in which they are working. Gibbard (2006, p.1) states, for example, that the strict limit of six sessions in her service was imposed not because of a lack of trust of clients or 'an organisational fear of the client, but more a mistrust of the counsellor, based on the past experience of the manager ... of other services which had become "clogged up" with small numbers of people in long-term therapy'. These are genuine issues to be discussed and managed. Clearly, for a self-regulating – or organismically regulating – service to operate successfully, all parties need to trust and to be trusted, and to co-create conditions whereby all parties can thrive.

   Having discussed the themes of time, and limits and limitations, and their implications, I turn in the last part of the chapter to two specific issues of brief person-centred therapeutic practice.

Practice

Here I discuss two issues or areas of practice which arise from the challenge of time, limits and limitations: the question of 'suitability' and assessment, and being conscious of time limits.

The question of 'suitability' and assessment

A common argument in the literature on brief therapy questions the suitability of brief or short-term therapy for certain clients with particular issues who, it is argued, need longer (see, for example, Feltham, 1997). For some clients, the argument continues, having a few sessions is irrelevant; for others, it may even be positively deleterious. From this point of view, it follows that there is a necessity for an assessment which, in effect, screens people in or out of therapy. Feltham (1997) proposes certain 'fallible guidelines' as to who may benefit from time-limited counselling: those who perceive their concerns as quite circumscribed; those who have little commitment; those whose problems are mild to moderate; those who are open to focal work; and those who are well-motivated and ready. In my view, these guidelines certainly are fallible. First, from a holistic perspective it is hard to see how concerns can be so circumscribed. Indeed, arguably, such circumscription could itself give cause for concern. Second, a guideline that argues therapy as something to be sampled without commitment implicitly undermines the therapeutic process. Third, categorising problems as mild or moderate is as scientific as determining the length of the ubiquitous piece of string. Fourth, I don't imagine many clients would know what 'focal work' is, let alone be in a position to be 'open' to it, a guideline which reveals Feltham's perspective on selection as entirely a therapist-centred one. Finally, from a person-centred perspective, as all human organisms are motivated in some way or another (see Patterson, 1964/2000), it makes no sense to distinguish between people on this basis. Rather than uncritically accepting criteria for selection, therapists need to question them, and the assumptions on which they rest. Writing 40 years ago, Berne (1966), the founder of transactional analysis, was sceptical about selection criteria, originally in the context of selection for group treatment. He (p. 5) comments: 'the real issue ... is not the one commonly debated, "What are the criteria for the selection of patients", but the underlying, usually unstated assumption "Criteria for selection are good" '.

The logic of defining people by diagnosis or types of problem implies, indeed, *requires* selection and, therefore, assessment. Henderson (1999, p. 94), for example, is certain about the value of selection: 'Whatever the theoretical base, the counsellor needs tools and skills for agreeing a focus for brief work with a client ... or their intervention may not fit what the setting (or the patient) requires of them'. The influence of the medical model on Henderson is apparent, and she clearly prioritises the setting: the intervention may not fit what the *setting* requires of the counsellor. This reflects a view that counsellors in health care settings are unquestioning agents of the medical system and a medicalised view of therapy, a perspective which is vigorously challenged by person-centred practitioners such as O'Hara (1999), Sanders and Tudor (2001), and Sanders (2005, 2006). Person-centred therapy and therapists generally are sceptical about assessment by the therapist, principally because of our wish to honour the client's authority. However, as Wilkins and Gill (2003) point out, there are a number of differing perspectives on assessment, and on diagnosis, within the person-centred approach. They also report on some research which shows that, despite perceived theoretical differences about assessment (p. 174) 'practitioners of psychodynamic therapies do not differ fundamentally from person-centred practitioners in their attitudes to, and practice with, their clients in the early stages of therapy'. Whatever the differences, both within the approach and between different theoretical orientations, it seems clear:

1   That, to paraphrase Rogers' (1951) view of diagnosis, a person-centred approach to assessment views therapy as an ongoing process of assessment, and one which goes on in the experience of the client, rather than in the intellect of the therapist – a perspective which is consistent with the evidence that 87% of the variability in therapeutic outcomes is accounted for by the client (see Bohart and Tallman, 1999).
2   That, from the therapist's perspective, the question of assessment is one of a self-assessment as to whether he or she can hold and embody the principles of the approach, and co-create the therapeutic conditions necessary and sufficient to help the client to change. See also Shlien's frank comments on criteria for accepting or rejecting clients (in Chapter 5) which, similarly focus on the therapist's limitations rather than those of the client.

In my view, the only argument for excluding clients from access to therapy, however brief, is if there is evidence that the particular therapy is contraindicated, and likely to be damaging. This said, the literature on contraindications for brief therapy needs to be read carefully as much of it makes unwarranted and negative assumptions about the client, especially regarding his or her lack of 'ego strength', and is therapist- and service- rather than client-centred.

A second argument on selection focuses on assessing the client as suitable for a particular service, and goes something like this:

1   Because of limitations of resources an organisation assesses people in order to decide who should have access to the services it is offering. (For various reasons, to do with history, philosophy, politics and social policy, the National Health Service, at least in the UK, does not offer a complete range of health services.)
2   Because the organisation offers limited services of a particular nature such as brief cognitive behavioural therapy from psychologists and health care workers, or a limited number of sessions from counsellors, the organisation assesses people to 'fit' the service or the 'treatment'.

Stated thus, this argument is revealed as promoting a service-centred rather than a client-centred service. This, in turn, raises the issue of access to resources, such as counselling services and, therefore, of equity for all clients, an argument represented by Gibbard (2006). If we take the principles of accessibility and equity seriously, and assuming that a client wants to engage in therapy, however brief or limited, then he or she should be able to, and person-centred practitioners should resist assessing clients *in order to* select them for a service.

Consciousness of time limits

Just as life is time-limited, so all therapy is time-limited. I think that it is better to be conscious of this and to live with it, than to ignore the existence of time, limits and limitations, to deny our awareness of these aspects of therapy and their significance, or, in some way, distort our perceptions of them – processes which represent the three defence mechanisms identified in person-centred psychology (see Rogers, 1951). In this sense, a time limit is like any other limit to therapy of which both therapist and client need to be aware. Indeed, Taft herself (1933, p. 20) talks about limiting treatment in time as 'one of the most valuable single tools ever introduced to therapy'. However, for reasons discussed (above), the external imposition of a time limit seems to pose more problems and to evoke more reactions than the 'imposition' of any other boundary. I'm curious that therapists who hold very clear boundaries about, for instance, starting and finishing the session on time, and holding to the agreed length of time, can get agitated and oppositional about working to a time-limited number of sessions. One explanation is that, predominantly, it is the therapist who decides the length of the session, usually 50 minutes, and usually, in effect, imposes this on the client. By contrast, it is an external authority (a GP, a Primary Health Care Trust, an employee assistance programme) which decides the limit of the number of sessions, and imposes that decision on both client and therapist. Perhaps, therapists need to be more conscious of all limits and limitations, including their own and those of others. Following her positive view of time limits, Taft (p. 20) warns that:

> A time limit is a purely external, meaningless and even destructive device if used by someone who has not accepted limitation in and for himself. It becomes then merely a weapon turned on the other, or a salvation to be realized through and by the other.

She concludes that, in this and other instances, therapy depends on the personal development of the therapist (p. 21) 'and his ability to use consciously for the benefit for his client, the insight and self-discipline which he has achieved in his own struggle to accept self, life and time, as limited'. Of course, there's a time and place for both client and therapist to challenge limits and limitations and, to negotiate additional sessions. I think, however, that both Taft (1933) and Rogers (1942) offer strong arguments for being conscious of time limits and their therapeutic benefits.

The practice of assessing people, and especially for their 'suitability, implies a number of assumptions which some clients and lay people as well as some therapists hold about therapy. These are, notably:

• That change is difficult and, therefore, necessarily takes a long time. We hear this in everyday sayings such as 'You can't teach an old dog new tricks'. Sometimes in response to a confrontation, people say: 'That's me', 'It's just how I am', 'It's my personality'. For a critique of this view of change see Gladwell (2001) and Tudor (2007b).

- That therapy, it follows, is, by definition, long-term. This is an historical view which dates back to the psychoanalytic origins of psychotherapy, and is one which is perpetuated in some people's claims that psychotherapy is long-term as distinct from counselling which is short-term (see, for instance, Woolfe *et al.*, 1989).
- That the nature of some clients' problems and/or pathologies are not resolvable in a short time, e.g. people with certain personality disorders (see Gabbard, 2005), and hence there is a need for assessment of their 'suitability' for 'treatment'; and that, in this way, the therapist acts as assessor of the client and as gatekeeper to therapeutic services.

These assumptions are, in my view, often based on a lack of trust in the client, for instance, that she can derive some benefit from a few sessions, and an inflated view of the role and responsibilities of the therapist. An alternative is for a therapist to deconstruct these assumptions by sharing with her clients her awareness of and concerns about her clients, their problems, and the limits and limitations of the therapy. This perspective is supported by organismic and person-centred psychology which views the individual human organism as in an interdependent relationship with its environment, including environmental limitations. In *Time-Conscious Psychological Therapy*, Elton Wilson (1996) makes this point about consciousness, and designs a way of working with it. She offers her model to practitioners and (p. 7) 'especially those critical of short-term work, as an invitation to use a range of considered options, to *design*, in consultation with their clients, an appropriate and practical package of focused psychological change'.

In this chapter, I have discussed some of the complex challenges for person-centred practitioners working in time-limited contexts who aspire to remain philosophically congruent with the fundamentals of the approach (see Tudor and Worrall, 2006) without becoming fundamentalists (see Tudor, 2007a); who want to be responsive to a changing environment, including the social and political environment in which services are provided, whilst honouring their clients' emerging and changing needs.

References

Balint, M., Ornstein, P.H. and Balint, E. (1972) *Focal Psychotherapy: An Example of Applied Psychoanalysis*. London: Tavistock.

Barkham, M. and Hobson, R. (1989) 'Exploratory therapy in two-plus-one sessions', *British Journal of Psychotherapy*, 6(1): 79–86.

Berne, E. (1966) *Principles of Group Treatment*. New York: Grove Press.

Bohart, A. C. and Tallman, K. (1999) *How Clients Make Therapy Work: The Process of Active Self-Healing*. Washington, DC: American Psychological Association.

Boswell, J. (1887) *Boswell's Life of Samuel Johnson, Vol III* (G.B. Hill, ed.). Oxford: Oxford University Press (Original work published 1749).

Coghlan, D. and McIlduff, E. (1990) 'Structuring and non-directiveness in group facilitation', *Person-Centered Review*, 5(1): 13–29.

Cornelius-White, J.H.D. (2003) 'The effectiveness of a brief, non-directive person-centered practice', *The Person-Centered Journal*, 10: 31–8.

Davies, P. (1995) *About Time: Einstein's Unfinished Revolution*. Harmondsworth: Penguin.

de Shazer, S. (1985) *Keys to Solutions in Brief Therapy*. New York: W.W. Norton.

Elton Wilson, J. (1996) *Time-Conscious Psychological Therapy*. London: Routledge.

Feltham, C. (1997) *Time-Limited Counselling*. London: Sage.

Gabbard, G.O. (2005) *Psychodynamic Psychiatry*. Washington, DC: American Psychiatric Association.

Gendlin, E.T. (1981) *Focusing* (rev edn). New York: Bantam.

Gibbard, I. (2004) 'Time-limited person-centred therapy: Non-directive aspects', *Person-Centred Practice*, 12(1): 42–7.

Gibbard, I. (2006) 'Time-limited person-centred counselling in primary mental health care', *Person-Centred Quarterly*, 1–4.

Gladwell, M. (2001) *The Tipping Point: How Little Things Can Make a Big Difference*. London: Abacus.

Gleick, J. (1999) *Faster: The Acceleration of Just about Everything*. London: Abacus.

Griffiths, J. (2000) 'Local time', *Resurgence*, 199: 32–4.

Hawking, S. (1998) *A Brief History of Time* (2nd edn). London: Transworld.

Henderson, P. (1999) 'Supervision in medical settings', in M. Carroll and E. Holloway (eds), *Counselling Supervision in Context* (pp. 85–103). London: Sage.

Honoré, C. (2004) *In Praise of Slow: How a Worldwide Movement is Challenging the Cult of Speed*. London: Orion Books.

Kübler-Ross, E. (1970) *On Death and Dying*. London: Tavistock.

McCann, D.L. (1992) Post-traumatic stress disorder due to devastating burns overcome by a single session of eye movement desensitization, *Journal of Behavior Therapy and Experimental Psychiatry*, 23(4): 319–23.

MacDonald, P. (2006) 'Person-centred therapy and time-limited therapy', in G. Proctor, M. Cooper, P. Sanders and B. Malcolm (eds), *Politicising the Person-Centred Approach* (pp. 37–43). Ross-on-Wye: PCCS Books.

Malan, D.H. (1963) *A Study of Brief Psychotherapy*. London: Tavistock Publications.

Mearns, D. (2002) 'Response from the Lanarkshire Counselling Service' [Letter], *Healthcare Counselling and Psychotherapy Journal*, 2(1): 2.

Mearns, D. and Thorne, B. (1999) *Person-Centred Counselling in Action* (2nd edn.) London: Sage.

O'Connell, B. (1998) *Solution-Focused Therapy*. London: Sage.

O'Hara, M. (1999) 'Moments of eternity: Carl Rogers and the contemporary demand for brief therapy', in I. Fairhurst (ed.) *Women Writing in the Person-Centred Approach* (pp. 63–77). Llangarron: PCCS Books.

Patterson, C.H. (2000) 'A unitary theory of motivation and its counseling implications', in C.H. Patterson. *Understanding Psychotherapy: Fifty Years of Client-Centred Theory and Practice* (pp. 10–21). Ross-on-Wye: PCCS Books. (Original work published 1964.)

Pearson Education (2007) *Life Expectancy Rates*. Information available at: www.infoplease. com/ipa/A0762380.html

Rennie, D.L. (1998) *Person-Centred Counselling: An Experiential Approach*. London: Sage.
Rogers, C.R. (1942) *Counseling and Psychotherapy: Newer Concepts in Practice*. Boston, MA: Houghton Mifflin.
Rogers, C.R. (1951) *Client-Centered Therapy*. London: Constable.
Rogers, C.R. (1959) 'The essence of psychotherapy: A client-centered view', *Annals of Psychotherapy*, 1: 51–7.
Rogers, C.R. (1959) 'A theory of therapy, personality and interpersonal relationships, as developed in the client-centred framework', in S. Koch (ed.) *Psychology: A Study of a Science. Vol. 3: Formulation of the Person and the Social Context* (pp. 184–256). New York: McGraw-Hill.
Rogers, C.R. (1978) *Carl Rogers on Personal Power*. London: Constable.
Rogers, C.R. (1980) *A Way of Being*. Boston, MA: Houghton Mifflin.
Sanders, P. (2005) 'Principled and strategic opposition to the medicalisation of distress and all of its apparatus', in S. Joseph and R. Worsley (eds), *Person-Centred Psychopathology: A Positive View of Mental Health* (pp. 21–42). Ross-on-Wye: PCCS Books.
Sanders, P. (2006) 'Why person-centred therapists must reject the medicalisation of distress', *Self and Society*, 34(3): 32–9.
Sanders, P. and Tudor, K. (2001) 'This is therapy: A person-centred critique of the contemporary psychiatric system', in C. Newnes, G. Holmes and C. Dunn (eds), *This is Madness Too: Critical Perspectives on Mental Health Services* (pp. 147–60). Llangarron: PCCS Books.
Taft, J. (1933) *The Dynamics of Therapy in a Controlled Relationship*. New York: Macmillan.
Talmon, M. (1990) *Single Session Therapy*. San Francisco, CA: Jossey-Bass.
Thorne, B. (1999) 'The move towards brief therapy: Its dangers and challenges', *Counsellings*, 10(1): 7–11.
Timulák, L. and Lietaer, G. (2001) 'Moments of empowerment: A qualitative analysis of positively experienced episodes in brief person-centred counselling', *Counselling and Psychotherapy Research*, 1(1): 62–73.
Toal, K. (2001) 'An exploration of person-centred brief therapy', *Person-Centred Practice*, 9(1): 31–6.
Tudor, K. (1995) 'What do you say about saying good-bye?: Ending psychotherapy', *Transactional Analysis Journal*, 25(3): 228–34.
Tudor, K. (2001) 'Change, time, place and community', in P. Lapworth, C. Sills and S. Fish, *Integration in Counselling and Psychotherapy* (pp. 142–51). London: Sage.
Tudor, K. (2002) 'Introduction', in K. Tudor (ed.) *Transactional Approaches to Brief Therapy or What do you Say between Saying Hello and Goodbye?* (pp. 1–18). London: Sage.
Tudor, K. and Worrall, M. (2006) *Person-Centred Therapy: A Clinical Philosophy*. London: Routledge.
Tudor, K. (2007a, 26 January) *Person-Centred Therapy: Foundations, Fundamentals and Fundamentalism*. Keynote speech. Annual Congress of the VCgP, Amersfoort, Holland.
Tudor, K. (2007b) 'Making changes', *ITA News*, 34(1): 3–7.
Wakefield, M. (2005, August) 'Person-centred practice in primary care: Evidence that without time limits the majority of clients opt for short-term therapy', *Person-Centred Quarterly*: 1–5.
Wilkins, P. and Gill, M. (2003) 'Assessment in person-centered therapy', *Person-Centered and Experiential Psychotherapies*, 2(3): 172–87.
Woolfe, R., Dryden, W. and Charles-Edwards, D. (1989) 'The nature and range of counselling practice', in W. Dryden, D. Charles-Edwards and R. Woolfe (eds), *Handbook of Counselling in Britain* (pp. 3–27). London: Tavistock/Routledge.

PART I
INTEGRATING PERSON-CENTRED AND EXPERIENTIAL THERAPIES

2

Integrative Experiential Psychotherapy in Brief

Mia Leijssen and Robert Elliott

The person-centred approach has long included an interest in brief therapy, even before Shlien *et al.*'s (1962) ground-breaking research. Since then, various sub-orientations within the large person-centred family have emerged, some taking a strong interest in short-term work. One of the most important of these sub-orientations can be grouped under the broad heading of experiential therapy, consisting primarily of focusing-oriented therapy (Gendlin, 1996), and process-experiential (also known as emotion-focused) therapy (Greenberg, *et al.* Elliott *et al.*, 2004). Experiential therapy tends to emphasize facilitation of productive client process, referred to as process guiding, within a person-centred relationship. Supporters of experiential therapy argue that process-guiding enables it to be more efficient, and, therefore, to be particularly appropriate as a brief therapy.

Because there are different kinds of productive client process, depending on the client's presenting issues and immediate goals for a given session, the therapist may do different things at different times in order to facilitate different client processes. For example, at some moments, it may be important for the client to approach difficult, painful experiences, while at other times, it may be more appropriate to help the client create distance from these experiences. The choice of what to do when is inherently a product of the collaboration between client and therapist, guided by a combination of research and clinical experience, and located within a set of integrative frameworks. Emotion theory is the framework that has been written about most often, but other frameworks also guide this work, including the domains of process stagnation model we present here. Thus, experiential therapy is inherently integrative (Gendlin, 1996), and over time, experiential therapy has assimilated methods from other varieties of person-centred/humanistic therapy, including, in particular, gestalt and existential therapies.

In this chapter, we provide an overview of the main elements of an integrative experiential approach to brief therapy, including our combina-tion of classical person-centred ways of working with a range of broadly humanistic therapy processes. We then offer a brief review of the main research evidence. We follow this with an extended case study of relatively short-term but complex therapy for trauma, and conclude with a few thoughts about current developments.

Strands of integration in brief experiential therapy

Brief integrative experiential therapy draws systematically from several sub-orientations of contemporary client-centred therapy: classical, focusing-oriented, emotion-focused, interactional, and existential. Each of these different sub-orientations has translated the Rogerian basic therapeutic conditions into differentiated therapeutic helping processes and has its traditions of therapeutic methods or tasks based on these basic attitudes. Each sub-orientation can be recognized by how much it accents certain processes, pointing to kinds of work representing discrete domains of human functioning in which the client may be experiencing process stagnation, i.e. stuckness:

1   *Life narrative* disruptions – which are dealt with from a client-centred relational base.
2   Interruptions in *intrapsychic organization* – which call for an experiential approach, and which make up most of our work.
3   *Interpersonal* impasses – which indicate an interactional approach to resolve them when they occur.
4   *Existential* stuck-points – which, when they happen, suggest that an existential approach may be useful.

The relational and task-oriented principles are also applied in different ways as a function of the client's issues. The expertise of the therapist involves recognizing areas in which client process is stuck and, therefore, where the opportunities for forward movement or change are, using specific process-guiding responses and tasks. At the same time, the therapist always starts by actively trying to build a good working relationship. In order to facilitate a fast-developing, positive working relationship, it is important that the therapist be – and be perceived as – empathic, caring, authentic, involved, and competent.

1   Client-centred relational base for life narrative disruptions

The original Rogerian idea is most developed in the classical wing of the person-centred approach, also known as the 'orthodox' or 'non-directive' approach. The accent lies here on the authentic, accepting, empathic supporting, and exploring relationship as the central instrument in the change process (Rogers, 1957).

From this part of the tradition, we draw our basic therapeutic principles, first, of always beginning with active empathic attunement to the client's experience, and, second, of clearly and genuinely communicating our empathy and acceptance to the client. Beyond this, we draw on this empathic exploratory way of working as our baseline position, the way in which we normally work in the absence of indications or markers for a different, more process-guiding mode. Further, the relational conditions have a decisive role in all the different ways that we work, even when we are using particular procedures for helping clients work on specific tasks based on the client's issues, the setting and the phase of the therapy. Finally, we find that at times of client intense vulnerability, it is essential to take this even further than usual, in order to provide a clear empathic prizing presence to our clients (Elliott *et al.*, 2004).

However, we have found that working exclusively in this way, fulfilling as it is, in many cases does not appear to be the most efficient way of working. Therefore, in order to help clients move forward in dealing with their problems more rapidly, we have come to draw on other branches of the broader person-centred/experiential tradition.

2   *Experiential work for intrapsychic organization interruptions*

Importantly, the experiential wing of the tradition has developed different methods to facilitate the experiencing process, in order to help clients gain better access to their immediate experience and stuck places, and to process constructive solutions in a more active way (Gendlin, 1996; Leijssen, 1996; Greenberg *et al.*, 1993).

From this part of the tradition, we draw our particular interest in the client's immediate experiencing and in distinguishing different forms of productive or unproductive client process. For us, a key part of what enables us to work as brief therapists is our recognition of common ways in which clients get stuck, and ways to help them to get unstuck and to move forward again. For example, Leijssen (1996) identifies four ways in which client experiencing can become stuck and structure-bound: missing object or situational context; missing bodily reference; missing conceptualization; and missing action tendency. Furthermore, we have drawn on the writings of Gendlin (1996) and others (e.g. Grindler Katonah, 1999) to develop 'clearing a space' as a separate therapeutic task (Elliott *et al.*, 2004), and to describe multiple ways of helping clients to find a productive working distance from difficult or painful experiences (Leijssen, 1998). We have also adopted active expressive two-chair and empty chair exercises from the related *gestalt* tradition to help clients address stuck inner critic processes and unresolved issues with important others. This work typically forms the heart of our work as therapists.

3   *Interactional work for interpersonal impasses*

The interactional-interpersonal part of the tradition has been developed by writers as diverse as van Kessel and Lietaer (1998), Schmid (2002), and Cooper (2005) and, from slightly outside the tradition, the closely related work of Safran and Muran (2000) on the repair of alliance ruptures. These writers emphasize collaboration, encounter and dialogue as key aspects of the tradition.

We have also taken up key insights and ways of working from this inter-actional wing. Here, we have found useful a process-guiding style similar to the focusing-oriented approach, but with interpersonal perceptions and actions as the subject of therapy and as an entrance to the client's more general issues or emotion schemes (Elliott *et al.*, 2004). Therapist presence in the form of meta-communicative feedback in the context of an open and caring dialogue is used as the most important way of working, as formulated in the process-experiential task of relational dialogue for alliance ruptures (Elliott *et al.*, 2004). On the one hand, relational impasses and unspoken client dissatisfaction can seriously hamper the progress of therapy, while, on the other hand, we argue that explicitly including interactional processes where called for can contribute importantly to helping therapy be brief. Nevertheless, while we clearly see this work as important for some clients, for many clients it does not come up.

4   *Existential stuck points*

In the existential wing, a deeper layer of experience is touched upon by looking more closely at the meaning of the difficult or painful experiences that clients face in relating themselves to the givens of human existence, such as loneliness, responsibility, meaning, and death (Yalom, 1980; Cooper, 2003).

We have found that at times clients become stuck in the face of the intractable basic facts of their lives, struggling with isolation from others, difficult decisions, senseless events, and paralyzing fear of death. The basic person-centred relational conditions are brought to bear on these existential givens, with therapist authenticity, caring and empathy providing the basis on which the therapist joins the client in facing the difficult, inescapable facts of human existence. At times, also, we have found it useful to rely on particular ways of working with the emotional pain that stems from senseless, traumatic life events, using a therapeutic task, the 'creation of meaning for meaning protest', characterized by an intense sense of injustice or unfairness (Clarke, 1991; Elliott *et al.*, 2004). While many brief therapies never reach the point of addressing such existential issues, we have found that drawing the existential part of our tradition enables us to help our clients work with these issues in a direct, focused way that can readily be handled in a brief therapy.

Research on brief experiential therapies

What is the nature of the research evidence that supports the kind of work we have been describing? Elliott (2001) reports a meta-analysis of 28 outcome studies of brief, individual outpatient experiential therapy, between five to 20 sessions and involving at least 10 clients in each study. These included eight controlled studies and 14 comparative studies (involving comparisons with non-experiential treatments). Seventeen of the studies involved client-centred/non-directive therapies, while 12 involved contemporary process-guiding experiential therapies, primarily process-experiential.

These analyses were consistent with those reported elsewhere (e.g. Elliott *et al.*, 2004). First, there were large pre-to-post therapy changes, of about 1.1 standard deviation (sd) units; these changes were maintained or enhanced at follow-up, for an overall mean effect size (ES) of 1.2 sd. In addition, these effects were consistent across the three main types of client problems studied: 'neurotic' (15 studies, ES = 1.02 sd), depression (six studies; ES = 1.61), and anxiety (five studies; ES = 1.16). For these results, it made little difference whether the therapy was experiential (process-guiding) or classical person-centred (non-directive).

Analyses of the eight studies using waitlist control groups indicated an equally large advantage over untreated clients (ES = 1.14). Moreover, analyses of comparative treatment studies showed that clients in experiential therapies changed as much as clients in non-experiential therapies (ES = −0.04 sd). In the comparative studies process-guiding experiential therapy did better when pitted against non-experiential therapies, primarily cognitive behavioural therapy (CBT) than non-directive therapy did, although this may be due to the fact that almost all the studies of non-directive therapy were carried out by CBT researchers!

In the face of current challenges to client-centred/experiential in several countries, this relatively small body of research is in immediate need of expansion in the form of a combination of randomized clinical trials, as emphasized by scientific review bodies such as the National Institute for Clinical Excellence and large-scale practice-based research reflecting the use of brief client-centred/experiential therapies in real-world practice settings (e.g. Stiles *et al.*, 2007).

An even more appealing approach for practising therapists is intensive single case research. One such strategy is tracking change in key client issues across the course of therapy, as is done in Stiles' assimilation model (Honos-Webb *et al.*, 1998). A different, but complementary development, is the emergence of interpretive single case designs. These approaches use rich single-case records of both quantitative and qualitative data, then apply systematic interpretive strategies to evaluate non-therapy explanations for client change (e.g. Elliott, 2002). These case-based approaches offer the possibility of clinically useful therapeutic knowledge built on research-based understanding rather than the simple accumulation of facts.

Time limits as impulse for quality

Time is inextricably interwoven with the different forms of process stagnation. Life narratives are fundamentally organized within and across time. Time is always either implicitly or explicitly part of the therapeutic process, and needs to be addressed along with diagnosing specific process stagnations and fitting interventions to the issues to be addressed. In fact, the very concept of process stagnation is a temporal one, since stagnation refers to a key life process having become stuck in time short of its natural temporal unfolding. Given this, time can be used therapeutically by making explicit agreements about the number of therapeutic sessions. When discussing the time limit, the therapist can help the client with specific questions and negotiations. Rather than asking: 'How much time will you need to deal with that issue?', which is something neither the client nor the therapist can know, the important and answerable question becomes: 'How many sessions are we going to work on this issue?'

Realizing that the number of sessions is limited makes therapists more creative, more energetic and more optimistic. Clients also experience having an end point as a hopeful sign. For a brief therapy, the time limit for the whole treatment is decided at the very beginning. For long therapies or for treatments, where it is difficult to estimate how long will be needed, it is useful to work within shorter timeframes. Thus, evaluations can be set for every five or 10 sessions, each time involving an exploration of how therapy is going and what further is needed. Working with clear timeframes has the function of maintaining awareness of progress and the quality of therapy, thus preventing it from falling into endless talking.

Time and finiteness are also of course important existential themes; the way people deal with time points to core themes in their life. Working with time limits requires realism and being strong enough to deal with limits in a constructive way. To deal therapeutically with client disappointment, frustration and even anger, as well as to make realistic estimates of how many sessions will be needed to make adequate progress on specific issues, requires significant therapist expertise and careful consultation with the client.

Furthermore, it is important to keep in mind that clients often find the early steps of the change process enough for their needs. It is much more often the therapist who finds the result unsatisfying, because the therapist is still painfully aware of the unreclaimed, raw problem areas and the unrealized further possibilities for growth. To respect the limits of time implies that many problems do not have to be solved; however, it does mean that the client has to be able to mobilize enough means to continue with the change process he or she has started in therapy. On the other hand, the therapist does need to make sure that the time limit does not lead to so much pressure that it ends up paralyzing either client or therapist. In general, this can easily be dealt with by offering one to three extra sessions.

Case study of brief therapy for complex post-trauma difficulties

The following case study[1] is a concrete example of how a short-term integrative experiential psychotherapy is carried out in practice. It illustrates both the integration of therapeutic work over different life domains by drawing on the different person-centred experiential sub-orientations, and the issue of managing and using time limits to enhance the effectiveness of therapy. We realize that in many contemporary clinical contexts, a 25-session therapy would not be considered to be brief, but, in fact, this case consists of a series of 2-to-8 session phases, each in effect a separate therapy focusing on a different form of process stagnation, any one of which might have taken considerably longer in a non-time-limited format. More typically, we would expect only one or two of these forms of stuckness to come up, resulting in a comparably brief therapy. Presenting a case of this complexity allows us to illustrate what brief work on each of the forms of process stagnation looks like.

Phase 1. Client-centred base: Establishing a productive working alliance; bringing the narrative to life (sessions 1–2)

SESSION 1
A 40-year-old woman comes to see the therapist (ML), saying that she has already been in therapy three times and that all these previous therapies failed, including one with a psychiatrist who had made sexual advances toward her. The client's father was an alcoholic who abused her, while at the same time being respected by others for his high level of professional functioning. The family kept up appearances, even while she was being traumatized. The client is currently married to a partner who also abuses her and their children. Her partner has pressured her into giving up her successful career, and now she is financially dependent on him. She has come to therapy because she cannot control her restlessness and feelings of fear, and because she feels overwhelmed by frightening memories from the past.

---

[1] We thank the client for giving permission for publication. Non-relevant data have been changed or left out to guarantee the client's anonymity.

She talks about all this during the first session, in which the therapist mainly confines herself to being attentively present, giving supportive empathic reflections, and from time to time asking for clarification or concrete examples. In this way, during the first session, the narrative construction of the client's identity comes to life. Her narrative shows that she has already thought and talked a lot about her life and that the acute problems for which she is seeking help predominantly belong to the experiential and interpersonal domains.

At the same time, the therapist becomes aware that she feels a bit intimidated by the client's beautiful appearance: clothes, jewellery, and accessories, to all of which she has paid attention. She does not, however, talk about this interactional element yet, but keeps it in the back of her head.

Because her long story takes up the entire first session, client and therapist do not get to the point of discussing a working contract. Thus, the therapist proposes looking at that during a second exploratory session.

Session 2

The client enters the second session in very agitated state. Because the client is panicking, the therapist suggests they try 'clearing a space', a calming task from the experiential repertoire. She facilitates the client through this process, in which the client names elements of her painful past and says she is afraid to go back to those traumas. At the end of the session she says that today's approach appeals to her. She has the feeling that her 'wounds are being bandaged' and that 'there is someone who understands her and brings her to safety'.

The therapist offers to work mainly with focusing during the beginning of therapy, explaining that this approach can help the client deal differently with what scares her and makes her restless. The therapist also lets the client know that the problems she has with her violent partner will not be solved with these individual therapy sessions. Because her partner wants nothing to do with therapy, they agree that they will need to look for a way in which the client can deal differently with his aggression. Based on the complexity of the client's issues, including her history with boundary-violation and being overrun by others, and her perfectionism, the therapist suspects it will be good for the client to have a significant but clearly marked space for exploration, and proposes a working contract of 20 sessions.

At this point, this client is also asked if she is interested in participating in a study. During a subsequent interview with the researcher[2], the client reports that she appreciates that everything was clearly explained from the

---

[2] We thank Jutta Schnellbacher for doing the interviews and transcribing them.

beginning; that she knew what to expect and how she and the therapist would work during therapy. She said that the first contact gave her hope for improvement: 'The fact that the therapist wanted to work with me was a very special moment. One way or another I had the feeling that this was going to work. I had so many problems and all of a sudden I saw light at the end of the tunnel.' About her feelings regarding the time limit, she told the researcher: 'The proposal of a therapy consisting of 20 sessions gave me the feeling that my problems could be solved. For the first time I thought "aha", there's an end to it!'

Phase 2. Experiential work: Developing a healthy internal self-relationship (sessions 3–10)

From session 3 on, at the start of each session attention is paid to: 'What is calling for attention right now?' and 'What do we select from all that to work on?' For this client, the all-consuming fear, caused by her traumatic past and the aggression of her current partner, is always at the surface during the first phase of the therapy. That is why the sessions mostly start by clearing a space, so that client and therapist can look at the problem from a safe distance.

They work with the image of the 'hurt child' who has been through a lot, but does not dare to talk about it. Because this hurt child often stops functioning and becomes overwhelmed with fear, the client gladly accepts the proposal that 'the hurt child can stay at the house of the therapist during the week'. She feels herself beginning to feel better as a result of this idea and notices during the following week that she is not so much thrown off her balance while fighting with her aggressive partner.

SESSION 6
In the sixth session the client reports feeling 'a lot of tears' during the focusing exercise, even though she does not cry. When asked what she needs most now, she answers: 'To get rid of the scary images from the past'. The therapist realizes that they have to proceed carefully because the client has previously warned her of her inclination to flee. The therapist asks her which images from the past she wants to lose. She describes two frightening, unbearable images. The therapist gently guides the client to attend to the images as though they are in a film that the two of them are watching together and from a safe distance. This is instead of allowing the client to drown in the traumatic experience of the abused child. Instead, the therapist carefully observes the client's expressions and verbally communicates her own strong presence.

At the end of this session the therapist proposes that the client 'put the tape with the film of the horrible images in the closet in the therapy room'. The therapist feels touched by the client's need for acknowledgement of the sadness she was never allowed to express, but restricts herself to giving warm verbal support of the client's openness, out of a sense that doing more might threaten the client's independence.

SESSION 7

In the next session the client reports having felt much calmer and safer during the week, but that the 'tapes with the film have been in the back of her head the whole time'. When asked what is so important on those tapes that she needs to keep with her, she answers: 'My child is in there; everything I am right now is connected to it'. The therapist suggests that together they carefully watch the film again, while the client also attends to her body for expressions of what it needs. She says immediately that she needs to protect her child in the film. The therapist asks her to take the child in her lap and watch the film alongside the therapist. Doing that immediately gives the client a warm feeling and she reports that 'the film shrivels up'. She now describes how the child in her lap has endless fear, pain and sadness, and how it needs never-ending consolation. This image of the child leaning against her shoulder stays very strong while she recounts parts of what the child has been through. 'But', she says, 'it does not have to explain all that; it is enough that it feels comforted and that this comforting will continue as long as it is needed'.

At the end of the session the client says she 'no longer needs to leave the hurt child behind with the therapist', because she is now aware of how she can comfort and protect it. In fact, 'her child has fallen asleep leaning against her shoulder'. She tells how exhausting everything has been for the child, while she herself was never allowed to rest, she always had to stay alert for approaching danger. She leaves the session 'holding the sleeping child'.

SESSION 8

The client starts this session by recounting that she had a 'week full of love'. 'The sleeping child' stayed with her the whole time. The horrible images from the past have not come back and her fear has disappeared. It feels good to her to give this child a place in her life alongside her real children.

SESSION 10

This is a previously arranged evaluation of the therapeutic process: 'Where are we now?' The crucial change in the client after session 7 has stayed with her; the horrible images from the past have not come back. The client says she found it very helpful that she was taught a method to point her attention to her bodily felt sense without being overwhelmed.

Later, when the therapy has ended and she is being interviewed by the researcher, the client points to this as the crucial phase in which she learned 'once and for all to point her attention to what her body has to say and that she experiences that as very helpful and as making her stronger'. During this later interview she also says it touched her that 'the therapist was always carefully thinking and feeling with her'.

Meanwhile, in session 10, the therapist asks her, 'Where do you want to go?' She answers that she continues to make herself dependent in relationships, and that she is afraid of the physical violence of her partner. She wants to be able to handle men who dominate her.

Phase 3. Changing maladaptive interpersonal patterns (sessions 11–18)

When the complaints have mostly to do with problematic relationships in the life of the client, then the interactional domain becomes a priority and the interpersonal approach becomes most relevant. The therapist focuses on the relationship between herself and the client, so the client can see and become aware of her own part in the interpersonal difficulties she experiences in relationships. The genuineness of the therapist becomes a stepping stone to change. Here genuineness means that the therapist does not communicate any mixed messages and is also aware of her own reactions, using these as diagnostic instruments for registering what the client elicits in her. The feedback through which the therapist puts her own observations, feelings and views into words is concrete: the therapist describes which behaviour leads to what kind of reaction. This metacommunicative feedback acts as an invitation to a new way of communicating.

SESSION 11
As the client talks about a fight with her husband, the therapist's eye is caught by how she is sitting cross-legged, feet off the ground. The therapist becomes aware of how easy it would be to push the client so she would fall back. She brings up this behavioural feedback and asks the client to try to feel how she is presenting herself in this interaction. The client – to her own surprise – acknowledges that, in most fights with her husband, she sits cross-legged and that, without much protest, he pushes her over and then beats her.

SESSION 13
In this session, the therapist discloses the honest feedback that, in response to the way the client presents herself and looks at the therapist, the therapist sometimes feels that she is herself not well enough dressed. The client discloses that her husband often reproaches her for looking down on him, and this stimulates him to humiliate her even more. She reveals that she

learned from her family never to show vulnerability, and always to act as if everything is under control.

Unexpected events can also bring about relevant interactional starting points. After session 15, the therapist was unexpectedly taken into the hospital, so she couldn't keep her appointment with the client. The therapist's husband contacted the client by telephone to let her know the session was cancelled. It later came out that the client had interpreted the cancelled appointment as a 'punishment' for being too much of a hassle; the therapist then explained the nature of her medical problems. Later, during the interview with the researcher, the client said:

> The clear and honest communication of the therapist had a very important modelling function. Sometimes I think: 'I have to cancel something', and then I think, 'How would the therapist do this if she were in my position?', and then I do it that way.

SESSION 18

The 18th session is again a previously arranged evaluation session within the working contract of 20 sessions. The client thinks she has become much stronger and more authentic in several situations; only with her husband does she still continue to feel like a dependent child. She is not beaten as often anymore, but her relationship is still very unstable, and her husband often threatens and is still verbally abusive toward her and their children. The client sees that she has never really been herself in her marriage and does everything in service of her husband. She has never dared to put boundaries on his unreasonableness because she is very afraid being abandoned. She acknowledges in this session that her financial dependence makes her particularly vulnerable to her husband. She decides she wants to look for a job and to take more responsibility for what she will be doing with the rest of her life.

Phase 4. Existential work: Choosing a new existential position (sessions 19–25)

These sessions mark a new phase in the therapy. It is not realistic to expect that the client can fulfil the changes she is thinking about during the two sessions left. The therapist also thinks that it would be irresponsible to stop the therapy right at the moment when the client is untying herself from her partner. The client and the therapist decide there will be five to 10 more sessions, with a bit more time between the sessions. The idea is that during this last phase of the therapy the client will start envisioning a clear design of her 'new life'. Thus, they enter the domain of existential issues of responsibility, meaning and loneliness.

SESSION 19

As this final phase of therapy begins, client and therapist explore the tension between the client's need for dependence and belonging with her husband, and her need for autonomy and for developing her own identity. During a guided fantasy about her marriage she describes the image of a tree without roots, a tree that is grafted onto another tree. She experiences how she has completely become a part of her husband and how frightening it is to let go of that bond. She also sees the immense loneliness she experienced as a child and how she tried to put that behind her during puberty by offering her body to every man who approached her. Emotional intimacy and being wanted in a sexual way were very often the same to her. Continuing to work with the tree imagery, the client visualizes herself as the young cutting, ready to grow roots herself. Client and therapist try to find out what would be good soil for her to develop in and what she would need to be able to grow.

SESSION 21

She talks about the many lies in her marriage. She now reports that she has confronted her husband with the fact that she knows that he has been unfaithful to her. She confessed that she has known the truth for a long time, but didn't dare to bring it up before because she was afraid of his reaction. She has made her choice: she no longer wants to live with a man who cheats on her and beats her. She wants to go her own way if he does not choose an honest loving relationship with her.

SESSION 22

She can now think of several positive sides of 'being alone'. She redefines the difficulty with her husband as a chance to grow stronger herself. She tries to find realistic steps in the process of loosing herself from him. She wants to travel roads that do not harm her children. A complete independence, however, is emotionally and financially too much.

SESSION 23

She takes up classes that she can combine with a part-time job. On the Internet she finds an older lady looking for a younger family to share a 'kangaroo house'. Client and therapist agree that the client is well on her way to a more authentic way of life and that she is now living more in agreement with her own values and beliefs. She has not yet separated from her husband and knows the battle with him is not over yet, and that she is still vulnerable – also because of contact with her husband through their children – to violations of her new-found boundaries. We see that in this phase of dealing with her problems she has gone beyond the existential to the practical, and is now more in need of a good lawyer than of a psychotherapist. A combination of the two is financially too heavy for the client. Therapist and client plan to end the therapy after two more follow-up sessions.

SESSION 24
The client cancels the 24th session (the first scheduled monthly follow-up session) by leaving a message on the therapist's answering machine. The therapist contacts the client to set up a new appointment and asks what the 'cancelled session' was about. The client judged everything was going fine and she didn't 'feel like' going to a session. When they explore this, she admits she wanted to run away from the therapist, before it turns out that the therapist 'would never want to see her anymore'. She wants to prevent her image of the therapist as a caring person from changing into a vision of someone who does not care for her. During the interview with the researcher she says she found it very special that she wasn't punished for this dishonest action. She learned from this that small incidents are also meaningful and worth discussing.

SESSION 25
During the last session (second follow-up after three months) she recounts that she has now separated from her husband and how her newly acquired freedom is sometimes enriching and sometimes frightening. The conflicts with husband are not finished either. But she does have the feeling of having enough resources to face her future with more openness and hope.

Conclusions and future directions

Experiential therapy is in the midst of a renaissance of theory development, practical application and research. In terms of theory development, the most recent and ongoing developments involve further elaboration and clarification of emotion theory (Elliott *et al.*, 2004); the integration of affective self-regulation and attachment theory into the experiential approach (Johnson, 2004); and post-modernist conceptualizations of Self (e.g. Elliott and Greenberg, 1997).

Clinically, integrative experiential therapies have now most clearly demonstrated their value as a brief treatment of trauma/abuse (e.g. Paivio and Greenberg, 1995; and our present case study) and of depression (e.g. Greenberg and Watson, 1998). Several general experiential therapy treatment manuals have been published, including books by Gendlin (1996), Mahrer (1996/2004), and Elliott *et al.* (2004). These books manage to capture the specific qualities and main forms of therapist in-session response, while at the same time communicating the essential and general person-centred therapist attitudes and stance with clients.

References

Clarke, K.M. (1991) 'A performance model of the creation of meaning event', *Psychotherapy*, 28: 395–401.

Cooper, M. (2003) *Existential Therapies*. London: Sage.

Cooper, M. (2005) 'The inter-experiential field: Perceptions and metaperceptions in person-centered and experiential psychotherapy', *Person-Centered & Experiential Psychotherapy*, 4(1): 54–68.

Elliott, R. (2001) 'Contemporary brief experiential psychotherapy', *Clinical Psychology: Science and Practice*, 8(1): 38–50.

Elliott, R. (2002) 'Hermeneutic single case efficacy design', *Psychotherapy Research*, 12(1): 1–20.

Elliott, R. and Greenberg, L.S. (1997) 'Multiple voices in process-experiential therapy: Dialogues between aspects of the self', *Journal of Psychotherapy Integration*, 7(3): 225–39.

Elliott, R., Greenberg, L.S. and Lietaer, G. (2004) 'Research on experiential psychotherapies', in M.J. Lambert (ed.), *Bergin & Garfield's Handbook of Psychotherapy and Behavior Change* (5th edn) (pp. 493–539). New York: Wiley.

Elliott, R., Watson, J., Goldman, R. and Greenberg, L.S. (2004) *Learning Emotion-Focused Therapy: The Process-Experiential Approach to Change*. Washington, DC: APA.

Gendlin, G.T. (1996) *Focusing-Oriented Psychotherapy: A Manual of the Experiential Method*. New York: Guilford.

Greenberg, L.S., Rice, L.N. and Elliott, R. (1993) *Facilitating Emotional Change: The Moment-by-Moment Process*. New York: Guilford Press.

Greenberg, L.S. and Watson, J. (1998) 'Experiential therapy of depression: Differential effects of client-centered relationship conditions and active experiential interventions', *Psychotherapy Research*, 8(2): 210–24.

Grindler Katonah, D. (1999) 'Clearing a space with someone who has cancer', *Focusing Folio*, 18: 19–26.

Honos-Webb, L., Stiles, W.B., Greenberg, L.S. and Goldman, R. (1998) 'Assimilation analysis of process-experiential psychotherapy: A comparison of two cases', *Psychotherapy Research*, 8(3): 264–86.

Johnson, S.M. (2004) *The Practice of Emotionally Focused Marital Therapy: Creating Connection* (2nd edn). Philadelphia, PA: Brunner-Mazel.

Leijssen, M. (1996) 'Characteristics of a healing inner relationship', in R. Hutterer, G. Pawlowsky, P.F. Schmid and R. Stipsits (eds), *Client-centered and Experiential Psychotherapy: A Paradigm in Motion* (pp. 427–38). Frankfurt am Main, Germany: Peter Lang.

Leijssen, M. (1998) 'Focusing microprocesses', in L. Greenberg, G. Lietaer and J. Watson (eds), *Handbook of Experiential Psychotherapy* (pp. 121–54). New York: Guilford.

Mahrer, A.R. (2004) *The Complete Guide to Experiential Psychotherapy*. Boulder, CO: Bull. (Original work published 1996).

Paivio, S.C. and Greenberg, L.S. (1995) 'Resolving "unfinished business": Efficacy of experiential therapy using empty chair dialogue', *Journal of Consulting and Clinical Psychology*, 63(3): 419–25.

Rogers, C.R. (1957) 'The necessary and sufficient conditions of therapeutic personality change', *Journal of Consulting Psychology*, 21(2): 95–103.

Safran, J.D. and Muran, J.C. (2000) *Negotiating the Therapeutic Alliance: A Relational Treatment Guide*. New York: Guilford.

Schmid, P.F. (2002) 'Knowledge or acknowledgement? Psychotherapy as "the art of not-knowing" – Prospects on further developments of a radical paradigm', *Person-Centered & Experiential Psychotherapies*, 1: 56–71.

Shlien, J.M., Mosak, H.H. and Dreikurs, R. (1962) 'Effect of time limits: A comparison of two psychotherapies', *Journal of Counseling Psychology*, 9: 31–4.

Stiles, W.B., Barkham, M., Mellor-Clark, J. and Connell, J. (2007) 'Effectiveness of cognitive-behavioural, person-centred, and psychodynamic therapies as practised in UK primary care routine practice: Replication in a larger sample', *Psychological Medicine*. Published online 10 September 2007. doi:10.1017/S0033291707001511.

van Kessel, W. and Lietaer, G. (1998) 'Interpersonal processes', in L. Greenberg, G. Lietaer, and J. Watson (eds), *Handbook of Experiential Psychotherapy* (pp. 155–77). New York: Guilford.

Yalom, I.D. (1980) *Existential Psychotherapy*. New York: Basic.

3

Getting the Most from the Therapy Hour: Integrating Experiential and Brief Therapy

Bala Jaison

... all living creatures make perfect sense if we can enter their world. This is the cornerstone of our unflagging respect for our clients.

(Marion Hendricks)

Our world, mired with instability and uncertainty, has become increasingly complex. The therapy room is a microcosm of the world in which we live, reflecting these complexities. Many clients come to therapy yearning to find depth, purpose and meaning, not only in their personal lives (connected to their presenting issues), but in facing the myriad of adjustments to the unpredictability of our times. Simultaneously, clients are looking for solutions, action-steps, ways out of their quagmires, as quickly and effectively as possible. So how, as clinicians, do we address this both/and – being *deep* and *brief* – in our work?

This chapter demonstrates the blending and integration of two therapy modalities: focusing-oriented therapy (FOT), a deep method of therapeutic practice developed by Eugene T. Gendlin (1996) and solution-oriented therapy (SOT), a brief therapy model that carries the depth of our work into immediate, practical and useful applications. The blending, integration or 'solution' (so to speak) comes in the form of a 'both/and' approach to therapy.

I have often ruminated about the diversity of our field and how many variations exist on original models of a therapeutic style: from Freud to Jung, Rogers to Gendlin, and Erickson to the various models of brief therapy. As clinicians, I believe that we gravitate toward therapeutic models that feel congruent with who we are as individuals. For clients, their gravitation is not toward models, but rather toward finding clinicians with whom they feel valued, resonant, connected, understood, and safe. This is the therapeutic relationship. From this we may derive two premises:

- Premise one – There is no one, or right way, of practicing psychotherapy. For clinicians, it is about finding ways of working that feel natural and 'in-synch' with their character. For clients, it is about a sense of feeling unconditionally valued by the practitioner. Thus, the therapy flourishes from the connection between the client and therapist.

- Premise two – Clinicians can be eclectic in therapy, integrating any number of models or styles. For me, however, the tenets of experiential therapy, such as empathic attunement and the focus on the client's in-the-moment experiencing, are foundational for seamless integration. In addition, the solution-oriented adage 'If it works, do more of it' allows practitioners to embrace a willingness to do whatever will be helpful to facilitate meaningful change.

The integration of FOT with SOT creates a therapeutic marriage, which, like any good marriage, makes a more: something bigger, richer, more time efficient, and more profound than either model could achieve on its own. I call this approach SOFT: solution-oriented focusing therapy (Jaison, 2007).

In the beginning: Carl Rogers and client-centered therapy

Let's begin (briefly!) with the foundations of client-centered therapy as outlined by Carl Rogers before segueing into Eugene Gendlin's elaborations into focusing and FOT. There are a number of key words (in italics) that highlight and exemplify Rogers' propensities and approach to psychotherapy. Consider the implications of being *client-centered*. The underlying or implicit meaning is that the orientation of this therapy is *centered around the client* who is the ultimate authority and expert regarding his or her own process (as distinct from the therapist as expert or interpreter). Therefore, this model is *non-directive*, that is, the *client guides* the direction of the session according to what spontaneously emerges within his or her *experience* during the therapy hour.

One of the cornerstones of Rogers' approach is his view of therapy as an *experience*. Rogers (1951, p. 65) observes: 'the probability of therapeutic movement in a particular case depends primarily not upon the counselor's personality, nor upon his techniques, nor even upon his attitudes, but upon the way all these are experienced by the client in the relationship'. It is through *being in* the relationship that clients change.

Consequently, the foundation of the *therapeutic relationship* is built on the premise that the therapist is authentic and real. Rogers (1951, p. 30) believes that 'for therapy to be effective, it must be genuine'. This authenticity includes: *listening deeply* and *reflectively*, with an attitude of what he termed *unconditional positive regard* (Rogers, 1957); being with a client in an atmosphere of *respect, caring*, and *empathic connection*. By listening *non-judgmentally* and *non-intrusively* to the client, who already *knows interiorly* what is *right*, based on his or her own '*sensory and visceral* and *gut-level feelings,* the client will begin to experience *congruency*' (Rogers, 1951, p. 97). Through the therapist's valuing and respecting exactly how clients internally experience their own realities, clients find their true sense of *self-acceptance* leading to a more accurate *self-concept*, that is, how he or she would like to authentically *be* versus an imposed false self-concept, perhaps how others would like him or her to be. Rogers believes that for genuine healing to occur, clients, and, I might add, people in general, need to feel a sense of affirmation and positive regard from others (Rogers, 1959).

Eugene T. Gendlin and Focusing

Eugene Gendlin was a student and later a colleague of Rogers. In many ways their foundations and philosophies are similar: emphasis on the value of the *therapeutic relationship*, and viewing the client with *caring, respect, empathy* and *unconditional positive regard.*

Focusing and, subsequently, FOT, evolved from research conducted by Gendlin and a group of colleagues in the 1960s at the University of Chicago. They wanted to know *why* psychotherapy worked when it did, and what made it *not* work when it didn't. Was it something the therapist was doing or something the client was doing? They studied thousands of hours of tape-recorded therapist – client interactions of various models of psychotherapy. The results were astounding. They could tell within the first two sessions – and later in the first few minutes! – which clients would have successful outcomes and which would not. Some of their startling revelations were:

- That the success of any particular therapy session had more to do with the client than the therapist.
- That the model of therapy being employed was not significant to a successful outcome.
- That change occurred through something that clients did, *naturally* and *internally*, often without awareness, that was:
  (a) So obviously it could be spotted immediately; and
  (b) Easily *explainable* and *teachable*, to both students and clients (Gendlin, 1978).

What was this special thing that clients were doing? It was making contact *inside*, with a *feeling* or *sense*, that either *exactly matched* their *experience* of an issue: 'It *feels* like sinking in quicksand … yes, that's *exactly* what it *feels like*'; or didn't match at all: 'My *head* says, it's no big thing, but my *body* isn't buying it'. Gendlin (1978, p. 10) named 'this special kind of internal bodily awareness … the *felt-sense*' (or *bodily felt-sense*) and developed a distinctive process for helping clients notice whether what they were feeling and thinking '*fit*' or *matched* their *direct inner experience.* Recognizing how to interact consciously with this *bodily felt-sense* of an issue or experience is what he called *focusing.*

One aspect of the theory behind the model is based on the premise that, from birth, everything we experience is registered by the body in a cellular way, whether or not we consciously remember it. By *being with*, and *keeping company* with the *felt-sense of our experience*, which already contains all there is to be known, and by *listening attentively* to *what this felt-sense has to say*, it is possible to get new and valuable information that is *more* than one receives from the cognitive mind alone.

Over time, Gendlin developed a model to teach and convey the essence of focusing, both to students and clients – with the radical idea that if clients understood what they were doing, they would be better and more informed clients! Some of the key components of the focusing process are:

- *The focusing attitude* – This describes a *way of being* with clients that includes: gentleness, acceptance, allowing and permitting *whatever inside wishes to speak* with no judgment, blame, or criticism. This idea is not unique, therapists listen this way all the time. What is unique is that clients learn to develop this fundamental attitude *towards themselves*, both in and outside the therapy room.

- *Paying attention inside* to whatever might be there – By *paying attention* and *staying with* the unclear *bodily felt-sense* of an issue, situation, or person, movement or steps forward will occur that produce *change*, not necessarily of the particular issue or problem, but in one's *relationship* to the issue, thereby creating a feeling of relief, or *felt-shift*.

- *Finding a felt-sense* – This is the *body's experience* of a situation or feeling. It takes about 30 seconds for a felt-sense to form. A *felt-sense has* a *life* of its own, *separate from our thoughts*. It has its own *aliveness*, *rhythm*, *frequency*, and *unique quality*, directly *connected* to our *immediate/present* experience. Focusing works best when we are in a *right*, i.e. non-critical *relationship*, with the felt-sense: close enough to get a *feel* for the issue, but not so close as to get overwhelmed. This varies with each individual issue or concern.

- *Listening* – The client is asked to get very quiet inside, *inviting* the felt-sense *to speak, to tell its story*, with no blame or judgment, while *listening deeply* and *empathically*, with *caring* and *concern*.

- *Asking* – There are *gentle questions* we can ask that help the felt-sense unfold, expand, grow, and eventually *shift* to a better place. There are some model questions for asking:

  (a) Questions that ask the felt-sense what's wrong: What's the worst of this [whole thing]? What is it that feels so … [fill in felt word, e.g. queasy, uneasy, yucky, sinking]? What's between me and feeling really good?

  (b) Questions that ask what would be right: What does this (felt-sense) need? What feels like a bit of relief? If this whole thing had a voice and could speak to me, what would it want me to know?

- *A felt-shift* is the *'aha' experience,* where *our relationship* to the issue *changes* or *shifts* as we *carry* the issue in a different way. The issue may not be totally resolved, but our *relationship* with it has changed.
- *Receiving:* Taking time to *welcome, receive,* and say an *inner 'thank you'* for whatever *came inside.* This is a moment to appreciate the process of *processing* and to *internally mark the spot* to revisit, at a later time.

This step is also a juncture where the integration of a solution-oriented approach fits well, adding some possible action steps:

- Is there a word or an image that will help me remember the sense of all this…?
- What's my sense of how this would affect my life … if I could do it … or do it more often?
- Where do I imagine this working best …?

Like Rogers, Gendlin believed that clients *inwardly know* the next right steps toward creating change. By empowering clients to guide the direction of their therapy, following their own 'sensory and visceral experiences' (Rogers) or 'bodily felt-sense' (Gendlin), clients will find 'the surest route to the issues which have importance' (Rogers, 1942, p. 131).

Gendlin carries Rogers' work forward

In pondering the Rogers/Gendlin connection, I tend to think less about how they differ, and more in terms of *direction:* how Gendlin *carries forward*, or takes Rogers' work to *another level.* The following briefly outlines Gendlin's method of moving the work of Rogers on with focusing and FOT.

How therapists respond?

Rogers revolutionized the practice of psychotherapy with his concept of 'reflection of feeling'. The key shift in Rogers' approach was that therapists listen and respond 'to the feeling which is being expressed, rather than giving sole attention to content' (Rogers, 1942, p. 131).

Gendlin builds upon Rogers' model of listening with *experiential responding, which assists clients in understanding their own intricately felt meaning of an issue by engaging the client's felt sense directly.* Gendlin (1968, p. 214) eloquently describes this process:

> An experiential response points at, and brings the client's attention to his felt experiencing … Thus, one of the best possible client reactions to what a therapist says is: 'No, not at all, it isn't like that; it is rather more like …' Often, my saying how I guess 'it is' enables the client to say much more exactly how it really is … that is what I want, for my response is not a factual statement that seeks to be true,

but a pointing statement that seeks to bring into clarity and help carry further what he feels.

This direct experiencing of felt meaning leads clients toward change.

Therapists' use of self

Rogers emphasized the importance of the therapist being genuine and congruent in relationship with clients. Gendlin furthers this concept with the process of *experiential listening*. Therapists listen, using their *own felt sense as a barometer* to *directly sense the client's meaning*. By using one's self as a felt mirror to reflect *one's own sensed meaning* (of what the other is saying), the therapist can *sense* a lack of congruency in the client, and reflect it back without interfering.

Example

Client:	I really feel like this will work out, so I'm not that worried about it. [Based on a previous discussion, the therapist's *own felt sense* is that the client is not entirely sanguine 'that this will work out', and is perhaps minimizing or denying the issue. Using experiential listening, the therapist might address the client's seeming incongruence in this way.]
Therapist:	Your sense is that it really is OK with you. There's *no worry there* ... and you *feel comfortable* that this will all work out.
Client:	Well, when I heard you say 'no worry' and 'comfortable' ... well, maybe I do have some feelings, concerns about it.
Therapist:	So you might have *a few* concerns, that is, it's not *entirely* comfortable *in there.*
Client:	You know what. I'm not comfortable *at all!!* In fact, I'm *really miffed* with my boss ...

The point is that the therapist reflects back his/her own felt-sense to *mirror* the client's *meaning*. Concern about intrusion is unnecessary: if the reflection is incorrect, the client will inevitably correct it. Gendlin always says (with humor): 'Never be afraid of getting it wrong ... the *wronger* you get it, the *righter* they'll get it!'

Directionality

This is my experiential word for 'directive'. If you asked a focusing-oriented therapist whether focusing was 'directive', s/he would be horrified and answer emphatically: 'No'. If you asked a Rogerian or classical person-centered therapist the same question, s/he might say that focusing is too 'directive'. So yes, as in focusing there is an 'asking' step, questions are *gently* posed to assist in either *deepening* the felt sense, or *moving* stuck places forward. These 'questions' have a particular quality to them, and are posited as 'suggestions' not as direct questions, and phrased in a way that encourages clients to be accountable to the *self*, rather than to the therapist:

- Can you ask yourself what this felt-sense is wanting, right now?
- Maybe check and see if it would be right to …
- Take as much time as you need to sense what your body might want to say.

As a result of this phrasing, the focusing-oriented therapist feels freer to make 'suggestions' without 'interfering' because: (a) the right *attitude* (the *focusing attitude*) is already in place; and (b) by using the phrase 'ask yourself', the client's process takes precedence, the implication being that the client is accountable only to his/her unique felt experience. For some, just this step of asking may be too directive. Yet, as Embleton Tudor *et al.* (2004, p. 32) clarify: 'being non-directive describes *the attitude*, rather than the *behavior*'. This is an instance of a both/and approach: *doing* more with clients while *being* non-directive.

Teaching (Psycho-education)

Rogers (1961, p. 280) noted that: 'significant learning is facilitated in psychotherapy and occurs in the relationship'. Rogers believed that clients learned as a 'reciprocal of the therapist's attitudes' (p. 63), that is, as a client 'finds the therapist showing a consistent and unconditional positive regard for him and his feelings, slowly he moves toward taking the same attitude toward himself, accepting himself as he is' (p. 63).

Gendlin builds on Rogers' approach, adding the dynamic idea that by actually taking time to teach clients skills, clients would understand better what they are doing, and why. Hence, there are *teaching pieces* that focusing-oriented therapists use during the course of therapy: explanation of '*parts*', *listening* skills, *focusing attitude*, etc. Gendlin believed that educating clients about their own inner process would equip them with valuable tools that could be employed *outside* the therapy hour.

Gendlin has given the professional therapy community, as well as students and clients, the ability eloquently to name, label, understand, and articulate deeply complex feelings. The language of focusing has an inherent quality that points to *forward movement*. By making focusing available in a myriad of forms, Gendlin has given people the capacity not only to say: 'I know', but to say '*I know* that I know'!

Brief therapy

If we imagine experiential therapy as an umbrella under which there are many models (Rogers, Gendlin, Perls, Satir, etc.), then brief therapy may also be seen as an umbrella under which there are numerous models: strategic therapy (Haley, 1963; Madanes, 1981); solution-focused brief therapy (Berg, 1991; de Shazer, 1988); solution-oriented therapy (O'Hanlon and Weiner-Davis, 1989; Cade and O'Hanlon, 1993); narrative therapy (White and Epson, 1990; Freedman and Combs, 1996); possibility therapy (O'Hanlon, 1997); and, of course, the genius of Milton Erickson, whose work is probably the meta-umbrella under which all other brief approaches follow.

Whichever model appeals to the reader, I think it would be accurate to say that the original purpose of brief therapy was, as the rubric implies, to be *brief*. However, over time, the work has evolved and has been adapted by so many different clinicians, from so many different traditions, that the whole genre stands on its own as an extremely valuable and respectful way of practicing therapy, whether the intention is to work more rapidly, or to integrate some very effective *brief pieces* into other modalities.

The purpose of this next section is to demonstrate how to partner or marry two models, FOT and SOT, so that practitioners of long-term experiential therapy can integrate relevant parts of solution-oriented work into their practice, while maintaining the foundations of focusing; and, conversely, how brief therapists can learn to integrate components of FOT.

Note for brief therapists: Because of the direct, in-the-moment '*aha*' shifts that clients experience through experiential work, brief therapy actually goes faster with the addition of an experiential process!

Focusing-oriented and solution-oriented therapy: A partnership of processes

To begin, it is possible to take any brief therapy model and make it *experiential* through the use of phrasing, timing, and linguistic applications. Conversely, FOT can be formatted to work more *briefly*, by revising SOT questions to fit the experiential style.

When thinking of a partnership or marriage, we might imagine two people standing side by side, or, as noted couples' therapist Terry Real often says, 'standing toe to toe'. Lining up the two models, let's explore some of the parallels.

Similarities between the models

ORIENTATION

The key word that joins or weds the two models is 'oriented', which implies *leaning toward, in the direction of, so inclined*. Both models are *oriented* toward change:

FOT: in how the client *carries* the issue or problem *inside*.
SOT: in how the client *views* the problem *differently*.

Both models are *oriented* toward wellness, meaning that they each avoid focusing on pathology by helping the client move in the direction of:

FOT: what *feels* right, and life-enhancing for the client.
SOT: *what works*, what will be *helpful*, *hopeful*.

PHILOSOPHY AND ATTITUDE

Both models have an attitude and philosophy that includes a deep belief that clients already have within them the knowledge, inner resources, life experience, and natural competencies which can be accessed to find the *solution* or *right way*. By therapists affirming, listening, and assisting clients in drawing upon what is already intuitively and instinctively known, clients will gradually learn how to tap into their own innate capabilities. While SOT does not specifically 'name' what we call the *focusing attitude*, each model emphasizes a way of being with clients that is respectful, non-judgmental, caring, and above all, that acknowledges the client as the ultimate expert or authority regarding his/her own process and development. SOT does not use the term 'client-centered', yet, I have always viewed the model as client-centered in *attitude*.

Similar and different

Paralleling FOT and SOT, we see a number of areas where the approaches are different, yet the outcome is the same or very similar.

THE I/IT RELATIONSHIP

An underlying principle in FOT is that of essential wholeness: quintessentially we are well, whole, and 'all OK', but *'things come that stand between'* us and experiencing our essential wholeness. Hence, if a client says, *'I am really unhappy'*, the focusing-oriented therapist would not reflect back: *'So you are really unhappy'*; rather, the reflection would be: *'So there's a "part" of you that's feeling really unhappy, right now'* or, alternatively, *'There's "something there" feeling really unhappy, right now'*. The implication is that there is a *part* ('it') that *feels* really unhappy and there is another *part* ('I') that is all OK, and not unhappy. The focusing orientation helps the client develop the healthy 'I' that can assist the 'not OK part' toward healing.

The solution-oriented approach does exactly the same thing, by finding the 'exception to the problem':

- When was the last time things were better, or a little bit better?
- What was happening then that seemed different?
- What did you notice about those times?
- What were you doing differently then?

Focusing avoids direct questions by asking the client to '*ask yourself*'. However, the above questions can easily be *experientialized* in order to give the client the time to *take in, sit with,* and find a *felt sense*:

- Maybe take some time to *sense* the last time things *were better*, or *a little bit better*.
- See if you can get a *feel* for what was happening then, that seemed different.
- *Sense* what you notice about those times.
- Maybe *ask yourself*: 'What was I doing, *feeling differently* then?'

When a client is given the time to *fully experience* these questions, *the ability to shift comes faster.*

LANGUAGE: TOTALLY DIFFERENT, SAME OUTCOME

Each model has a specific way of using language, unique to its style, and phrased for a particular effect. At first glance, it would seem that the different phraseologies would steer clients in totally different directions. Remarkably, by weaving the two styles together, the client gets to exactly the same place of *knowing*.

Parallels and integrations

- A hallmark of the FOT approach is a brilliance in *listening experientially* for the most subtle nuances.
- A hallmark of the SOT approach is in *asking questions* that are brilliantly phrased to pick up subtle nuances.

FOT language is expressed in the present tense: clients can experience *in the moment* how they are feeling about an issue:

- Maybe *take a moment* to just *be with*, *all about this whole issue*, noticing what wants to form.
- If this issue could speak to you, *right now*, see if there's anything it would like you to know.
- Check with yourself: what is it, *now*, that *makes* this feeling of discomfort *there*.

SOT language is expressed in the future tense: the client can explore the world of *possibilities, how it could be*:

- When it is right, what *will* that look like?
- What do you imagine *will be* different when this issue is no longer happening?
- What do you suppose *you'll do differently*, when it's better?

COMBINING

FOT: *Taking the time* to let the issue form, to explore it more deeply, *in the moment.*

SOT: *Exploring possibilities*, using SOT questions, *experientially.*

Thus:

- Can you *sense inside*, what *it will* look like, *feel like* when it is right?
- See if there's a *feeling there, right now* about how *it will be when* the issue is no longer happening.
- Notice what *comes in your body* when you see yourself *doing it differently*, when it's *better.*

Combining the *asking* of SOT questions in a FOT style, then *listening experientially*, takes both models further.

More on language

FOT is specifically vague, fuzzy, and unclear. Its *value* is to let clients *sense*, and *explore* from the body, the *exact right words* that fit their *felt meaning.*

SOT is specifically intentional and clear. Its *value* is to enable clients to *pin down exactly* what they are *meaning* and *wanting.*

Example (Vague and fuzzy – the therapist takes time to find out what the issue is really about)

Therapist: There's *something* about that … that leaves you *feeling* …
Client: Angry. I feel angry.
Therapist: So there's a feeling *there* … that's like … angry …
Client: Well, it's actually not quite angry. It's more like frustration, fed-up. Yes, that's it! I've had enough, I'm just *fed-up* with the whole situation.

Example (Specific and clear – the therapist looks for forward moving steps)

Therapist: So, if this was somehow resolved, and you weren't *fed-up* anymore, what do you imagine *will be* different when it's right? What *will you notice?*
Client: I'd take some action. I'd tell him how I feel. I'd probably give him an ultimatum.
Therapist: So you'd *want* to take some action: address the problem, talk about it, express how you're feeling.
Client: Yes, and I'd probably make a plan to get out!

Different yet compatible

GOALS

FOT is not goal-oriented. While it is *positive* in orientation, it is *non-directive*, following the client in whichever direction the process wants to go.

SOT is goal-oriented: intentionally *solution focused* rather than *problem focused*, working with clients on specific goals and outcomes, stated by the client, either long-term, or for the current session.

Integrating the two approaches

Eliciting the best of both approaches, the therapist helps the client to find a goal at the beginning of a session, *experientially*:

> *Maybe take a minute now, to take a breath, just to be here* (give the client a minute to do this) *then, checking inside, maybe ask yourself: 'What feels important to me today?' or 'Is there anything that wants my attention, right now?' or 'How would I really like to use this time?'*

A case example of the SOFT approach

The client, 28 years old, was raised by an alcoholic single mother. As a child, he spent much time hiding (staying at school or at friends' houses for as long as possible) to protect himself from his mother's erratic and often abusive behavior. As an adult, he has difficulty with long-term relationships, both personally and professionally. He cannot distinguish feedback from criticism, and tends to personalize (negatively) even the most constructive feedback. He is often defensive, even when others are talking about their own experiences. His first reaction is: 'It's not my fault'. Although aware of the problem, he sees himself as getting 'triggered', and has 'no clue' about how to break the cycle of defensiveness. He is a nurse in a large hospital, and often has problems both with staff and his supervisor. He came to therapy wanting to work out his relational issues. We met for a total of six months, moving from weekly to bi-weekly, to monthly sessions.

Second session (starts with FOT approach)

Client: My supervisor says I need an anger management course, but that's *not it*.

Therapist: So although she's naming it 'anger management', that *doesn't feel right*, it feels maybe like *something else*.

Client: Yeah, it's like she's picking on me, she's out to get me.

Therapist: So there's a feeling *there*, like picking on you, out to get you. [Note: In FOT, two commonly used words to help clients connect with their felt sense are '*something*' and '*there*', sometimes used together as in 'There's *something there*', and sometimes used separately: '*Something* about that makes you feel' or 'You feel it *there*.']

Client: Yes, but then, part of the problem is that I never *really know* what's my stuff, and what's somebody else's. I get confused because I get so easily triggered.

Therapist: You're saying that because you get triggered it's really hard to *know* what's your stuff, and what is someone else's.

Client: Yeah, that's why I'm here. I need to find a way to not get so hooked. [The client was clear in the first session that he wanted 'some direction'. He's also not *yet* responding from the felt sense. The therapist asks a SOT question, *gently*, in an *experiential* FOT style.]

Therapist: It sounds like there is *something* that *you are wanting*, about not getting hooked, triggered. I'm wondering if you have any *vision* of what it would *look like*, *feel like*, *if it was right*. [SOT calls 'vision' the '*solution picture*']

Client: Ummm, I see myself as being more in control, less defensive, more aware of what I'm saying and doing.

Therapist: So you're *wanting* to *feel* more in control, less defensive, more aware of what you're saying and doing.

Client: Yes. [The SOT approach tends to pursue more: '*What else* will work?' Because the client is less connected to his *direct experience*, the therapist still emphasizes experiential language.]

Therapist: *Anything else* you might notice when you are *feeling* more in control?

Client: I think I'd be able to step back more.

Therapist: *Something about* stepping back, that would allow you to feel more in control, less defensive, more aware of what you're saying and doing.

Client: Yes, 'stepping back' *really fits* here. [This is the first time he has responded experientially, an important place to take more time.]

Therapist: Would it be OK to take a minute to sit with: '*What comes up for me when I really allow the whole of "stepping back" to form*'.

Client: [Shifts in the chair, slightly leaning forward, from the waist up. His hands come together in his lap with his fingers lightly touching. With surprise he exclaims:] I just changed my position didn't I?

Therapist: Mmmm, yes, it looks like you did.

Client: It's like, sitting more forward puts my abdomen more back. I *feel* more protected.

Therapist: So this change, with your upper body more forward, and your abdomen more back, *carries a feeling* … of being more protected.

Client: Ummm, the feeling reminds me of being a child, like getting suddenly punched in the stomach with no warning … how I always felt with my mother. I didn't realize 'til just now, but did you see what I did with my hands? [noticing that his fingers are lightly touching.] [Here is a therapeutic 'judgment call'. One might respond to the powerful feeling he had with his mother. The therapist *senses* that the 'fresh air' is more connected with his hands.]

Therapist: *Something about* your hands.

Client: It's like I'm protecting myself, it's kind of subtle, like keeping my fingers slightly touching is some private way between me and myself, of staying protected, of not feeling so vulnerable.

Therapist:	So it's like some kind of special and private protection.
Client:	[pondering] You know what! It's like when I get triggered, I *act* like a child, and when I sit like this, I *am* an adult! [The client has just experienced a *felt shift*: being an adult vs. being a child. Note: What the felt shift is in FOT parallels the 'exception to the problem' in SOT, a juncture where *change is happening.* The therapist sees an opportunity here to bodily 'anchor' the shift/exception. Again, the therapist poses SOT questions, FOT style.]
Therapist:	Would it make sense, right here in this spot, to ask yourself: '*What* are some of the first things I'll *notice* when I'm *feeling* like an adult?'
Client:	Ummm, the first thing that comes, after *stepping back*, is that I'm more of an *observer*, watching, listening, more detached.
Therapist:	This is *really important* [the 'anchoring' piece]. First, you '*step back*' and *that helps you* become *more of an observer.* Then you can begin *watching, listening, being more detached.*
Client:	Yes, indeed!
Therapist:	Anything else?
Client:	Well, part of 'observing' is being able to notice where *others* are coming from. I don't do that very well. It's like when I get triggered, I forget to see where the *other* is at, it becomes all about me, where *I'm* coming from. [SOT tends to stay with *what's right,* avoiding a negative reflection such as: 'I forget to see …' Notice (in italics) the added emphasis on the positive.]
Therapist:	So part of *being able* to observe, *really well,* is about *taking the time* to *really notice* where *others* are coming from and maybe *stopping,* or *stepping back* to *take that in.*
Client:	Yes, this *feels very right,* to take some time to really observe. If I did that I'd feel so much more in control.
Therapist:	[Reflects above experientially, then adding a SOT piece, pursues further:] Maybe see if there's more …
Client:	I'd listen in a different way.
Therapist:	*Some way* you'd be listening differently.
Client:	Yeah, I'd sort of be more open to what the other person was *meaning.* [In FOT, there are junctures where the therapist pauses for *teaching pieces.* Integration: FOT addresses the *felt trigger responses* (adult/child); SOT addresses what the client *wants* to do *instead.*]
Therapist:	This might be a good spot to make some lists *sensing* what you *used to do and say,* and what *you'd like to do and say more of now,* in a new way.
Client:	Well, before, I reacted immediately. Now I would reflect back what the other person said.
Therapist:	So before, you reacted immediately. Now you would *take the time* to reflect back what the other person was saying.
Client:	Yes. Before I was so over-reactive. Now, I'd be more detached, more observing.
Therapist:	You *see a change* here. Before you were over-reactive, now you *see yourself* as being more detached … more observing.
Client:	I like this idea of labeling and naming. It helps me to *understand* what's really going on for me.

Therapist: So you like the idea of labeling and naming because it *helps you to understand more accurately* what's going on inside of you.
Client: Exactly!
Therapist: Anything else, *there?*
Client: Humor! I take things *too seriously.* I'd like to use my sense of humor.
Therapist: That's great! ... adding some humor [client is smiling] OK, let's see how this fits:

Before you	*Now you would*
Used to react immediately	Take *some time* to reflect back what the other said
Were over-reactive in your responses	Be more detached, more observing
Would misread another's meaning	Name and label what is going on
Took things too seriously	Add in your *sense of humor*
Does that sound about right...?	

Client: Yeah, it sounds great. I think work will be very different tomorrow!

Some closing thoughts

Using a combination of the two approaches, this client made tremendous movement forward, learning:

Through FOT:

– To take time to *be with* and *experience* his genuine feelings.
– With teaching pieces about *parts*, to discern more clearly between the 'adult' and 'child'.
– To validate and affirm his authentic self.

Through SOT:

– To look for the positive: what's *right*, what he *wants*.
– To be *less reactive* and *more responsive*.
– To work on small, helpful, manageable steps.

Clearly, there is no 'one way' to work with a client, in large part, because each one is so uniquely different. The foundation is: *respect* for the client's innate wisdom and inherent competency, and an *attitude* of empathy and unconditional positive regard.

This brings me to an interesting epiphany about integrating FOT and SOT. The differences between the two models are more connected with *style* rather than *outcome*. SOT doesn't 'teach', it 'models'. SOT doesn't use experiential language; it doesn't talk about 'parts' or the 'authentic self', yet, in its own respectful way, by finding out *what works*, *what's right*, and *what's real*, the model takes the client to the same place of 'fresh air'.

I feel strongly that for *deep processing*, especially of very negative and traumatic events, clients need a referent for the 'adult', other than the therapist, in order to feel empowered to deal with dysfunction and consequent healing. It is therefore important that the client and therapist construct some semblance of the *authentic self,* even if very small at first, to help clients better understand:

–   Who they *actually are* (beneath the judgment and criticism).
–   How they *view* the *best* of themselves.
–   How people who love them view them, e.g. 'If your best friend was here, what do you imagine she'd say she loves about you?'

Through the constructive building of a 'vision', the *solution picture* of '*How I want to* be', the SOT approach helps enhance the client's inherent and natural resources, laying a foundation for the deeper work of FOT. So, we come back again to the both/and perspective:

FOT helps the client 'grow' the self, by taking the time, experientially, *to be with* what's *inwardly known* as *feeling right.*
SOT helps the client 'grow' the self, by pointing to *what's right and possible.*

Both embrace the concept of 'taking small manageable steps':

–   FOT, the steps that the body '*buys*',
–   SOT, the steps that feel '*doable*'.

SOFT (solution-oriented focusing therapy) makes room for both!

References

Berg, I. (1991) *Family Preservation: A Brief Workbook.* London: BT Press.
Cade, B. and O'Hanlon, W.H. (1993) *A Brief Guide to Brief Therapy.* New York: W.W. Norton.
de Shazer, S. (1988) *Clues: Investigating Solutions in Brief Therapy.* New York: W.W. Norton.
Embleton Tudor, L., Keemar, K., Tudor, K., Valentine, J. and Worrall, M. (2004) *The Person-Centred Approach: A Contemporary Introduction.* Basingtoke: Palgrave Macmillan.
Freedman, J. and Combs, G. (1996) *Narrative Therapy: The Social Construction of Preferred Realities.* New York: Norton.
Gendlin, E.T. (1968) 'The experiential response', in E. Hammer (ed.) *Use of Interpretation in Treatment* (pp. 208–27). New York: Grune and Stratton.
Gendlin, E.T. (1978) *Focusing.* New York: Bantam Books.
Gendlin, E.T. (1984) 'The client's client', in R. Levant and J.M. Shlien (eds) *Client-Centered Therapy and the Person-Centered Approach: New Directions in Theory, Research and Practice* (pp. 76–107). New York: Praeger.
Gendlin, E.T. (1996) *Focusing-Oriented Psychotherapy: A Manual of the Experiential Method.* New York: Guilford Press.
Haley, J. (1963) *Strategies of Psychotherapy.* New York: Grune and Stratton.

Hendricks, M.N. (2002) 'What difference does philosophy make? Crossing Gendlin and Rogers', in J.C. Watson, R.N. Goldman and M.S. Warner (eds) *Client-Centered and Experiential Psychotherapy in the 21st Century* (pp. 52–63). Ross-on-Wye: PCSS Books.

Jaison, B. (2007) *Integrating Experiential and Brief Therapy: How to do Deep Therapy – Briefly and How to do Brief Therapy – Deeply* (2nd edn). Toronto, ON: Focusing for Creative Living.

Madanes, C. (1981) *Strategic Family Therapy*. San Francisco, CA: Jossey-Bass.

O'Hanlon, W.H. and Weiner-Davis, M. (1989) *In Search of Solutions: A New Direction in Psychotherapy*. New York: W.W. Norton.

O'Hanlon, W. (1997) *A Guide to Possibility Land*. New York: W.W. Norton.

Real, T. (2002) *How Can I Get through to You?* New York: Simon and Schuster.

Rogers, C.R. (1942) *Counseling and Psychotherapy: Newer Concepts in Practice*. Boston, MA: Houghton Mifflin.

Rogers, C.R. (1951) *Client-Centered Therapy*. Boston, MA: Houghton Mifflin.

Rogers, C.R. (1957) 'The necessary and sufficient conditions of therapeutic personality change', *Journal of Consulting Psychology*, 21(2): 95–103.

Rogers, C.R. (1959) 'A theory of therapy, personality and interpersonal relationships, as developed in the client-centered framework', in S. Koch (ed.) *Psychology: A Study of Science, Vol 3: Formulation of the Person and Social Context* (pp. 184–256). New York: McGraw-Hill.

Rogers, C.R. (1961) *On Becoming a Person*. Boston, MA: Houghton Mifflin.

White, M. and Epson, D. (1990) *Narrative Means to Therapeutic Ends*. New York: W.W. Norton.

4

Traumatic Incident Reduction and Applied Metapsychology Techniques: Operationalising Rogerian Theory in a Brief Therapy Practice

Henry J. Whitfield

I am always ready to learn although I do not always like being taught.

(Winston Churchill)

Traumatic Incident Reduction (TIR) and its related techniques is a form of brief therapy for Post Traumatic Stress Disorder (PTSD) and other trauma-related conditions. The techniques of TIR were originally developed within a humanistic approach to general counselling and personal growth and, specifically, metapsychology as a study of the principles that underlie all psychologies and human experience, as viewed by the individual.[1] During the 1980s, metapsychology practitioners began using an Applied Metapsychology technique to help Vietnam veterans suffering from PTSD. This technique became known as Traumatic Incident Reduction. During the 1990s, a number of empirical studies were also completed, testing TIR's efficacy with PTSD (Figley and Carbonell, 1994; Bisbey, 1995; Coughlin, 1995; Valentine, 1997). Since that period, TIR and its related metapsychology techniques have been best known as a brief therapy for PTSD (Bisbey and Bisbey, 1998).

This chapter examines the person-centred approach as it is understood and applied in the practice of TIR. It also offers an analysis of how TIR practice succeeds in applying a structure that does not compromise the client's own unique process. Finally, I also address how a number of elements of Rogers' work might be structured in TIR in order: (a) to enable clients to engage deeper and faster into therapeutic process, thereby reaching their therapeutic goals in less time; and (b) to enable practitioners to help a wider range of client populations. Thus, this chapter demonstrates how therapy might be briefer and yet equally thorough and effective, whilst honouring the key principles of the person-centred approach.

---

[1] 'Applied Metapsychology' (AM) refers to the technical subject which is taught to therapists; 'metapsychology', often written in lowercase to distinguish it from AM, refers to the abstract philosophy which lies behind it.

Despite being a structured therapy that makes extensive use of directive techniques, Gerbode (1995) describes the philosophy and practice of TIR as person-centred. I highlight this point because many person-centred therapists struggle to reconcile terms like 'structured techniques' and 'directive' with the person-centred approach, even though Rogers (1957) clearly acknowledges that techniques can be used *if* they serve as channels for his therapeutic conditions. Elsewhere, Rogers (1970, p. 53) also acknowledges that he works in a directive way in that he is more interested in certain kinds of content than others:

> There is no doubt I am selective in my listening ... I am unquestionably much less interested in the details of the quarrel with his wife ... than in the meaning these experiences have for him now and the feelings they arouse in him. It is these meanings and feelings to which I try to respond.

Since Rogers' early work on client-centred therapy, many practitioners and theorists have examined how to reconcile the use of techniques and the application of structure with the person-centred approach. The most notable of these was Eugene Gendlin whose work gave rise to focusing-oriented and experiential psychotherapy. Gerbode ([1988, 1989], 1995) describes the subject of Applied Metapsychology as a person-centred approach to stress-reduction and personal growth, and in my view, TIR therapy has reconciled person-centred philosophy and principles with structured techniques in that structures are used systematically to operationalise person-centred values, such as client self-determination and choice; and those attitudes or conditions considered helpful and therapeutic, including Rogers' six 'necessary and sufficient' therapeutic conditions. In TIR and related techniques, the client remains the authority on the content of his experience, what direction or issue to take, what pace to go at and, to a lesser extent, and what exercise to experience. The latter is to a lesser extent because the therapist usually has more knowledge about such exercises, but only offers them as possibilities that the client may or may not choose to engage in. Furthermore, the exercises or techniques are presented in a thoroughly transparent way so that the client is in a good position to decide if they fit within his or her unique frame of reference. Power issues stemming from the therapist's professional/expert setting are at least partially addressed by placing regular emphasis on the client's perceptions, asking questions that have no obvious answer, and giving the client choices of techniques (with no hints as to which would be more effective or relevant).

The following analysis of TIR and related Applied Metapsychology techniques aims to cover the more notable similarities and differences between TIR and (1) Person-centred therapy (PCT), and (2) Focusing-oriented therapy, a more directive or 'instrumental' form of the person-centred approach. I then examine metapsychology techniques for operationalising therapeutic process as Rogers' described it in his (1958/1961) paper on 'A process conception of psychotherapy'.

TIR and PCT

Rogers (1957) states boldly that six conditions are necessary and sufficient for therapeutic change to occur. In the same paper, Rogers also states that the therapist's direction of the client's process is both undesirable and unnecessary. Since then, much debate has ensued around both the necessity and sufficiency of these conditions. Putting aside the debate of whether Rogers' six conditions are sufficient alone, let us examine how these six conditions may or may not be present in TIR counselling.

In the Appendix I are described some detail eight exercises used to train TIR therapists to manage the session environment in a particular way. The eight exercises systematically operationalise at least five of Rogers' conditions. For example, three of the exercises help the therapist develop her ability to be present and maintain empathy. Another exercise practises the ability to acknowledge a client clearly and authentically. TIR practitioners are expected to acknowledge everything the client says or does without exception. This is a thorough application of the sixth condition, that the client perceives the therapist's empathic understanding of the client's internal frame of reference.

Structuring person-centred values

Any action that is completed more than once could be argued to form part of a structured process. For example, a therapist that does anything regularly is following a definable pattern, even if it is loosely defined. Examples of this in PCT are: reflecting back to the client, using the client's perspective, and checking one's understanding of the client's internal frame of reference. These are all things that the therapist does regularly, even if they are an embodiment of qualities. Whilst these latter may not be done using rote sentences, there is nonetheless a pattern and, therefore a structure present. Perhaps one could even go as far as saying that anything that is clearly defined is a form of structure. Coghlan and McIlduff (1990, p. 20) similarly argue that:

> A staff decision to 'let the participants decide' on whether and when to form small groups or to remain in a large group is, in itself, a form of structure … These are some examples of structuring that are typically not perceived to be inconsistent with the values and operations of the person-centred approach.

A significant part of the 'technique versus no technique' debate relates to a dichotomy between abstract and concrete, that is, a principled dichotomy between a 'being' therapy (abstract), and an instrumental 'doing' therapy (concrete). TIR theory and practice also values the flexible use of principles over rigid systems. A difference, however, is that TIR practice also has a major focus on the 'skilled doing' and appropriate application of general principles, in the form of many learnable techniques, questions and non-verbal behaviours (see Appendix 1 for more details of such non-verbal actions).

Receiving the client

Metapsychology theory teaches that the genuine comprehension by the therapist of a client's viewpoint is therapeutic for the client. Furthermore, the genuine empathy, presence and interest of the therapist can gently encourage the client to look even further or deeper. This is comparable to Rogers' (1958/1961, p. 130) description of the 'basic condition' for therapeutic change: 'that the client experiences himself as fully received'. Receiving the client and the condition of empathic understanding are examples of clear similarities in TIR and PCT practice.

The client's unique inner process

Another emphasis of TIR practice is this: during moments when the client is actively engaged in accessing, identifying, and describing his inner material (or 'direct-referents'); it is very important not to do anything during the client's engagement in this process. After the client has completed a particular 'viewing' of his inner experience, it is then equally important to indicate *nothing*, other than that you received his communication. That is, one avoids adding anything to colour what the client has said. In TIR, saying anything that colours the client's experience is thought to be potentially interfering with the client's unique inner process. This commitment to honouring the client's unique perceptions and inner process is another prominent similarity between TIR and PCT. Both approaches emphasise the importance of these elements. However, there is also a prominent difference regarding what sabotages this unique process. Person-centred therapists offer their perceptions of the client's unexpressed material; TIR therapists do not. For example, observing that a client is smiling while describing something sad, a PCT practitioner is likely to indicate her observation of this to the client. In TIR, pointing out such an incongruence (or any other exterior viewpoint) is considered to be interfering with and potentially stopping the client's unique process. This is because the TIR viewpoint fears that clients may start looking from the therapist's viewpoint rather than their own.

A therapist with intentions

I believe that placing person-centredness in the context of therapist intentions is yet another way of displaying the style of practice found in TIR. PCT leans towards the therapist not intending anything in particular to happen in the session, as intending could be a form of directing the client's process. TIR makes extensive use of structures for bringing about particular therapeutic conditions that engage the client in doing something experiential. The TIR therapist has intentions to engage the client in experiential exercises that either accelerate or unblock the client's unique process. I argue that such experiential exercises do not conflict with Rogers' (1957) view; in other words, that such exercises often serve as a channel for the conditions. For example, if a client is repetitively focusing on some anxiety-inducing memory, the second condition (that the client is in a state of incongruence, being vulnerable or anxious) will be maintained more consistently during the session, than if the client is left to wander with much less structure. Again, Coghlan and McIlduff (1990, p. 21) argue that: 'if structuring facilitates client or group self-determination in achieving the client's or group purposes, then it is in accordance with person-centred values'. This is the style of person-centredness found in TIR theory and practice.

In summary, TIR and PCT are both consistent with the person-centred values of self-determination and choice, and the importance of the client's authority on his process and experience. TIR and PCT differ in opinion regarding what interrupts a client's unique therapeutic process. Finally, whilst TIR makes use of a higher degree of structuring and technique, both are structured therapies that align with Rogerian theory.

TIR and focusing-oriented therapy

Focusing-oriented psychotherapy, which has emerged from the work of Eugene Gendlin (1996), forms a major offshoot of PCT. Rogers (1958/1961) himself acknowledges the importance of Gendlin's influence on his own work. However, there is a principle disagreement between the two schools of thought: PCT therapists hold that instructing the client to do anything might affect her unique therapeutic process, and represents a movement towards the therapist being an expert who knows better than the client. Gendlin and his many colleagues in person-centred experiential therapy hold that instruction or technique may be applied whilst remaining within the client's 'experiential track', that is, as Gerbode (1995, p. 5) puts it: 'It is possible to direct a person's attention without telling the person what he is to perceive'. According to Gendlin, techniques are not necessarily theory-centred and can be client-centred. Moreover, both Gendlin and his colleagues believe such instruction is necessary with some clients so that therapists can help: 'make interaction happen where it isn't' (Gendlin, 1964, p. 172). The TIR approach occupies the same viewpoint: that Rogers' six conditions are not sufficient with all clients and that structured exercise can be used to empower clients and even accelerate the therapeutic process.

TIR and FOT have a lot in common, having a similar emphasis on the client 'viewing' or contacting his inner world, moment to moment. They both consist of experiential techniques that help bring about a mindful relationship between the client and his inner 'online' experience as it unfolds, moment to moment. Gendlin's (1978) 'focusing' method consists of six steps that instruct the client how to connect and communicate with her inner experiential entities. A difference is that TIR is generally less 'instructive'. The TIR client does not feel he is expected to develop or learn a new ability, even though he usually does. He will tend to feel he is simply being asked to do things he is already able to do.

Process facilitation in TIR

TIR and related techniques offer many strategies for enhancing the client's ability to perceive his inner experience. In fact, to this end, quite a spectrum of styles and techniques are employed. Some of these techniques (illustrated below) are structured exercises that suggest little, or nothing, to the client. At the other end of the spectrum, there are methods comprising theoretical models that are tentatively offered to the client as a new angle from which to examine an experience. For example, a technique known as 'Wrong Indication handling' is based on a theory of how a person can become deeply upset when his self-concept is threatened or challenged by a person whose opinion the client values. A girlfriend tells her partner he is a liar, when the partner considers himself very honest. If the therapist perceives a wrong indication has occurred, the therapist may choose to offer an explanation of the mechanics of the Wrong Indication model, and then ask the client if such a thing occurred in his experience. Spotting the mechanics of the upset can bring relief, a clearer, more detached awareness for the client, and render a client more able to face situations that threaten self-concept.

Purton (2004), a notable contributor to FOT, points out that:

> people *are* helped by psychological theories. Someone reads Freud, or Jung, or Rogers and what they read throws new light on their situation. Things which they hadn't thought of bringing together before, now illuminate each other; things that previously looked much the same now are differentiated through the new concepts which the person has acquired.

TIR and related metapsychology techniques consist of a very wide palette of styles and technique types, for a broader overview on which see Volkman (2003), and French and Malnati (2002).

Most of the theories behind these techniques relate to an extensive phenomenology of entities chosen for their commonality with all human experience, and therefore fit into any internal frame of reference. For example, all human beings spot similarities and differences between separate phenomena. A client can therefore be asked to explore these similarities and differences, without anything being suggested about the nature and content of the client's world. For a full description of this phenomenology, see Gerbode (1995).

Here I examine those methods that most clearly operationalise the work of Rogers. Before doing so, however, it is useful to mention the most common technique type within TIR and metapsychology practice.

Unlayering

'Unlayering' techniques consist of repetitive questions or instructions that are asked as long as the client is interested and feels the repetitive process is likely to be of use. This is usually continued until the client makes some kind of clear experiential shift in her mental environment. All unlayering techniques are applied within the framework of the eight communication exercise, and the 13 rules of facilitation (see Appendix 1). Repetition, advocated by Raimy (1975), is a useful way of intensifying and operationalising whatever a training considers therapeutic in a therapy session. This is of particular relevance to brief therapy, if one considers that the presence of certain therapeutic conditions facilitates a more efficient form of therapy. Repetition is a way of bringing about those conditions more often. Gerbode and French (1992) highlight beneficial factors of the use of repetition. Here are two of them:

1   It achieves a thorough and penetrating awareness of a particular topic – if a client contemplates or experiences a private event or inner experience several times, they are likely to be more intimately aware of it than if they only look once or twice.
2   It strengthens abilities – repetitive practice enhances that ability, whether it is the ability to 'focus' as Gendlin (1978) teaches, to be mindful, or the ability to play the C major scale on a piano.

When a client understands the purpose of repetition, he or she will nearly always be happy to look at a topic over and over again in a repetitive manner, provided that new material or new experience continues to surface. Repetition gives clients the opportunity to look at old situations with newness, taking each contemplation 'as though you were looking for the first time'. Furthermore, the movement to another contemplation exercises the ability of letting go of the previous contemplation, so that another, newer viewpoint can be formulated. From the TIR viewpoint, the principle condition to operationalise is that of intimate, yet detached awareness of one's inner environment; intimate awareness disentangling the client from his thoughts and feelings. The emphasis is less on how the client relates to the therapist, and more on the client's relationship with his mental/bodily environment. The TIR client has very little attention on his therapist when he is engaged in a therapeutic exercise. Similarly, Kornfield, in his endorsement of Gendlin's (1978) book on *Focusing* notes that focusing offers a 'deep parallel to the practice of mindfulness meditation'.

The instruction 'Tell me something you can really do' is an example of a simple unlayering technique that any client may or may not find interesting to answer many times, giving a different answer each time. Doing this raises a client's awareness of his abilities. It is an ego-strengthening strategy. A cli⁻⁻⁺ ⁻ ht find 60 answers to this question in 15 to 20 minutes. This   ʼ is designed to elicit open-ended responses, and suggests very   than that the client is able to do a number of things, whi   ⁻eople if you include smaller actions, such as smiling, brea   ɘrapist and client collaboratively end such a repetitive 'unl   ʼs soon as a client feels they have made significant pro₹   lly evidenced by the emergence of insights or a posi   ʼient's emotional state, and is termed an 'end poir   ⁻een used as an indicator of change in empirical stud   1951). Again it can be left to the client to deci   ed. Working to end points is another major aspect of TIR work which maximises or accelerates progress. Ending every session at an 'up' point increases client willingness and trust in engaging in experiential therapeutic exercises. The next section examines how unlayering can be applied directly to therapeutic processes as Rogers describes them.

Rogers' process of therapeutic change

Rogers gives a detailed account of how therapeutic change manifests in a number of publications. In a chapter on 'A process conception of psychotherapy', Rogers (1958/1961) provides a seven point scale in the form of 'seven stages of process', the seventh level being the higher level at which a client may function in therapy and in life, with regard to awareness of his inner experience.

Examining the lower levels of Rogers' seven stages of process brings to light some of the more difficult situations in which therapists find their clients. Conversely, Rogers' higher levels of therapeutic process highlight positive qualities in clients that make a therapist's job much easier. Towards the end of his chapter, Rogers (p. 156) states that: 'It would occur very rarely, if ever, that a client who fully exemplified stage one would move to a point where he fully exemplified stage seven. If this did occur, it would involve a matter of years'.

Applied Metapsychology has been developed to facilitate precisely such large shifts within a relatively short period of time, i.e. one to two years, using an extensive programme of exercises or techniques known as the metapsychology curriculum. Some of these techniques are found in TIR treatment plans for case preparation.

In his paper, Rogers acknowledges that clients who are in the lower stages of processing ability are likely to make slower progress than those in a higher stage of process. One can argue therefore that 'brief therapists' with modern time pressures are likely to wish that clients in stage one, two or three were able to (at least temporarily) develop the qualities found in clients at stages five, six or seven. In theory, this can be done by asking clients, remaining within their own experiential tracks, to exercise these abilities directly. I now examine how this is done in TIR and metapsychology practice.

Tudor and Worrall (2006) have further developed Rogers' process conception, placing more emphasis on elements of process than the stages of process. This is useful and more comprehensive in that the seven principle elements Rogers mentions, are, according to Tudor and Worrall, present or absent in all stages of process. Examining Tudor and Worrall's expanded version of Rogers' conception of therapeutic process, I give examples of how TIR/Applied Metapsychology techniques can be used to exercise the seven elements of process that Rogers distinguishes in his seven stages.

A loosening of feelings

In their expanded table of Rogers' seven stages of process, Tudor and Worrall (2006, p. 259) first address the element of 'A loosening of feelings' in terms of a continuum: 'From a process of experiencing a continually changing flow of feelings … to remote, unowned feelings, not present'. If an inability to experience or 'own' one's feelings is perceived in a client, there are many exercises that could be applied to address this directly, whilst remaining within the client's frame of reference and interest.

The basic TIR technique is a form of regression done completely within the client's experiential track, in the absence of judgement. Repetitive re-experiencing of a past incident, positive or negative, is often successful at raising the client's ownership of her experience. The majority of questions in this regression technique ask for details of the incident that are universal to any incident, for example: 'Where were you at the time?' as all incidents have to occur somewhere. If the client either doesn't know the answers or only has vague answers to these questions, this is not a problem: any answer, no matter how vague is accepted as fine. There is, however, a question in this technique that could be described as theory-driven. That is: 'Is there an earlier similar incident?' This question is based on the theory that earlier incidents can be associated with, and affect later incidents. However, this question is only asked when the client gets stuck with an unchanging experiential process, and does not spontaneously find other inner experience that he is able to process.

If a client still describes the incident from a dissociated viewpoint and considers he is not making progress, a client can be gently encouraged to connect with his feelings by asking a question such as 'How did you react at the time?', 'What were you feeling at the time?', 'Did you express it?' and 'How?' (Bisbey cited in Volkman, 2003, p. 12). Clients may also access more distant incidents by getting them to express in the present what they did not express at the time of the incident (French and Malnati, 2002):

Therapist (T):	If you had expressed that anger to her at the time of the incident, what would you have said exactly?
Client (C):	I would have said that I hated her. [Here the client did not do exactly as asked but this would not be pointed out to the client.]
T:	Thank you. [The therapist still receives the client with unconditional positive regard, as though everything the client did was perfect, and simply asks the client again.] How would you have said that if you had said it at the time of the incident?
C:	I would have said: 'I hate you'. [The client is still not connecting with his experience at this point.]
T:	Thank you. Just as an exercise, I'll ask you to say that a number of times if that's OK with you?
C:	OK.
T:	OK. Say that again.
C:	I hate you.
T:	Thank you. Say that again.
C:	I hate you! [Emotion begins to surface.]

This would be done until any emotion that surfaced had then dissipated. The client could then systematically do this for any other emotions or other inner experiences that he had at the time, as long as he feels the exercise is worthwhile. After a certain amount of this, experience has shown that clients often then become able to regress into the incident. The theory behind this is that some clients may not feel able to experience certain inner events due to the amount of emotional charge (fear, anger, upset) connected to the experience. For the client to reduce the emotional charge by initially using a lighter or less demanding way of facing it, in turn, enables a client to look more fully at an experience. This is an example of applying the principle of a gradient of 'viewing' actions (Volkman, 2003). The principle of facing inner experience gradiently is thoroughly applied in TIR and metapsychology practice.

A change in the manner of experiencing

The next of the seven elements, Tudor and Worrall (op cit., p. 260) define as the continuum which goes: 'From living freely and acceptantly in a fluidity of experiencing … to a fixity and remoteness of experiencing'. More specifically, Rogers (1958/1961, p. 134), in his second stage of process, states that: 'experiencing is bound by the structure of the past'.

From the TIR point of view, all unlayering methods are designed to create an experiential opportunity for movement from one structure to another, within the client's unique experiential track, and in the absence of suggestions or judgement that could influence the client. As a client regularly experiences this he will realise without any suggestions from the therapist that his viewpoints can change significantly.

The techniques described in response to 'a loosening of feelings' (above) would also apply to a loosening of experiencing. Here is an example of an unlayering technique that can directly address the ability to experience any area of experiencing that the client deems problematic.

If a client believes that he or she has difficulty with experiencing emotions, a TIR practitioner is likely to offer the use of a technique known as Unblocking. Unblocking is a theory-driven technique that can be used within the client's experiential track. The client is first asked to explore at some length what the area of concern is. Following this exploration, the client is asked repetitive questions as to whether there has been any: suppression, judgement, avoidance, distancing from or other forms of mental defence, relating to the assessed area. Bisbey and Bisbey (1998) present a list of 60 such concepts for use in unblocking lists. Here is a short example of using such a technique:

T: Regarding 'your emotions', has a judgement been made?
C: Yes, I don't like them, they are so upsetting.
T: Thank you. Regarding 'your emotions', has a judgement been made? [This is repeated with genuine interest, as though it is the first time the question is being used.]
C: I can't bear the fear, I lose all sense of myself. [This same question would be asked repetitively until either there were no more answers or until there is an insight. Then the next question would be asked repetitively, such as: 'Regarding "your emotions", has anything been disregarded?']

Such a method is an effective way of enabling a client to disentangle themselves from their mental barriers to awareness. The concepts used are all common ways in which human beings stop themselves from being fully aware of their experience. A thorough awareness of this avoidance, paradoxically reconnects the client in a detached, yet intimate way to his experience.

Constructs

Tudor and Worrall (2006, p. 261) describe a seven staged continuum relating to constructs thus: 'From developing constructions which are modifiable by each new experience … to construing experience in rigid ways'. Again, from his description of the second stage of process, Rogers (1958/1961, p. 134) specifically states that: 'Personal constructs are rigid, and unrecognised as being constructs … "I can't ever do anything right"'.

From the point of view of ability, a term often used in TIR and metapsychology, the creation of any belief or construct is something the client does whether he realises it or not. This ability can be exercised so that the client is more in touch with how she or he makes constructs. Simply, the therapist asks the client repetitively to create the construct that he has already created, but purposefully. For example:

T: You mentioned that you 'can't ever do anything right'. Would you be interested in having a look at that?
C: Sure.
T: OK, I'm going to ask you to imagine, just for a moment, that you 'can't ever do anything right'.
C: OK, did that. That was easy.

Asking the client to create this construct under his own volition a number of times is likely to create distance as well as familiarity with what this construct really is. However, classic TIR practice would usually add another step:

T: Thank you. What would be an alternative way of seeing that idea? [Note the use of the word 'idea' here. Words like belief or construct are not used because they could be considered to be an opinion on the client's content. 'Idea' is a more neutral word.]
C: I suppose I might get things right sometimes.
T: Alright. Imagine that you 'get things right sometimes'.
C: That's difficult to imagine.
T: See if you can get it, just for a split second.
C: OK.
T: Alright. Imagine you 'can't ever do anything right'.
C: Did that.

The therapist gets the client to imagine both ideas one after each other repetitively. The client is likely to have an experiential shift in relation to both ideas after completing just a couple of minutes of this exercise. Some clients may take longer if they are heavily burdened with many worries and concerns, or are at a low stage of process. Techniques in TIR are also graded in terms of how much ego strength they require. Therefore, a TIR therapist will choose techniques that a client at stage two or three will find easy enough to do, before offering more demanding exercises. In TIR, this is known as 'case preparation'. With regard to working with clients at this stage Rogers (1958/1961, p. 134) states that: 'we have a very modest degree of success in working with them'. The use of these very targeted strategies is a way of achieving a higher degree of success with this client type.

The individual's relationship to their problems

Tudor and Worrall (2006, p. 262) describe this as: 'From living problems subjectively, and being responsible for their part in the development of problems ... to problems being unrecognised (and, therefore, the individual having no desire to change)'. Rogers (1958/1961, p. 133) specifically states that, with regard to problems, at stage two: 'There is no sense of personal responsibility in problems'. The ability to take responsibility for problems can be exercised experientially with the following two repetitive questions:

T: Tell me a problem you have had with ... [insert area of concern].
C: My boss thinks I'm stupid.
T: Thank you. Tell me a part of that problem for which you might have been responsible.
C: I suppose I have done some stupid things in front of her that might have made her see me that way.
T: Alright. Tell me a problem you have had with ... [insert same area of concern].

The two questions are repeated in a loop until an end point, or positive experiential shift evidences as experienced by the client.

The metapsychology curriculum for clients, exercises the general ability to take responsibility for problems. An extensive battery of such techniques are employed, that focus on a client's relationship to problems from a range of perspectives. These perspectives are chosen for their universality to all people. Just as metapsychology theory considers 'problems' as universal to human experience, so are: facing problems, solving problems, using unworkable and workable solutions to problems, comparing problems and communicating about problems. These are some of the perspectives from which a client can examine her relationship to problems, generally.

Communication

Tudor and Worrall (2006, p. 261) describe this element in terms of a continuum: 'From a willingness to communicate a changing awareness of internal experiencing ... to an unwillingness to communicate' and give the example: *'I'm OK, really, and even if I were not I'm not sure what good it would do to talk about it'*. The willingness to communicate self in the context of a therapeutic relationship can be exercised or explored thus:

T: What would it be safe for you to tell me about yourself?
C: It would be okay to tell you about my car.
T: Thank you. Who could you tell me about that exactly?

C: Umm ... it's red.
T: Thank you. What would it be safe to tell me about yourself?

As the client experiences himself received unconditionally by the therapist, whatever he reveals about himself to the therapist, he becomes increasingly comfortable, and reveals more and more. A client that was not ready to answer questions directly about self, could be asked a less directive set of questions such as: (1) Recall a time you communicated to another, (2) Recall a time you didn't communicate to another (asked repetitively 1, 2, 1, 2, 1, etc. until an endpoint manifests). I argue these are less directive in that they do not focus on a particular topic such as self. Some clients may therefore find these easier to answer than the previous set. After completing lighter exercises, clients tend to feel safer and become able to address more challenging issues.

Congruence

This element describes a process from congruence ... to incongruence. The type of incongruence to which Rogers refers in his conception of therapeutic process is an incongruence between the self as perceived, and his organismic experiencing, that is, a discrepancy between how one sees oneself, and how one actually is. As we saw earlier, most TIR methods actually avoid pointing out such discrepancies directly to the client. The emphasis is on letting the client awake to these incongruences, of her own accord, through the practice of repetitive awareness-expanding exercises. Within the coaching methods of metapsychology, as distinct from the repetitive focusing of awareness exercises, hitherto presented, one finds methods that engage the client in defining her values, and then comparing these values to her actual behaviours. For example, a client may realise he has the value of 'living healthily' and yet have the behaviour of smoking 10 cigarettes a day. Clients with more burdened cases may find it easier to focus on external entities, than more subtle inner phenomena. Such metapsychology coaching may therefore be particularly appropriate to clients at lower stages of process. Some clients may benefit from the following two-part unlayering technique, asked in a 1, 2, 1, 2, loop:

T: How have you perceived yourself?
C: Hardworking.
T: Thank you. How has another perceived you?
C: Struggling to get the job done.

The individual's manner of relating

The final element that Tudor and Worrall (2006, p. 262) isolate in Rogers' (1958/1961) conception of therapeutic process is that of relating. They define the continuum across the seven stages: 'From living openly and freely in relation to others … to avoiding close relationships'. A client's awareness can be directly focused on how they relate thus:

T: Tell me who I am in relation to you.
C: You're the guy my doctor referred me to.
T: Thank you. Tell me how you have related to another.
C: I feel my mother understood me sometimes.
T: Alright. Tell me who I am in relation to you.
C: You seem to be someone who it is safe to talk to.

If a client avoids close relationships, the TIR practitioner is likely to ask the client to explore any inner experiences the client has (such as unwanted emotions), that surface in response to close relationships. The unblocking technique (described earlier) is also regularly used to address 'relationships'.

Final discussion and conclusions

A magician, who knows many tricks, may still be unconvincing if his basic presentation is not well-tuned. In learning anything, it may be useful to make a distinction between basic qualities that enhance success, and models or structures that clarify, or help teach when and how the trainee practitioner actually responds in the moment, even if such structures merely serve as initial stabilisers to prevent the inexperienced trainee from making mistakes. *Both* being and doing can be addressed in a counselling training programme. Most activities can be broken down into a number of parts, some of which may have a sequential relationship. For example, in the Basic TIR regression technique, the theory-centred question: 'Is there an earlier similar incident?' is only asked after a client's own process of change has become fixed and unchanging.

In this chapter, I have described TIR and related metapsychology techniques as an experiential person-centred therapy which has much in common with focusing-oriented therapy. I also examined a range of defined methods or structures used: (1) to intensify the client's natural therapeutic process with repetition; a repetitive process as an accelerated and more thorough process; (2) to redirect the client's process when it has become stuck; and (3) to strengthen specific mental faculties of the client, such as the ability to make and let go of constructs, particularly when an absence of such an ability is a barrier to change. In the second half of this chapter, we examined a range of techniques that were chosen in response to specific process elements, as described by Rogers. This has partially described the broad palette of methods that form TIR and related metapsychology techniques. Humanistic therapists often frown upon structured techniques, seeing them a bit like the inflexible bureaucratic procedures that hold an impersonal corporation together. However, I have argued that techniques need not be that way and that client-responsive person-centred techniques are both possible and effective.

Flexible precision tools can elegantly match the issue they were designed to address, and also respond momentarily to a unique process. Note that these 'tools' still honour person-centred values because they are handed tentatively to the client for the client to use, in a very transparent and non-manipulative way. They are not 'done to' the client, they are invitations that the client may or may not take up. They exercise the client's self-actualising tendency in a structured way.

To continue the analogy of a wide 'palette' of tools, one can argue that the wider the therapist's pallet is, the more precise he can be in matching a tool to the momentary situation. Modern computerised paint palettes can analyse the constituent primary colours of any of thousands of colours, and then immediately mix that colour with precision. Perhaps modern therapy tools sets could respond similarly to specific client variables. These variables would be both qualitative and quantitative, such as the client's stage of process, ego strength, and his or her viewpoint or conceptualisation of the issue. In addition, a methodology for unblocking clients' unique barriers to therapeutic change is also likely to increase the number of client populations we can help. Most of the structured 'techniques' that are referred to in this chapter are likely to be compatible with FOT. Some may be palatable to person-centred therapists, such as the structures that do not obviously present any particular theory. Either way, TIR and related techniques offer methods of working that honour the client's unique, self-directing process and yet also facilitate therapeutic change within a short time frame.

References

Coghlan, D. and McIlduff, E. (1990) 'Structuring and non-directiveness in group facilitation', *Person-Centered Review*, 5(1): 13–29.

Coughlin, W. (1995) *Traumatic Incident Reduction: Efficacy in Reducing Anxiety Symptomatology*. Unpublished doctoral dissertation, Union Institute, Cincinnati, OH.

Bisbey, L. (1995) *No Longer a Victim: A Treatment Outcome Study of Crime Victims with Post-Traumatic Stress Disorder*. Unpublished doctoral dissertation, California School of Professional Psychology, San Diego, CA.

Bisbey, S. and Bisbey L.B. (1998) *Brief Therapy for PTSD: Traumatic Incident Reduction and Related Techniques*. Chichester, UK: John Wiley & Sons.

Figley, C.R. and Carbonell, J (1999) A systematic clinical demonstration of promising PTSD treatment approach, Florida State University. *Traumatology*, 5:1 Article 4.

French, G.D. and Malnati, R. (2002) *Traumatic Incident Reduction for Case-Planning and Life Stress Reduction: A Training Manual*. Menlo Park, CA: IRM Press.

Gendlin, E.T. (1964) 'Schizophrenia: Problems and methods of psychotherapy', *Review of Existential Psychology and Psychiatry*, 4(2): 168–79.

Gendlin, E.T. (1978) *Focusing: How to Gain Direct Access to Your Body's Knowledge*. London: Rider Books.

Gendlin, E.T. (1996) *Focusing-Oriented Psychotherapy: A Manual of the Experiential Method*. New York: Guilford Press.

Gerbode, F.A. (1995) *Beyond Psychology: An Introduction to Metapsychology* (3rd edn). Menlo Park, CA: IRM Press.

Gerbode, F.A. and French G.D. (1992) *Traumatic Incident Reduction Workshop Manual*. Menlo Park, CA: IRM Press.

Purton, C. (2004) 'Focusing-oriented therapy', in P. Sanders (ed.), *The Tribes of the Person-Centred Nation: An Introduction to the Schools of Therapy Related to the Person-Centred Approach* (pp. 45–66). Ross-on-Wye: PCCS Books.

Raimy, V. (1975) *Misunderstandings of the Self*. San Francisco, CA: Jossey-Bass Publishers.

Rogers, C.R. (1951) *Client-Centered Therapy*. London: Constable.

Rogers, C.R. (1957) 'The necessary and sufficient conditions for therapeutic personality change', *Journal of Consulting Psychology*, 21: 95–103.

Rogers, C.R. (1961) 'A process conception of psychotherapy', in *On Becoming a Person: A Therapist's View of Psychotherapy* (pp. 125-62). Boston, MA: Houghton Miflin. (Original work published 1958).

Rogers, C.R. (1970) *Encounter Groups*. Harmondsworth: Penguin.

Tudor, K. and Worrall, M. (2006) *Person-Centred Therapy: A Clinical Philosophy*. London: Routledge.

Valentine, P.V. (1997) *Traumatic Incident Reduction: Brief Treatment of Trauma-Related Symptoms in Incarcerated Females*. Unpublished doctoral dissertation, Florida State University, Tallahassee, Florida.

Volkman, M.K. (2003) *Traumatic Incident Reduction – Expanded Applications Workshop Manual* (rev. edn). Kansas City, KN: AMI Press.

PART II
PRACTICE IN CONTEXT

5

Time-Limited, Client-Centered Psychotherapy: One Case[1]

Madge K. Lewis, Carl R. Rogers and John M. Shlien[2]

Introductory comments by Carl R. Rogers

It is a privilege to be invited to introduce these two cases, each representative of client-centered therapy, and each dealt with by an experienced therapist. I will make some comments about the process of change in these clients, and some comments about the therapists, which may give more meaning to the case material which follows.

Client-centered psychotherapy: The process in the clients

In one sense I approached this material in exactly the same manner as the reader of this chapter. I knew nothing of the clients here described – Mrs. Teral [and Mr. Tapa] (pseudonyms, of course) – or of their therapy. Yet, as I read the accounts of the course of their interviews I found all of the phenomena which have gradually come to stand out in my experience as evidences of therapeutic movement. In each of these clients, certain characteristic trends occur. Let me list a number of them.

> The client moves from guessing what his feelings are, to remembering them in the past, to experiencing them fully in the immediacy of the therapeutic moment.
> He moves from fearing and defending himself against his feelings, to letting these feelings *be* and exist, acceptedly, in him.
> He moves from a role relationship (a 'client' in relation to a 'therapist') to a real relationship (person to person).

---

[1]For reasons of space I have only included one of the original two cases; the other case was the report by Lewis of a longer piece of work, over 38 sessions. Apart from this, the chapter has been reproduced with its original spelling, footnotes, and conventions regarding references.

[2]The authors are indebted to the Wieboldt Foundation for generous support of research in its early phase. Further analysis is made possible by the grant of the Ford Foundation (Psychotherapy Research Program) to the Counseling Center, University of Chicago.

He moves from living by values introjected from others to values which are experienced in himself in the present.

From existing only to satisfy the expectations of others, and living only in their eyes and in their opinions, he moves toward being a person in his own right, with feelings, aims, ideas of his own.

From being driven and compelled, he moves toward the making of responsible choices.

From poor communication within himself – being out of touch with some aspects of his experience – he moves toward free inner communication, a greater awareness of what is going on from moment to moment within.

Likewise he moves from poor communication with others to freer, more real, and direct communication.

He moves from a distrust of the spontaneous and unconscious aspects of himself to a basic trust of his experiencing, of his organism as a sound instrument for encountering life.

He moves from rigidity and defensiveness to an inner flow of experiencing in the moment.

From behavior which is at odds with what he consciously desires, he moves toward behavior which is an integrated expression of a more integrated self.

Each of these clients, in my estimation, illustrates in specific fashion each of these trends … This material will repay very careful study.

It is of interest to me that though each of these clients was limited in the hours he could spend in therapy, as is explained by Dr. Shlien, the process in each seems *very* similar to that in unlimited therapy, except that certain aspects become intensified.

The attitudes of the therapists

In reading the client material, I am, as I stated, in the same position as any reader. In regard to the therapist responses I am in a very different position, since I have known each of these therapists for a number of years. I believe that a few comments about each of them – which *they* cannot very well make about themselves – may give more meaning to the recorded client–therapist interchanges.

These are most assuredly not therapists who are using the *techniques* of client-centered therapy. They are therapists whose own attitudes are such that a client-centered orientation is a natural and congenial expression of their own genuine attitudes. Let me be more specific.

Dr. Shlien, in his relationship to his client, seems to me to feel a deep interest, and a thorough-going confidence in the client that rarely wavers even when the going is roughest. He accepts the client as he is. He feels a tenderness or even compassion (in its literal sense of feeling with) toward the client in his struggle to meet life …

Both of these therapists are very warm individuals in their therapeutic relationships, Dr. Shlien perhaps more openly so, but both with a genuine human concern for the other person.

As individuals, aside from therapy, each has his own difficulties, tensions, achievements, and failures, his own satisfactions, fulfillments, and disappointments. In short, they are very human, but in therapy their humanity exhibits itself much as I have tried to describe.

I have given this personal sketch because I believe it will enable the reader to gain a much more accurate picture of the relationships … It occurs quite frequently in each of these cases, that the counselor is so deeply involved in the relationship that he speaks from *within* the client's world, not as an outsider.

All this description, however, is but a poor substitute for the raw material of therapy. Let us permit the therapists and their clients to speak for themselves.

Case I   Mrs. Teral: A case of brief, time-limited, client-centered therapy – John M. Shlien

There is no special 'strategy' in typical client-centered therapy. There is only the general effort to provide a steady empathic understanding of the feelings and perceptions of the client (and this is no small thing if it can be achieved). The specific elements of this therapeutic behavior have recently been given a specific statement by Rogers.[3]

This is not quite a typical case. There is no special strategy, but there is a special structure, one which is a radical departure from customary procedure. Usually, the client determines the general course of therapy, the pace, and the point at which he wishes to terminate. This has been an effective policy, one in keeping with our over-all philosophy. In the present case, the termination is set in advance. The client was offered a maximum of 20 interviews, at the suggested rate of two per week, to terminate at the end of 10 weeks. She was told, truly, that this limit was imposed because of the practical necessity to meet our long waiting list. This client was the first of many who were offered therapy under one of three conditions: (a) a maximum of 20 interviews; (b) a maximum of 40 interviews, with a 10-week 'vacation' after the first 20 sessions; (c) without limits, to terminate voluntarily. A case from the second group is included in this volume.[4] A case, 'Mrs. Oak', from the third group

---

[3]Rogers, C.R. (1957) 'The Necessary and Sufficient Conditions of Therapy', *Journal of Consulting Psychology*, 21: 95–103.

[4]The case of Mr. Tapa, reported by Madge K. Lewis.

is described in another volume.[5] The over-all design of this research, and its purposes, are described elsewhere.[6] It is enough to say here that the basic aim is to evaluate and compare time-limited cases, longer and shorter, with unlimited cases, longer and shorter. Mrs. Teral, though she did not know it, was the first person offered therapy under the first research condition.

Some theoretical considerations

There is more to the background of this research than the need to provide service for more people. A long and controversial history of opinion on termination contains some profound theoretical problems. Can the 'end' of therapy be advanced in time? What is the end? When is the end? Is there ever an end? Can termination be more than an accidental point in time coinciding with the decision to stop?

Otto Rank was the first exponent of end-setting. He chose to limit time mainly because it was so opportune and unavoidable an issue with which to mobilize the patient's will. Students and interpreters of Rank have stated that the practice of end-setting has connections with Rank's theory of birth trauma and separation anxiety, though Rank himself seems less interested in time than in limits, and would have challenged the will by 'forbidding the patient certain foods, smoking, or sexual activity', had not time seemed a more generally applicable category.[7]

Freud wrote of his experiment in setting an advance termination and called it 'a blackmailing device'. He believed it would be effective in overcoming certain resistance, but would at the same time drive important material underground, where it would be 'lost to our therapeutic efforts'.[8]

Rogers has taken the position that time limits are valuable for two reasons: (1) They furnish an aspect of reality to which the client must adjust. (2) They enable the counselor to function in a more open and responsive way, such as he could not do if he were bound to the therapeutic session for an unlimited period.[9] Rogers has spoken in favor of time limits only

[5]Rogers, C.R. (1954) 'The Case of Mrs. Oak: A research analysis', in C.R. Rogers and R.F. Dymond, (eds), *Psychotherapy and Personality Change* Chicago: University of Chicago Press.

[6]Shlien, J.M. 'An experimental investigation of time-limited therapy: Practical value and theoretical limitations', *Journal of Counseling Psychology*, in press. [Ed- This was Published in 1957 – see Introduction.]

[7]Rank, O. (1936) *Will Therapy* New York: Alfred A. Knopf, Inc.

[8]Freud, S. (1950) 'Analysis terminable and interminable', in *Collected Papers, Vol. V.* London: Hogarth Press, 316–57.

[9]Rogers, C.R. (1942) *Counseling and Psychotherapy* New York: Houghton Mifflin Company.

for the period of the appointment, not the duration of therapy, however. That, he believed, should be left to the client.[10]

More than anyone else, Rank's student and translator, Jessie Taft, has developed the theoretical significance of time-limits, which she calls 'one of the most valuable tools ever introduced into therapy'. She argues that time is supremely representative of all limitations in living. Her emphasis on the *quality* of therapy, as contrasted with the quantity, led to her famous statement on the 'single contact', in which she points out that unless the therapeutic quality is present, no amount of therapy will help; it cannot be time that heals, but a process taking place in time. Perhaps, then, to eliminate the reliance on time will heighten the quality of the process.

That process is more than a means to an end. *The process is a criterion in itself,* for it means that the individual is learning to come to terms with time, his lifetime, and his limitations. Insofar as he can use the given hour, from beginning to end, knowing that it cannot last forever, yet has all the value he can put into it, to that extent he has 'learned to live, to accept this fragment of time in and for itself, and strange as it may seem, if he can live this hour he has in his grasp the secret of all hours, he has conquered life and time for the moment and in principle'.[11] The writer, and many colleagues on the staff, were deeply influenced by the writings of Taft. It is in this context that Mrs. Teral's case is presented.

The Client

Mrs. Teral came to the Counseling Center after months of hesitation. In a preliminary interview, she agreed to participate in the research. She was 23 years of age, married to a young lawyer, and was herself employed as a grade school teacher. Why did she come for help? At first, she could not express herself. With trembling fingers, she tried several times to light a cigarette. The counselor said, 'Feeling awfully scared?' She nodded, looked determined, and said (as do many clients), 'What do you want to know about me?' When the counselor said he was ready to hear whatever she wanted to talk about, she began with information about her age, her job and its location, her education, and so forth. Then she began to talk about her 'problem'. They began simply and built up to a poignant crescendo.

First: I want to give up smoking. (It makes me nervous, I feel a slave to it, etc.)

---

[10]The opinions given are now 15 years old. It is worth noting that Rogers, while still holding that all limits are a function of the counselor's needs, was active and helpful in planning and carrying out this experiment.

[11]Taft, J. (1933) *Dynamics of Therapy in a Controlled Relationship.* New York: Macmillan Company.

Second: I can't read. Need to read, need to learn, want to know things, be a knowing person, but look at the same page for an hour. I don't know *what* makes me that way.

Third: I sleep all the time. I hate to wake up, and whenever I dare, I crawl into bed and sleep.

Fourth: I can't work. Can't clean the house, never finish anything, hate to start anything.

Fifth: I feel so worthless. Why should I even bathe? What difference does it make? If other people didn't insist, I wouldn't bother to keep myself clean.

Sixth: *[crying]* I don't know who I am, or what I am – I don't know if I'm beautiful or ugly. I just don't *know*. I have no idea.

In this initial interview, she ran the gamut from the usual 'presenting problems' (how can I stop smoking, lose weight, recover my wife, learn to study, choose a profession, etc.) to the basic, ultimate questions every human being in trouble asks of himself: Who am I? What am I? What am I to think of myself?

Early interviews

In the second interview, the client looked back at her early life, considered her family and school experiences, and *guessed* at how she must have felt – 'I must have been afraid, I guess I was shy'.

In the third interview, the client still looked back, specifically at her relation to her parents and sisters during childhood, this time *remembering* her feelings. After the interview, she took the appointment slip offered to her and looked at it silently for a minute. She said, 'I still can't believe that you are willing to see me again. How can I be worth your time?'

In the fourth interview, she began to report recent events, and intense feelings *experienced* in connection with them. Her sister blamed her for spoiling an occasion they had shared and the parents sided with her sister.

C 3:   Oh! And when ... that's all I needed. They kept repeating this about two or three times. And we took my folks home and I blew. I haven't spoken to my parents the way I did since ... for a long time. But I said ... I really blew up then and I said, 'If you're going to', ... I said, 'you can blame me for what I do, but don't blame me for what someone else does. She's old enough to make up her own, mind ...' Well, I was really ... it hit me down deep. And afterwards I told *[husband]* that if I was searching for a way to find out about the past, that did it, cause that just ... that knocked right down into me. Because to me it wasn't just a little insignificant thing, but it typified *every* thing that had been done in my lifetime in my parents' attitudes toward my sister and me. It really got down in there.

T 3:   That really struck so deeply it just brought out all the things you've been feeling now. You really *blew*.

C 4:   Oh boy! And to me it ... I mean my parents just going right along with her ... I mean, she's old enough to make up her mind what she wants to do. And to come down and say a thing like that – that really annoyed me. But for that I could pass it off as ignorance. I said, 'Don't blame me; you did what you wanted to do'. And to her … I told her that. Then my parents started with this business of, see? If you would have gone up there [*sister*] would have done it. And this is it; my sister's word was always it.

T 4:   That's … that's how it's been – that's the end, huh?

C 5:   I mean, my sister's word – whatever she did – went. And this feeling that came into me was just the feeling that I remember as a kid. That sometimes I remember feeling, 'I'm right, *I know* I'm right'. And yet they would just … they would always see her.

T 5:   And this is exactly what I've been through so many times before.

C 6:   Absolutely. I just … 'cause the feeling just welled inside of me. I hadn't felt this because the occasion hasn't … has never come up before since I've, you know, been at home … since I was at home and since I was … and this was the first time something like that happened. And it brought back all those feelings – that constant feeling that was within me. I just … I said to [*husband*] afterwards, I said, 'I'm glad it happened because it gave me a really … a good chance to see'. I mean, I was saying it before, but this time I really felt it. And is it any wonder that I felt so darn lousy when this was the way it was, that they would … they would give me … they did me a dirty deal plenty of times. And conversely, I was no angel about it; I realize that. But …

T 6:   And this is it. This is just what I've been talking about, and no wonder I've been feeling so lousy because look how they treated me. And I've … I'm no wonderful person in reaction to that kind of treatment.

C 7:   That's right.

Mrs. Teral had begun to be aware of her emotions, to express them, and to understand her experience – even to take responsibility for her part in it. Next she declared that she had been denied the chance to think independently.

C 16:   There was no need for me to make decisions. All my decisions were automatically made for me. My parents made them in the home … My mother made them in the home, my sister made them outside. There never … there was no room for my own opinions, there was no room for me to learn to think. There was no room for me to experiment and …

T 16:   So you're saying, *of course*, I never learned to have my own opinions. There just wasn't any chance.

She described a choice now facing her as a test.

C 33:   Um-hm. So I don't know what I'll do. [*Slight pause.*] I usually do wait till the last possible moment and then make a quick decision. [*Laughs.*] One way or the other.

T 33:   You're kind of saying you won't handle it very well.

C 34:   No, I won't; that's right. I'll do it the way I usually do it. Slip-shod. [*Pause; sighs.*] Could I use a cigarette now, oh! [*Trembling.*]

T 34:   Right this minute, that is just what you would want.

C 35:   [*Sighs; tears; pause.*] I guess I'm upset now. [*Sighs; pause.*] Having state visitors come and visit our school tomorrow and they put up such a big show. And everyone gets very excited and … big fuss. [*Pained, stricken look.*]

T 35:   What … what's hitting you now?

C 36:   I don't know.

T 36:   Something upsetting, something that makes you feel like crying?

C 37:   [*Pause; crying softly; words lost.*] I could use a little more self control, too.

T 37:   You don't like to have to cry.

C 38:   No, I don't. [*Pause.*] And I don't know why, either. I just got very upset [*still crying.*]

T 38:   Um-hm. Something just came over you and you really don't know what started it.

C 39:   [*Long pause; still crying.*] I must have been getting a little too close to something – I didn't want to talk about, or something.

T 39:   You really don't know what made this happen. [*Client looks for clock.*] You've still got about fifteen minutes.

C 40:   [*Pause; still crying.*] Something hit me [*laughs*].

T 40:   Hm?

C 41:   Something hit me.

T 41:   Something hurts.

C 42:   [*Long pause.*] Here I go again. [*Pause.*] I don't know what it was. I just … I'm completely gone now. My knees are shaking all over me.

T 42:   Um-h. [*Pause.*] You don't know what started this but it's really taken hold of you. [*Pause; client crying.*] Your whole … your whole body is in a turmoil.

C 43:   I really can't concentrate on what I'm doing. All I can concentrate on is the feeling that I'm not going to smoke, I'm not going to smoke [*laughs*].

T 43:   I don't know exactly what you mean there.

C 44:   I can't even try to think what it is because I want a cigarette so bad I just have [*laughs*] to keep myself going. I'm not going to smoke, I'm not going to smoke [*laughs*].

T 44:   All your energy is just bent toward that one thing, just … to keep yourself from having a cigarette, huh?

C 45:   Yes. [*Long pause.*] I'm not very – I'm upset cause I said something about being dependent on [*husband*]. Maybe I just didn't want to start talking about that. That could be it.

T 45:   Maybe that's kind of a tender spot.

C 46:   [*Pause.*] And that's something that's closest to me – right now. It's these other things that I've been trying to get at, but things that happen today are really very important to me. [*Words lost; cries hard.*] It scares me more than …

T 46:   That's really the touchiest thing, the most frightening thing, your relation to [*husband*].

C 47:   No, the idea of bringing it up, that's most touchy because it's the most immediate thing. My parents I have … I mean …

T 47:   They're things you can look back at [*both together*] …

C 48:   Back at, yeah.

T 48:   But [*husband's*] right with you, that's …

C 49:   That's something right now.

T 49:   … closer and somehow more immediate and more risky.

Now the present had come into focus. History was left behind for the current and more upsetting relations. The relation with the therapist was touched upon, in connection with time.

C 52:   [Laughs.] I mean, it didn't seem so to me, but now it … I guess now it [words lost; long pause]. Maybe I'd better not waste your time just sitting here and I could come back and maybe next Saturday I'll be able to be calmed down about it. I'm all upset now.

T 52:   Maybe you shouldn't just take my time being upset and …

C 53:   And just sitting here.

T 53:   Well, I'll tell you how I feel about that.

C 54:   Okay.

T 54:   I feel that this time is your time and you can do whatever you want to. You don't have to stay, but if you just want to sit there and do nothing, that's your privilege.

C 55:   [Pause.] It won't come out [sighs].

T 55:   Um-hm. I don't … maybe one reason you felt you shouldn't stay is that you feel as if you know what the next thing is but it won't come out, so, maybe you just better creep away and come back next time. Is that …?

C 56:   [Laughs.] Yes. I … I guess so, yeah. To me, I myself don't want to deal with these other problems. Excuse me [cries].

Then she declared that the past was relatively useless though the present was most difficult to face.

C 58:   I mean I got uncomfortable there; I guess that's the thing. I've been talking about my past, and I go at talk about the present. I am what I am. No matter what it is that I … why the reason is that I am the way I am now, or how I will be in the future is … that doesn't … now I am this way. And certain things that I … that have taken place and they exist right now and they will have to come out too and that's the biggest threat to me.

Finally, she makes the first mention of her awareness of the limits.

T 60:   Well, now our time is about up.

C 61:   Okay. Thank you.

T 61:   Shall we make it [date and time]? [Pause.]

C 62:   I was thinking – only 20 sessions – you gotta make use of all of them. But, sometimes it can't be helped.

T 62:   You feel sort of that it doesn't seem like an awful lot of time or …?

C 63:   No, I mean that, seems that since there is a time limit, that you don't wanta dawdle about, and let yourself waste the time. I mean I guess it …

T 63:   I see. You mean that there's a little sense of pressure, and that's part of what's upsetting to you.

C 64:   I don't know if that's upsetting me. I mean I just said that as an after thought, that it shouldn't be wasted. But then maybe it's not wasted, so …

T 64:   Um-hm. Well, I'll see you [*day*].
C 65:   Okay. My eves all red?
T 65:   They feel all red?[12]
C 66:   Yeah, very much.
T 66:   See you. [*Client waves.*]

Excerpts from the fourth interview give some flavor of the client's mode of expression and examples of the interaction between client and counselor. Henceforth, the material is compressed into summary statements.

Fifth interview

The client expressed much interest in the counselor and in herself in relation to him. She was surprised at his casual dress, showed much concern about whether he was above her or was an equal. She was surprised at her own daring to ask such questions.

Sixth interview

She was deeply depressed and despaired of accomplishing any change. She felt inadequate in her job, and guilty about mishandling the children. She felt that there were things it would be impossible to tell the counselor, but that it was hopeless to expect help without revealing them. After a long pause, she mentioned, almost inaudibly, an itching sensation in the area of the rectum, for which a physician could find no cause.

Seventh interview

She felt much encouraged and considerably changed. She expressed surprise and satisfaction that the counselor had not tried to reassure her in her most despairing moments. She felt that she had lived through that, and continued to relate very deep fears of utter inadequacy, possibly mental deficiency, sterility, and ultimate disaster. At the end, she asked, 'What interview was this?' And she said, as if to herself, 'I think I'm going to make it'.

Tenth interview

The time between the seventh and tenth interview was a very full and complex period of development for Mrs. Feral. 'I've never had so many feelings in my life', was her first statement. She wandered in a stupor downtown until she bought a dress she felt uncertain about. Her husband

---

[12]Some more 'directive' therapists have asked, in connection with *C: 85*, 'My God, can't you even answer yes or no to *that?*' One could, but there is no point in so doing. The counselor is not needed for such information, but is much needed for understanding of the feelings about herself.

didn't like it, and she spent a sleepless night. For the first time, she became hostile toward husband, and wished she could hurt him, make him miserable – but claimed, 'he doesn't react to me. I don't matter enough, I guess'. She had stopped smoking. The itching had now moved to her fingers. She sighed, expressed the wish she could talk about sex, and asked, 'What interview is this?' Fearfully, with great embarrassment, she whispered, 'I'm bad', and described undressing games, and playing with the genitals of a little boy and later with another girl during childhood, and the scorn her sisters had directed at her ('You're dirty, no good') for these acts of masturbation. She added angrily, 'They didn't tell me that they did it too!' She dreamed of being a prostitute. Emotionally, she couldn't accept sex, couldn't read about it, and was even ashamed to buy sanitary napkins, 'because I'm just bad, dirty, that's all'. After minutes of sobbing, she expressed confusion and uncertainty – 'I want to be desired, and feel it's okay, but I'm so ashamed – am I lovable? – or desirable? Is it bad and dirty? I think I'm oversexed inside and not sexy enough outside to attract the response I want. Oh, I don't know, outside, what I am – plain or what?' Later, 'Inside, at least, I know, I'm bad or at least *sexy*. I don't know what I want to be outside, or don't want to be, *I'd like to be the same inside and out*'. Beyond her yearning for sexual comfort and satisfaction, and her confusion about it, she expressed the basic drive for congruence and integration.

Twelfth interview

She remarked that she was no longer sleeping to escape. Now when she went home in the afternoons, she took a bath, and said she 'enjoyed it'. She had found much relief in talking about sex, and decided she wasn't just *born* to be promiscuous. She mentioned that the therapist didn't seemed [sic] shocked, but wondered if he disliked her for what she had revealed. Now the itching had returned, and she wondered if it was connected with guilt about childhood masturbation. After a period of discussing affection in her family, she said she wondered if the counselor liked her, and admitted she had been afraid to come in today. She wondered if the counselor was married, and felt that if she knew more about him, he would be less threatening. 'You're a man, a good-looking man, and my whole problem is men like, you. It would he easier if you were "elderly" – easier, but not better, in the long run'. She was very upset and embarrassed after she said this, and wondered how long it took before a client could fully trust a counselor. 'It's like being naked – I'm so revealed to you, and you're so unknown to me'. Mrs. Teral had now confronted the therapist with her feelings about him in a very honest and direct way. It made her uncomfortable, but also brought relief and intimacy.

Fifteenth interview

She began by talking about time. 'It always seemed so fleeting to me. Now a minute seems like an amount in which I can get something done'. She remembered always getting up late for school, and then said: 'I feel more that I want to use time as I have it rather than waiting until I'm sure there is plenty of it. Somehow, a minute has body to it. It was a second to me. It was a 'one'. Not big enough to use. And an hour was too much. I could never do enough to use up a whole hour'. Mrs. Teral turned again to an exploration of attitudes toward sex, and 'her concept of men'. She had never seen her father naked, but once she saw a man urinating on the street; another man displayed himself on a streetcar. 'I was so shocked, and scared, I stayed home all summer'. She feared being raped, also felt suspicious of herself and her desires. It seemed that all men were bad, 'out to get you', except Dad, who almost doesn't have a penis. Later, 'I wanted to hurt myself, so I started going with men who would hurt me – with their penis. I enjoyed it, and was being hurt, so I had the satisfaction of being punished for my enjoyment at the same time'. She felt very much ashamed of her enjoyment of sex. Her two sisters, the neat, respected daughters, could not have orgasms, 'So *again* I was the bad one'. Suddenly she asked, 'Or am I really lucky?' Beauty has always been equated with goodness for her. She felt bad and saw herself as ugly. She still thought herself plain, but possibly attractive. She believed she might be likeable, but not lovable, and thought she might become promiscuous had she been more attractive. She felt that her husband did not consider her pretty and that he was holding out for the same ideal of beauty she held, which made her lot all the harder.

Eighteenth interview

The stress of impending termination was apparent. Mrs. Teral said, truculently, that she still had tremendous problems, but didn't want to talk anymore. She had gone far, she said, but not far enough. She asked for a drink of water; then asserted that she would now go home. Sarcastically she asked if that would be 'all right for the damned research'. When the counselor reflected her feeling of anger and resentment, she said she was not being honest, and wouldn't dare to be, for fear of his disapproval. 'I don't want to talk about it, I'm just running away from it. I feel like number 20349'. The counselor said, 'You feel that I don't care anything about you as a person'. Mrs. Teral replied that a teacher should never get emotionally involved with a child, since the two must separate as soon as the child graduates. 'That's what is wrong with this', she said. The counselor replied: 'You mean it's like giving you something, then taking it away – having to say good-bye before you are ready makes you feel unwanted?' 'Exactly', she said. Having been understood, Mrs. Teral asked herself, 'Do I really want more time, or do I just resent not having the choice? I know I wouldn't stop now if I didn't have to. I feel awful'. She watched the clock for a while, said our time was up, and left after saying good-bye.

Nineteenth interview

Mrs. Teral postponed her regular appointment, delaying the termination. Some important themes in the next-to-last interview are summarized:

> It upset me to miss the appointment; showed me how meaningful therapy is, how dependent I feel.
>
> Last interview, I was hurt, indignant, self-pitying. I wish I could have told you then and there.
>
> I'd like to go on, on my own. I feel that you'd take me back if I needed more help. I know not all my problems are solved, though.
>
> I have, and need to have, faith in myself.
>
> I have felt I was making headway only because I was able to talk to you.
>
> I need to know that I can make it on my own.
>
> I brought a friend in today to see about the possibility of therapy for her. I talked with my husband about things I've wanted to discuss for a long time.
>
> It might take a lot longer to work through my sexual problems completely.
>
> At first, I was so afraid I couldn't finish, I didn't dare to start.
>
> I would almost like for this to be the last interview, for I have nearly closed off things. I'm afraid to have that 'unfinished feeling'.

Mrs. Teral had been preparing herself for the separation – by talking to her husband, by considering the value of independence, by recognizing the incompleteness of her therapy, and by making plans to continue personal growth. At the same time, she hesitated to open any new areas. She showed some confidence in therapy by bringing a friend, and in the therapist by expressing the belief that he would not refuse to see her if she returned for help at a later time.

Twentieth interview

Important themes in the last interview are summarized:

> [*Enters laughing.*] I did want to come, after all.
>
> It has always been my way to say that if I can't finish something, I'll just give up. Any gains I did make, I'd just lose – felt I hadn't done anything, not even what I'd *done.* Now I've done a lot, and I have hopes that I'll be able to move forward.
>
> I think I've hit the basic things – not everything but the substance, and I feel good enough about myself that I can go on thinking *for* myself.

I see myself now as a good, worthwhile person, but still *react* sometimes with old feelings of a no-good person. Those feelings still influence me. I'm changing more slowly than I want, but I know I'll go on changing.

Last week, I was so disgusted with myself, my self-pity and sulking that I just decided to stop it. I got down and scrubbed the floors. For the first time, I'm ready in advance for company coming tonight.

I feel so delighted to have come to know myself. Will I go on learning more, alone?

I didn't force myself to come back and say I'm happy – usually I can't bear to say good-bye, I really feel this way.

I'm not subservient to you any more. If I need to come back, I have the right to ask for more time. You might not have it, but I can ask.

I'm a person, with the right to disagree with you or anyone else, and to have my own opinions.

I've been reading, and enjoying it so. Now that I have the right to make decisions, I love to read; it's worthwhile to read. The time I used to spend sleeping I now spend reading.

'Well, that's it. Time to go?' Asked Mrs. Teral at the end of the interview. 'Yes', replied the counselor, 'and I want to say that you can call me or communicate anytime, and that the door isn't being slammed behind you'. Mrs. Teral's last words were: 'If something comes up and I have to see you, I'll call'. They said good-bye.

A review

In 20 interviews Mrs. Feral had accomplished much. Early in therapy the focus moved from past to present, and soon thereafter to immediate relations with significant people, including the therapist. Even later, when she returned to recollections of sexual episodes, the main value of the hours seemed to be direct confrontation of the painful embarrassment and shame, rather than the relating of any specific experience.

The emphasis changed quickly from others and their doings to self-explorations, and also from remembered feelings to directly experienced ones. These are changes to be expected in therapy; they seemed to be accelerated in this time-limited course.

Some measures of change

Considering the presenting problems, much movement may be observed. Mrs. Feral stopped smoking midway through therapy, as a test of her will. She no longer slept to escape life. Instead, she spent the time reading (with great enjoyment), which she had been unable to do, or taking a bath, which she had formerly felt too unworthy to do. She worked more effectively than before, particularly in her home. She felt that she knew herself fairly well, with prospects of knowing still better the person she had come to be, and found that person no longer ugly, certainly not unknown, but moderately attractive, and likeable.

A follow-up interview two years after termination found all these gains maintained. Mrs. Teral said she would like to have continued therapy, but that she felt at worst interrupted rather than deprived, and at best, given a great momentum toward continued growth. Now she was so preoccupied and happy with her family (a daughter was born, ending her fears of barrenness) that she could not take time away from it, though she had a great respect for therapy as a helpful experience. Relations with her husband had been both better and worse, and certainly more intense. Indifference was no longer a problem.

Did Mrs. Teral profit according to the criterion described by Taft, learning to live in the allotted time, and using it in such a way that she may be said to have grasped the principle of living? There is evidence that to some extent she did. Her awareness of time and the limits of the treatment showed as early as the fourth interview, and again in the seventh. There, and in the tenth interview, she seemed to feel the limits as pressure. In the fifteenth interview, her attitudes toward time were those of one who could use what was available without greed or despair about the amount. In the eighteenth interview, she struggled with the problem of limitations in the relationship (separation) rather than with time. In her final interview, she seemed to be ready to say good-bye, satisfied that her experience, though incomplete, had for her the full value it deserved. To a large degree, Mrs. Teral may be said to have come to terms, by meeting the limits, with time, and with some basic problems of time and limits in life.

Of the many research instruments, one outcome measure can be reported here. That is the self-ideal correlation. The method has been described and validated in previous research.[13] Stated simply, the correlation measures the degree to which one feels himself to be a person he desires to be. The higher the correlation, the greater the degree of congruence and comfort. To illustrate the change in Mrs. Teral, her scores are compared with those of a previously mentioned case, that of Mrs. Oak, who voluntarily terminated after 40 interviews. (Both clients were rated '8' by their counselors on a nine-point scale of success.) The self-ideal correlation is administered at pretherapy, after seven interviews, at the end of therapy, and six to 12 months after termination. The clients are plotted in Figure (5.1) against a scale showing the range of self-idea correlations, so that the extent of change is easily seen and compared.

---

[13] Butler, J.M. and Haigh, G.V. (1954) 'Changes in the relation between self-concepts and ideal concepts consequent upon client-centered counseling', in C.R. Rogers and R.F. Dymond (eds.), *Psychotherapy and Personality Change* Chicago, IL: University of Chicago Press.

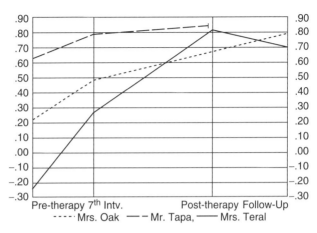

Figure 5.1   *Self-ideal correlations through therapy. For Mrs. Oak (40 interviews), Mrs. Feral (20 interviews), and Mr. Tapa (38 interviews).*

Mrs. Feral began therapy with a 'score' of −.26, a considerable disparity between her perceived self and desired self. After seven interviews, she moved to +.26, and at the end of therapy, to .82, a very high degree of congruence. Her follow-up level dropped to .70, which is not a significant decrease. Mrs. Oak started with a .21, a low level of congruence, though not so disparate as Mrs. Teral's, and moved after seven interviews to .47, and at post-therapy to .70. Her follow-up level increased to .79. Both cases were highly successful, according to this measure. Mrs. Teral achieved as much or more measured gain in half the time.

A caution

The presentation of the successful case does not intend a recommendation for arbitrarily terminated therapy. Like most innovations in therapy, this one must be thoughtfully explored for both values and flaws. Particularly, the therapist must be prepared emotionally to use this tool, for if it is imposed simply as a mechanical salvation for the overworked clinician, it may be useless, or even destructive. Used with a real acceptance of limitations on the part of the therapist, and with intelligence and good will, it may be, as it seems to have been for Mrs. Teral and her counselor, an experience to grow on.
[…]

Some measure of change

Mr. Tapa's self-idcal correlation scores are plotted in Figure (5.1) together with those of Mrs. Teral's and Mrs. Oak's. It will be noticed that Mr. Tapa's pretherapy score was .61, considerably higher than the scores of Mrs. Teral and Mrs. Oak; his post-seventh interview score .76; and his posttherapy score .84. No follow-up testing was done in this case. This represents a somewhat different pattern from that of Mrs. Oak and Mrs. Teral because the client's starting point was much higher. The trend is the same, however.

Addendum 1 – John M. Shlien

1   Optimally, what criteria do you use for accepting or rejecting patients for counseling?

Optimally – that is, when the counselor is operating with a very high degree of skill and security – the only criterion would be, 'Is this person dead or alive?' If alive, and wanting help of a psychological nature, there is no further consideration, except as scarcity of time might force a policy of 'to each according to his need'. Optimally, there is no basis for *rejecting* anyone. However, counselors seldom achieve this optimal state. Therefore, they need to ask themselves, 'Am I afraid of this person? Can I comprehend him? Do I like him well enough to commit myself to the task when the reward is dim or not forthcoming?' These questions frankly put the main limitations where they are, in the therapist, to be recognized and accepted. It is surely more therapeutic, and I think more professional, to ask these than to ask about the client, 'Is he psychotic? Can he respond to therapy?' and other such questions. The client is a candidate for therapy insofar as he wants to grow, and that is not a fixed quality. Though prognostic research is improving, and may produce useful criteria, I think that the mature therapist will always bear a large share of responsibility for the interaction which does or does not help the client.

2   Do you make a diagnosis before counseling begins?

No. Diagnostic techniques are not sufficiently valid, for one thing. Also, they do not help: if anything, they have an adverse influence on the relationship, since they tend to categorize the client in the counselor's eyes, and give the counselor an intimidating and unwarranted 'expert' status (he should be an expert, in fact, but not on that basis), and in general focus attention on artificial and impersonal issues. Finally, there is no specific treatment to be applied, so of what use would specific diagnosis be if it were accomplished? Psychotherapy is not medicine. Human misery is not an organic disease.[14]

   To clarify, diagnosis as discussed here does not mean the *judgment* exercised by the counselor at almost every step. Neither is it *prognosis,*

---

[14]No one has stated the case so well as Jung, C.E. (1954) 'The Practice of Psychotherapy', *Collected Works Vol. XVI.* New York: Pantheon Press.

which assesses the constructive resources and estimates the probability of achieving health. Diagnosis is the classical psychiatric classification and description which is static, and focused wholly on pathology. Therapy, in contradistinction, has a fluid tone and anticipates change. It will encounter the pathology ('what is wrong') but can rely only on 'what is right' with the organism.

We do indeed use measures of change in therapy, but these are for research to discover the facts about change in groups of clients, and these measures are not yet so keen as to be satisfactory for even that purpose, much less for individual diagnosis.

3 Do you attempt to persuade the patient or significant relative to change his (the patient's) environment?

No. Conceivably this might be wise and necessary, but usually the client knows it before the counselor, and would change it if he were psychologically or physically ready and able. More often, clients begin by asserting that they *must* change their environment, or have changed it many times. But it is the *internal* environment that matters most, though there are indeed life situations more strenuous than they are worth, and to tolerate such is only mock-heroism. When the external environment is clearly perceived, the client will make the best move in relation to it. The task of the therapist is to aid that perception.

4 How did you conceptualize the counselor's role in this case?

I did not. This is a question upon which I no longer dwell, certainly not as I enter into the therapeutic relation. Then my role is of no concern to me. It is almost habitual. However I may be seen: friend, enemy, mirror, doctor, judge, teacher, surgeon, authority, or fool, I have only one objective – from which it is easy to be distracted – to listen and to understand, without any prejudice whatever, the thoughts and feelings of another person. Sometimes, looking back at therapeutic experience, I feel that my role is like that of a gardener, who labors to provide the conditions for growth because it is his satisfaction to see the growing – but he knows, no matter how sophisticated a botanist or chemist, he cannot *make* the growth take place. That is up to the plant. I would also sometimes conceptualize my role as that of a child – innocent of preconceptions, trusting, and accepting even absurd distortions out of this grown mature adults. This last conceptualization will never become widespread. It offers none of the customary status satisfactions, and is quite opposite to the 'father figure' so often used to characterize the authority of the therapist. Yet I would assert that at his best a good therapist is much like a good child; a good child is a good therapist, and that in general children are by far the most therapeutic element in our culture.

5   What aspects of your theory of counseling were particularly apparent or useful in the case presented here?

In *general,* the introductory statement by Rogers answers this question very well. In *particular,* this case bears on the theory produced when Taft's question, 'If one cannot live forever, is it worth while to live at all?' is translated into terms of therapy. If one cannot continue indefinitely, is brief therapy of any use?

6   Do you feel that this case developed significant insight? If not, can improvement be maintained?

Yes, there is much evidence of that. But insight alone (understanding motives and patterns of one's behavior) does not assure improvement, much less maintenance of it. Achievement of 'insight' can become a dry and evasive exercise, or it can be a crushingly painful experience. With insight there must be an emotional acceptance of self to free one of self-conscious introspection, and allow for thought and action unhampered by preoccupation with self-analysis.

7   What aspects of your own cultural orientation facilitated or impeded the counseling of your case?

In general, I believe that therapy can transcend the powerful channels and constraints of cultural orientation, social class, sex, status, and even, to some extent, language. This is possible because, in therapy, a unique effort is made to *communicate, in one frame of reference,* without sham or defense. These communications, when achieved, constitute the most significant collaborative moments of therapy. Elsewhere in life, communication has somewhat the purpose of defending, maintaining differences, jockeying for position, sending subtle messages, etc. Were this not so, there would be no need for the specially designed and institutionalized communication of psychotherapy. While I believe this, I also recognize the existence of many aspects of cultural orientation which do operate and did influence both parties in the case, but are too complex for brief analysis.

8   If we consider that a continuum exists from superficial to deep counseling, where would you place your own case?

Moderately deep, with occasional profound moments, but not the huge and spectacular reorganization sometimes seen. At the same time, there was relatively little really superficial behavior.

*9   What did you think about the outcome of this case and what
criteria did you use for evaluating such outcome?*

Outcome, very satisfactory. The client accomplished a large part, but
not all, of her goals and developed enough momentum to carry on
productively beyond therapy. Main criteria used were the Q-sort, the
Thematic Apperception Test, and ratings by counselor and client, plus
a clinical interview two years after therapy ended. The tests were
administered immediately before and after therapy, and at two follow-
up periods, three and six months beyond post-therapy. It is interesting to
note that Mrs. Feral refused to take her second (six months) follow-up test.
She politely but firmly told the psychometrist that she had taken many tests
for us, appreciated her therapy, but was unwilling to submit to continued
examination. As a researcher one regrets the loss of data, but as a therapist
one can only revel in the new-found self-assertion of a girl who was once
so submissive and self-depreciating that she would not even take a bath for
her own sake!

10   How do you terminate counseling?

Ordinarily, in the same way we begin – by the client's expressed wish
to do so. In this case, of course, the very plan of the research called for
termination set in advance. In the light of our further experience, it would
seem that, ideally, the client should always have some considerable say
in the matter, and that if termination is set in advance, it should be by
mutual plan and agreement rather than arbitrary and unilateral decision. The
question of termination is truly a giant one; it involves decisions concerning
the whole of therapy, from a theoretical definition of ends and goals to a
development of means.
[...]

6

Working Sensitively with Time: Person-Centred Therapy in a University Counselling Service[1]

Paul McGahey

This chapter examines the relationship between the person-centred approach and time-sensitive or time-limited therapy in the context of a university counselling service. First, I introduce myself and the setting in which I work as a person-centred counsellor; next I look at the role of brief therapy in this particular counselling setting. Following this, I illustrate my work with two client vignettes; and finally I examine some of the arguments for and against brief therapy from a person-centred perspective. In this chapter, I approach the subject of brief therapy openly and critically, examining its potential strengths and limitations. As time-limited work has increasingly become the unquestioned norm in so many agencies, I reflect on the consequences of this for person-centred theory and practice. Part of my motivation in writing this chapter is to resolve or atleast clarify for myself some of the tension and confusion I sometimes experience as a practitioner with the concept of brief therapy. Also, I wonder if it is meaningful to talk about a model of person-centred brief therapy and, if so, what the philosophical and ethical implications of this might be.

The setting

I work as a counsellor, supervisor, and sometime trainer in a busy university setting in the United Kingdom. I am part of a dedicated team of counsellors who deliver a comprehensive counselling service to the students and staff of the university. I enjoy the ambience of working within a cohesive, stable team of counsellors of diverse theoretical persuasions. The day-to-day contact and close support of colleagues, with whom I can share experiences, helps me to stay grounded – and sane!

The main work of the counselling service is to provide a high-quality, professional, therapeutic service to both students and staff of the university.

---

[1] This chapter is dedicated to the memory of my mother, Kathleen Edith McGahey (1922–2007), who died just as I was completing it.

In recent years the university sector in the UK has changed beyond recognition, bringing with it huge challenges in the higher education environment. We constantly have to update our 'local' knowledge to be able to work effectively within the community we serve. One of the advantages of having a service on site is that students and staff can use it in the way that best suits their needs, as and when required. The service has an important proactive, preventative, and developmental role as well as providing a 'safety net' to catch those who fall. We are funded by the university to offer a free service to all students and members of staff who require our help. Of course, there are considerable resource implications for the university in providing and supporting such a service, which involves a significant commitment in terms of a sizeable budget, accommodation, staffing levels, and so on.

Within the wider organisation, the formal role of the counselling service is seen as preventative and educative: helping the university to develop ways of working that enable staff and students to fulfil their human and academic potential within a context of increasing demands and challenges occurring in the university sector. To this end, we have developed particular skills and sensitivity when responding to the needs of our client group within its institutional environment. The counselling service is used to the rhythms of the academic calendar of three terms or two semesters per year. There are particular times of peak demand for the service, especially around exams; these surges are predictable and can be absorbed by core and sessional staff as required. Also, there are natural breaks at the end of terms, and particularly at the end of the academic year. Again, we try to provide a consistent service, whilst dealing with these fluctuations in demand.

In addition, the counselling service performs a valuable function in providing a unique source of support for the university population as a whole. It is integrated within a comprehensive network of support, alongside other services such as the medical centre, mental health support, dyslexia support, careers service, student advice, and others. Our physical accessibility and position on campus symbolises a human and compassionate presence to which all our potential clients have recognised and legitimate access.

The role of brief therapy: Close encounters of the brief kind

Typically, the three to four years spent at university mark a period of strong developmental change for each student. It is usually a time of increasing independence and maturity: a relatively safe but crucial transition period between school and work and the fully adult world which represents that. Young people's lives change rapidly in their time at university as they mature very quickly. For many, it marks a period of new opportunities and experiences and the anticipation of what the future holds.

However, the demands and pressure of life within a contemporary academic institution can also provoke intense anxiety and distress, which sometimes results in personal crisis for some students. Universities can seem for some, initially at least, like big, impersonal, anonymous places. When a student or a member of staff is unable to make meaningful personal connections, there is a significant risk of social isolation; and feelings of loneliness, shame and failure can easily engulf the individual. Even young people who are very socially skilled can experience a confidence crisis and may seek help. Many clients we see tend to use the service when they are in some considerable distress, having suffered a setback and needing to talk to someone outside their immediate family or friendship group. They seem to value the role of the counsellor as someone who stands outside their immediate situation and who can maintain an interested but critical distance. This can help the client regain a sense of perspective when they feel too close and emotionally caught up with those around them. Many clients lack the opportunity to talk through their problems properly and seem to appreciate the time and space to be able to develop their personal stories in counselling. Unsurprisingly, many really seem to appreciate being treated with a respectful, non-pathologising attitude. Usually, with timely and sufficient support, many clients are resourceful enough to make use of the service and navigate their way safely past some problem or obstacle. I understand this to be evidence of the client's capacity to 'self-right' (Bohart and Tallman, 1999), and also of the power of the actualising tendency at work: 'All of the outcomes that we think of in regard to psychotherapy will gradually come about if the therapist can provide an affirmative facilitative climate, which permits the actualising tendency to take over and begin to develop' (Rogers, 1980/2007).

It is impossible to overstate the importance of the quality of therapeutic relationship in person-centred work. This strength and depth of relating can often be achieved quickly in the course of counselling by partners – counsellor and client – who are motivated and committed to the task. Therefore, rather than focusing only on the quantity of sessions, it is equally meaningful to focus on the *quality* of relational contact; whether this is one session or many. The quality and consistency of human contact in a person-centred relationship is, of course, absolutely crucial – if clients' feel are met and fully received in this way, it can be a powerful catalyst for change. With the help of experienced counsellors who are adept at forming strong helping relationships, clients can make very rapid progress and the work is usually highly productive. Many clients who are feeling stuck are highly resourceful in making the counselling work for them and can then manage to get on with their lives. In my experience, students rarely stay in counselling longer than is necessary, and once their immediate need is satisfied usually stop. The option to return later is available, if need be.

At this point, it is also important to emphasise that, although many clients seem to benefit from just a few sessions and can then move on in their lives, this does not describe the whole picture. Some clients, we see, come to us in such psychological distress that we make a decision to offer more intensive support, which may mean that the service provides more than a small set number of sessions of ongoing counselling. This flexibility allows us to discriminate and respond much more sensitively to the needs of each individual, especially where clients may be experiencing such states of desperation or despair that their lives may be considered at risk.

The service has, over time, developed considerable experience in terms of its responsiveness and flexibility in meeting its clients' needs. In managing our client caseload, counsellors have a policy of holding a 50/50 division between short- and longer-term work. Within the limits of what the service can offer, counsellors have considerable autonomy and latitude when using their professional judgement to decide collaboratively with clients what is in their best interests. This makes for a more discerning situation, where decisions are based on individual need and respecting of difference, not governed by the implementation of an impersonal, generic policy. We think that this is far better than treating each the same and giving them each, say, six or 10 sessions only. This ability to adapt and respond intelligently seems to work very well in our service; for the most part, though, the offer of up to six sessions seems to satisfy most of our clients' needs.

Over recent years, there has been considerable consistency in the average number of sessions per client seen. The majority of counselling contracts number around six sessions; this includes some who come for just a single session; a minority who come for the whole academic year, that is, over 30 weeks; and the rest who fall somewhere in between.

Client vignettes

The following vignettes illustrate the challenges and potential strengths of person-centred brief therapy within a university counselling service. The identities of both clients have been suitably disguised.

Sam

When Sam first came for counselling she was troubled by acute feelings of self-doubt. She would keep repeating 'I can't do it [followed by a long pause], but I can do it', like a mantra. Although she spoke in relation to her coursework, her doubt seemed to permeate her whole being and everything she did. Her quiet despair made her doubt if she could continue on the course. I also had a fear, from the way she expressed herself, that she was desperate enough and capable of harming herself. She seemed to me at first to be mentally at breaking point, and she felt such a failure that she was ready to drop out of her course. When she spoke she seemed to touch into such deep areas of vulnerability and sadness that it almost immobilised her. She described growing up and never feeling really wanted at home. Her younger sister was born soon after her, and Sam had never felt the exclusive love and attention of her mother. Consequently when her mum sent her to a neighbour to be looked after, she had felt rejected. Her feeling of alienation was so deep that as a young child she had wanted to die. By day she became skilled at pretending to be a happy child and, in bed at night, she would hold her hand over her mouth so that her family couldn't hear her sobbing. At school, children would make friends with her but she couldn't understand why – she just felt a gaping emptiness inside. She told me that since she was a child she hadn't been used to sharing her private feelings with anyone else. Although she was popular with school friends, who would confide in her, this felt one-sided as she wasn't able to talk about herself or her feelings. Deep down, she didn't believe that anyone could sincerely be interested in her. This type of relational pattern had continued into adulthood. Other people assumed everything was all right but they didn't know how she really felt: lost and lonely to the point of despair. Her extreme levels of self-doubt were so painful, and were moving to witness. The third session marked a turning point in our work together. She had missed the previous session so I had e-mailed her to see if she wanted to make another appointment. She did return and said she wasn't used to feeling important enough to have someone listen in a truly concerned and interested way. After a lifetime of keeping her feelings secret, she said that, in the first two sessions, she had felt quite exposed. Tentatively, at first, she began to explore and express her feelings, which were so painfully raw. Then gradually in the security of the counselling relationship she found the courage to begin making contact with some of her buried true feelings. Initially, the strength of those feelings frightened her and, for many of the early sessions, I witnessed her experiencing a deep emotional catharsis. Her deep sorrow seemed almost bottomless but despite my own anxiety I made no attempt to disturb or divert her from this process. By trusting her own healing process, something began to shift and slowly she emerged intact.

As she felt more secure in counselling, she seemed to enjoy the opportunity to talk and once she got started she didn't stop! Her earlier vulnerability began to disappear and, gradually, was replaced by a growing self-confidence. Within 12 sessions she had made such dramatic progress that she suddenly announced that she didn't need to come any longer. Her new-found confidence meant that she was able to take the decision to stop, and I had no doubt she would be all right.

Mark

I worked for a short time with a finalist who was on course for a first-class degree. For someone like Mark, who had very high academic expectations, the prospect of failure was unbearable. I made an assessment, and we contracted to meet for up to six sessions. Due to a family bereavement he found it difficult to concentrate and was confused and angry at both the timing of the death and with himself for not being able to focus properly on his work. It was late in the second semester and, as the exams approached, his final preparations were being disrupted. Also, he had embarked on a series of interviews with some of the best employers in his chosen profession and, after a couple of rejections, his confidence was beginning to suffer. Mark couldn't entertain the thought of failure which, in his terms, meant obtaining a 2:1 degree result. He described that, in his personal life, he was highly intolerant of others. I experienced him as opinionated and scathing in his contempt of fellow students, many of whom were dismissed as 'stupid' with such disdainful language that I found myself inwardly recoiling. Compared to *his* levels of high academic achievement everyone else lacked 'intelligence'. He hated the idea of being asked to help someone else: he saw others as intellectually weak and inferior, and was almost 'Darwinian' in his competitive belief that it was the strongest who emerged on top. He reinforced his perception with a whole series of dogmatic opinions. I found both his views and the force with which they were expressed extremely challenging. Initially, I wasn't confident that I could work with him successfully: I felt judgemental and frightened by his manner. However, to my surprise, in the safety of the counselling session he relaxed his defences and revealed another side. I found myself warming to him more than I expected, and he no longer seemed as fierce as before. In fact, I found myself beginning to like him and to respect the fact that he was so independently minded. Very quickly we formed a strong working relationship and, in the course of just four or five sessions, we achieved a level of relational depth that allowed him to explore aspects of self and experience previously ignored and unexamined. How did this happen? We didn't delve much into the past. He helped me to relate to him by inviting a more mutual type of contact that he said he wanted. He had stated at the outset that he didn't want a one-sided relationship where he had to do all the talking. I told him that I didn't work in that way: I preferred the challenge and satisfaction of entering a more mutual dialogue or encounter. By being real, following him empathically, and trying to keep in check my judgemental conditional regard, his trust in me and in the counselling process grew. His earlier apparent certainty started to dissolve: things became less 'black and white', and his need to control everything and everyone around him rigidly showed signs of weakening. If I had tried subtly to analyse or to 'guide' him in a moralistic way it wouldn't have been any use. We simply related to each other and I felt myself more and more accepting of him. I know that our relationship deepened, and the security of that therapeutic relationship allowed him to explore aspects of himself which hitherto had been undiscovered. Although initially he didn't seem very curious about himself, and didn't question his worldview at all, gradually he did become more self-questioning and more willing to be open to self-doubt. This allowed him to show more vulnerable aspects of himself, which at first hadn't been apparent. To my surprise, he seemed to trust and actually enjoy the opportunity afforded in counselling. As his personal crisis began to recede he was able to resume his studies and the counselling ended.

Brief therapy – For and against

In this part of the chapter, I examine some of the broader issues with regard to the person-centred approach (PCA) and time-limited therapies. The rise in popularity and prominence of models of brief therapy lies in the strong economic, political, ideological, and competitive forces in play that drive the trend towards making therapy more 'efficient' in terms of giving 'better' and quicker results. The various approaches to the development of brief therapy, represented by the different volumes in the series of which this book is a part, have evolved as a result of two main underlying forces. The first is the arrival of 'manual-based treatments' in the field of psychotherapy. These approaches are tested for efficacy in randomised controlled trials (RCTs), and are designed to be reproducible, and hence the importance of the manual. The second is the pressure of economic forces which is manifested in the managed care system that dominates health service delivery in the USA and, increasingly, in the UK through private sector contracts for National Health Service (NHS) services (see Milne, 2007), as a result of which there is probably going to be even more pressure to deliver therapy in less time. Another manifestation of the economic pressure is the increase in provision of therapy through insurance schemes and Employee Assistance Programmes (EAPs), whereby a specific number of sessions are funded. The approval for such funding is increasingly based on an 'evidence-based' approach to therapy. These two forces – research and economics – are not only linked but almost rely on each another for their further evolution. In the USA, many clinical trials take place within the managed care system. Here in the UK, as more psychotherapy provision becomes available for tender in the open market, the need for greater efficiency becomes almost inevitable due to the pressure of competition.

Arguments for brief therapy

Perhaps the strongest argument for time-limited therapy in a university counselling service is that, quite simply, for the majority of clients it seems to be effective. As mentioned earlier, brief therapy seems to 'work' in this context due to the particular needs of our clientele, mostly coinciding with what can reasonably be offered by the counselling service. Typically, the offer of between six to 12 sessions seems to satisfy the pressing or immediate needs of most of our clients. The explanation for this may lie in the fact that many young people do not view counselling in the first place as a long-term proposition or commitment. They come to us when something is wrong, when there is an 'interruption' in their 'functioning', or when they have a problem that they can't solve alone.

The other main argument for time-limited therapy seems to be one of pragmatism. University counselling services are not alone in trying to manage the dilemma of responding adequately to their clients' needs with finite resources. Brief therapy may be considered part of a strategy to cope with the anticipated take-up of counselling resources and, thus, a legitimate response to help balance potential demand and supply. It could be described as a form of rationing, ensuring an equitable distribution of available resources in a situation where counselling is not controlled by cost, as it is in the private sector. The adoption of a brief therapy model and system also ensures that there is a predictable turnover of clients, thereby making best use of counsellors' time and caseloads; and ensures more accurate estimates of waiting lists and times. It can also be seen as a way of managing the anxiety that a service could be overwhelmed if some such safeguards were not in place. The threat of unmanageable waiting lists is something which every service wants to avoid. In this sense, brief work could be described as a way of managing the imperfections of a system: it is the best – or least worst – solution to a situation that could feel too demanding. Put simply, it is a way of managing or economising on scarce counselling resources.

Waiting lists are a familiar and perhaps inevitable aspect of most counselling services. The waiting list functions as a temporary queuing system until a counsellor becomes available; and the goal of any service, is, of course, to minimise waiting times: a waiting list is perhaps an attempt to introduce an element of control and predictability into a system. From this viewpoint, brief therapy could be seen simply as a practical and necessary response to a very real situation of increasing client demand and limited therapeutic resources. Of course, if there is a limit to the number of sessions a service can offer, good professional practice dictates that this should be made explicit. This involves: skill and sensitivity at the assessment stage and beyond in order accurately to determine and monitor clients' needs; open communication as an integral part of the assessment process in which the client should be as informed as possible about what is on offer; and transparency of contracting.

Arguments against brief therapy

The rapid emergence and dominance of an evidence-based cognitive behavioural therapy (CBT), supported by quantitative research data derived from RCTs, has placed increasing pressure on other approaches like the PCA to 'deliver' therapy in just a few sessions (see Elliot, 2002, 2007). This situation has been exacerbated by the recent decision by the UK Government to finance and install within the NHS by 2011 thousands of new 'therapists' (one report suggests 3,500), who will be trained almost exclusively to deliver CBT, primarily as treatment for depression and anxiety. Depending on your viewpoint, this is either the road to the promised land of a happier society (Layard, 2007), or a dark age for mental health (Leader, 2007).

Person-centred therapy (PCT) has not traditionally been thought of as a brief therapy intervention. For instance, unlike a number of other brief therapies, there is no manualised version of PCT. I suspect that many person-centred practitioners regard brief therapy with some doubt and suspicion or, perhaps somewhat fatalistically. The term 'brief therapy', for its detractors, may simply represent surrender to the *zeitgeist* of quick-fix expertise and an over-simplification of the complexities of the therapeutic process. For many person-centred counsellors, the idea of brief therapy may sit uncomfortably. They see PCT as an organic process, which in its fullest expression aims to facilitate the unfolding or growth of the *whole* person and their potentialities. They may feel that the introduction of a non-negotiable fixed limit somehow goes against the 'spirit' of the person-centred approach, especially if the ultimate aim of person-centred therapy is the emancipation or empowerment of the client (Sanders, 2006a).

Conclusion

Although I can see the attraction of time-limited therapy for hard-pressed services, my sense is that we have to be careful about adopting it universally and uncritically. This could easily lead to a situation where expediency and the bureaucratic need to over-control could replace the therapeutic imperative that is the heart of our work. Central to this seems to be some deeply philosophical and ethical questions about how we view the purpose of therapy. From my biased person-centred perspective, I believe that therapy is ultimately about emancipation, actualisation, encounter, and authenticity rather than simply about a more narrow adjustment to the status quo. In political terms then, how do person-centred practitioners resist becoming as Sanders (2006b, p. 112) puts it: 'absorbed and commodified'? The challenge is to find ways of responding creatively and to resist being subsumed into an amorphous, medicalised type of brief therapy. What is irreplaceable about the PCA is its distinctiveness as a radical, critical and independent voice. The image of trying to compete with other models in the interests of fashion, or on the basis of being able to 'name that tune' in six or 12 notes is not a compelling one.

As I see it, these are some of the complex challenges for person-centred practitioners who aspire to remain true to their fundamental values, retaining their integrity, whilst honouring their clients' emerging needs.

References

Bohart, A. and Tallman, K. (1999) *How Clients Make Therapy Work: The Process of Active Self-Healing.* Washington, DC: American Psychological Association.

Elliot, R. (2002) 'Render unto Caesar: Quantitative and qualitative knowing in research on humanistic therapies', *Person-Centered & Experiential Psychotherapies*, 1(1&2): 102–17.

Elliot, R. (2007) 'Person-centred approaches to research', in M. Cooper, M. O'Hara, P. Schmid and G. Wyatt (eds), *The Handbook of Person-Centred Psychotherapy and Counselling* (pp. 327–40). Basingstoke: Palgrave.

Layard, R. (2007, 14 October) 'And now for the good news about therapy', *Guardian Unlimited Website.*

Leader, D. (2007, 13 October) 'A dark age for mental health', *Guardian Unlimited Website.*

Milne, S. (2007, 13 October) 'Only dogma and corporate capture can explain this', *Guardian Unlimited Website.*

Rogers, C. (2007) 'The basic conditions of the facilitative therapeutic relationship', in M. Cooper, M. O'Hara, P. Schmid and G. Wyatt (eds), *The Handbook of Person-Centred Psychotherapy and Counselling* (p. 2). Basingstoke: Palgrave. (Original work published 1980).

Sanders, P. (2006a) 'Politics and therapy: Mapping areas for consideration', in G. Proctor, M. Cooper, P. Sanders and B. Malcolm (eds), *Politicising the Person-Centred Approach: An Agenda for Social Change* (pp. 95–114). Ross-on-Wye: PCCS Books.

Sanders, P. (2006b) 'The spectacular self: Alienation as the lifestyle choice of the free world, endorsed by psychotherapists', in G. Proctor, M. Cooper, P. Sanders and B. Malcolm (eds), *Politicising the Person-Centred Approach: An Agenda for Social Change* (pp. 95–114). Ross-on-Wye: PCCS Books.

7

'In the World, But Not of It':
Person-Centred Counselling in Primary Care

Isabel Gibbard

The National Health Service (NHS) is an uncomfortable place for a person-centred counsellor. The NHS operates the medical model whereby people are regarded as patients who are ill. The medical practitioner is an expert who will diagnose diseases, disturbances and disorders, and formulate interventions and treatment plans to alleviate symptoms or bring about a cure. The person-centred counsellor, on the other hand, believes in helping whole people become more fully themselves by providing a relationship within which a person's intrinsic self-healing capacity and tendency to actualise is released, and the person can change and grow in a positive and life enhancing direction.

Person-centred counsellors and medical practitioners thus operate within completely different models. Effectively we inhabit different worlds. Some see the two as irreconcilable (e.g. Binder, 2007); others experience the medical world as dehumanising and oppressive (e.g. Freeth, 2007). I have managed to find ways of living with the discomfort of inhabiting two different worlds. My reasoning for this is that, for those of us committed to the person-centred approach and to public sector provision, it is important to engage with the medical world. If we do not, there is a real danger that the person-centred approach will disappear from the NHS: it will be sidelined by other therapies which are more in tune with the philosophy and methodology of the medical model, the most obvious being cognitive behavioural therapy (CBT). If this were to happen, people would be deprived of choice and a beneficial source of help through general practice and primary care.

The NHS, particularly in primary care, operates under enormous pressure to provide services to large numbers of people. As a consequence, most counselling in primary care is short-term and usually time-limited, although the number of sessions varies, typically from six to about 12. Time-limited counselling has provoked criticism from the person-centred community over the years (see Mearns and Thorne, 2000; Wakefield, 2005). There is general agreement that brief or short-term episodes of counselling can be of benefit to people and that often, if given the choice, clients will opt to stay only in a short time in therapy. However, this is brief or short-term counselling by choice or default rather than design. Where there is potential conflict between a time-limited form of therapy and the principles of the person-centred approach is the imposition of a designed time limit by an external authority. This is regarded as incompatible with the person-centred approach which supports the importance of the client's internal locus of control and, therefore, that he should be in control of the ending of therapy in the same way as he is in control of the direction therapy taken.

A primary care counselling service

The service for which I work began its life in 1999 as part of a Clinical Psychology Service, to offer counselling within primary care. To begin with, I was the only a counsellor, receiving referrals from 13 GP surgeries. I was given a time limit of six sessions, with further sessions a possibility, but only in exceptional circumstances and only after discussion with management. This was due, partly to past experience where services had become clogged up with small numbers of clients in long-term therapy, and partly to the demand for counselling which, it was anticipated, would quickly exceed my capacity to provide it. This limitation could be regarded as a typical but misguided response to gross under-resourcing. This may be true, but it is difficult to know what else to do when faced with the reality of limited resources and seemingly limitless need. This is something to which the human race is having to face up to on a global scale. We used to think that we could all use as much of the earth's resources as we wanted. We are now facing up to the damage we have caused and are causing and, if we are to survive, we will have to cultivate an attitude of conserving and sharing. Similarly, we have to make the most of the limited resources of the NHS and ensure it is distributed fairly. Quite simply, I could not offer counselling to everyone who would like it for as long as they would like to have it. When I worked out the capacity of the service I could offer, I found that, over a 12-month period, I could see approximately 100 people. This meant that each year 100 people would receive help that they would not previously have received, and I saw – and see – this as a good thing.

My training did not prepare me at all for this kind of work and dilemma. However, the last thing I wanted was to sacrifice my person-centred principles and to integrate techniques from other approaches. I began, full of anxieties about how on earth I was going to manage. Could I trust that the therapeutic process would work sufficiently within the six sessions? What if six sessions were not enough? What if it took time to build up relationships where clients could trust me enough to talk honestly about their problems? What if they only started to talk about their problems in any depth in session five or six? Would I have to abandon them in a raw and vulnerable state? What if they identified deep-seated, complex issues during the counselling? Would I be administering the equivalent of a therapeutic sticking plaster over deep psychological wounds? Would I have to limit myself to working with small, superficial and easily resolved problems?

Assessment and diagnosis is a key component of the medical model and is undertaken with the aim of formulating a treatment plan. I felt – and still feel – uncomfortable with this as it usually involves making a judgement and deciding what is wrong with a person. It seems to conflict with the person-centred approach as it locates power in the hands of the mental health professional and reinforces the externalisation of the client's locus of evaluation. The people who became my clients had been referred to the mental health services by their GPs. They were not considered complex or severe enough to need a psychiatrist, a community psychiatric nurse or a psychologist and, before my post was created, they would have been referred back to their GPs. In this sense, counselling was essentially a treatment plan formulated by someone else's assessment and diagnosis, but this left me free to meet the client as a person, to enter into a relationship with her, to hear and understand her own personal experiences and meanings. I could, therefore and at the same time, be both part of the medical model, and yet separate from it. To use a metaphor from the Christian religion, I could be 'in the world but not of it'. (John 17: 16–17).

The difference between the medical and person-centred models is immediately evident from the language used in referrals. To begin with I found it disconcerting to read of a prospective client with generalised anxiety disorder and depressive symptomology, as the person I met was invariably a person in distress with valid reasons for feeling anxious and low. Clients too picked up the language of disease, and often regarded themselves as having something wrong with them. They had 'got depression' or were 'suffering from anxiety'. I soon learned, however, that I could ignore all that and respond in ways which relocated the power back into the hands of the client, and helped facilitate the internalisation of her locus of evaluation. This was made easier by the fact that I have had no medical training. So, if a client arrived for their first sessions and said 'My GP thinks I've got OCD [obsessive compulsive disorder]', I could honestly reply 'I don't know – what do *you* think?'

It was clear straight away that I was not going to be dealing with problems which were small or easily resolved. Many people came with very complex and disturbing difficulties which they had lived with for a long time and I soon realised that the classical approach which allows the client to take their own time to find their own way through the therapeutic process was not going to work. I found that it was possible to speed up the process by being in the relationship in ways which I now realise could be located within the experiential and integrative developments of the person-centred approach (e.g. Baker, 2004, 2007; Worsley, 2004, 2007) respectively.

Experiential and integrative practice

In the 1960s, Rogers and colleagues undertook a large-scale research project intending to prove the effectiveness of person-centred therapy (Rogers *et al.*, 1967). The findings appeared to show that the outcome of therapy was dependent, not just on the therapeutic conditions, but also on the client's ability to engage with their experiencing. This experiencing is a continually changing process and includes the individual's perceptions, her thoughts, memories, feelings and also the meanings she attaches to them. At any one time an individual may be unaware of some of her experiencing even though she is affected by it. This has given rise to further developments within the person-centred approach, such as focusing or process-experiential practices, where it is acknowledged that the therapist is an expert in terms of the therapeutic process and the therapist may direct the client's attention towards his feelings and experiencing. There has been, and still is, considerable debate as to whether these practices can be considered within the person-centred approach (e.g. Brodley, 2006). Worsley (2007) writes of how it is possible for a person-centred counsellor to integrate different insights, not just from other models and theories but from the whole range of his own life experiences, the lives and experiences of others, and from therapeutic practice, literature and philosophy. In this way, Worsley links integrative person-centred practice to the process of personal integration; the growth of a counsellor as a whole person.

Working within a time limit

The NHS requires practitioners to provide treatments that are effective, where effectiveness is demonstrated by an improvement in the symptoms which brought the person to counselling. So an effective therapy is one which reduces a person's anxiety or lifts their depression, or simply makes them feel better. The person-centred approach, on the other hand, does not set aims and goals for therapy or make judgements about the outcome. It does not expect a client to 'get somewhere' by the end of therapy, for their symptoms to reduce or for them necessarily to feel any better. So I was faced with another conflict between the person-centred approach and the medical model. In primary care it is assumed that counselling will reduce our clients' distress and make them feel better, and we work under pressure to bring this about within the time limit.

    In my previous work, where there was no time restriction, there was time for a relationship to grow and for trust to develop, and it was quite reasonable for this part of the process to take weeks or even months. In primary care there was no time for this and, if counselling was going to be effective within the time limit, clients had to be prepared to trust me straight away. To some extent this was aided by my position as a mental health professional, as many clients were prepared to put their trust in me, in the same way as I would be prepared to trust a physiotherapist or a surgeon. The drawback was that clients often viewed me as the expert. At first, I found this was uncomfortable as, in line with person-centred philosophy, I rejected the role of expert. However, I accept that, although I am not and never will be an expert in any particular client or his or her process, I am a relative expert in the process of therapy. Clients arrive who have never experienced a counselling session before and have no idea what it entails or what might happen. For my part I have experienced thousands of counselling sessions with hundreds of clients, and have at least an idea of what the process might be. I learned that I could use this experience and expertise to explain what was expected of them and what might happen. I found this gave the client confidence and hope.

When I worked longer term or open-ended I had been able to practise my belief that the client knows best what hurts and, given the right conditions and sufficient time, will eventually talk about it. In primary care there simply was not the time. This gave a sense of urgency and intensity to counselling relationships. I think it is best described in the words of a colleague: 'Both client and counsellor know there is only a short time so they get stuck in and work their socks off!' I encountered little difficulty when clients arrived for their first counselling session knowing exactly what hurts, recognising their need to talk about it, and being prepared to do so straight away. However, there were those who arrived confused and bewildered about the reason for their anxiety or their depression. Some had many different problems which demanded attention, and others seemed to have denied or distorted their experiences to such an extent that they did not realise what their problems were and how much they were hurting. Still other clients had a good idea of what hurt but, quite understandably, because it hurt, they avoided talking about it.

When I worked longer term, clients could spend time talking around their problems until they identified what was significant and I could wait for important issues to emerge as time went on and the client felt ready. I would accept and respect a client's right not to talk about what hurts, believing that he or she would do so when the time was right. In primary care I was always aware of the danger that this would happen near the end of therapy, or not at all. In order to avoid this, clients had to be prepared to talk about painful and disturbing experiences sooner rather than later in the counselling relationship. I realised that I could play a very active role in making this possible by being very honest and direct in my responses. Just as I expected the client to trust me and take risks, I had to be prepared to do the same myself. I found I was responding at the very beginning of a counselling relationship in ways in which, in my previous work, I would not have risked until I knew the client much better and felt more comfortable with him or her. Now I found that it was possible to help a client to focus on themselves, to talk about what hurts, and to engage with their experiencing straight away.

Another difficulty I encountered was the concept of stuckness, where there is little observable change taking place in the client. When I worked longer term I accepted these periods as natural phenomena in the normal process of therapy, interspersed with moments of movement (Mearns, 1994). In this context I had the time for personal reflection and discussion in supervision to consider where the origin of stuckness lay, whether within the client, the relationship or with me. I could then take these insights back to the counselling relationship and wait for the next stage in the process to unfold. In the context of working in primary care I could not afford for a client to spend several precious sessions in a state of stuckness so, as soon as I became aware that a client was stuck, I started to introduce this into the content of counselling. This could result in a particular client making a conscious decision to explore an aspect of himself that he had been frightened of or unwilling to acknowledge or to make the changes in his life that he was resisting. Or it might mean that we terminated therapy with the option of returning at any point in the future when and if he felt ready to address whatever was frightening him. If the stuckness appeared to be a period of consolidation after a moment of movement then we would probably agree to finish counselling while he got used to where he was and while he readied himself for the next stage. I began to see the short-term work in which I was engaged as accompanying a client on a very small stage of his life's journey which I often describe in terms of climbing a mountain. A mountaineer rarely climbs straight from the bottom to the top. She climbs the first stage, then stops and rests. Maybe she has a drink, something to eat, and looks at the view until she is ready to move on again. Thus, moments of movement may be interspersed with moments of pause, and may involve returning to counselling, or may involve finding help elsewhere.

Just as a client might have to face up to their part in the stuckness, so did I. Just as I expected a client to face distressing and disturbing experiences early on in the relationship, I soon realised I would have to do the same myself. I had always tried to offer a high degree of the therapist conditions of empathy, respect, and congruence at all times (Rogers, 1957), but I had already experienced that sometimes I was better at this than at other times. In my previous work there was time to rectify shortfalls in my embodiment of the conditions at the beginning of counselling, and for this to have a beneficial impact on counselling as time went on. In primary care I did not have the time. Straight away I had to be willing to identify and to face up to those uncomfortable or disturbing aspects of myself which were hindering or preventing me from offering the conditions to the client.

Inevitably, there were clients who were eager to change and engaged quickly and extensively with the process, but for whom six sessions were not enough. Perhaps they had a number of pressing problems and we only had time to deal with some of them, or perhaps the damage was very great. I was then faced with a dilemma. Did I discharge them or try to negotiate more sessions with management? I decided on the second option and I found that the response I received from my manager depended on the language I used. If I spoke in person-centred terms of feelings and senses that six sessions were not enough and that more sessions would be helpful, this did not go down well. Neither did my reasoning that a therapeutic relationship was a unique and unpredictable process which would unfold in its own idiosyncratic way and in its own time. My manager would want to know how was I managing the therapeutic process within the time limit to ensure some benefit to the client. On what was I basing my feelings and senses? How many more sessions would be helpful and why? What did I envisage would happen? Was there anything I could have done to avoid this? Was there something I could do to avoid this happening in the future? Failure to give adequate responses seemed to confirm the stereotype of person-centred counselling as having little basis in theory and offering little more than 'a bit of supportive listening'. I quickly learned that if I was to be taken seriously I had to be very clear about the origin of the client's distress; how counselling in general and my involvement in particular was facilitating change; where we were in the process; and how I thought more sessions would be of benefit. At first I found this hard, as in my previous work I had been left very much to my own devices and had never been in the position of having to explain what I was doing or what was happening in a counselling relationship. However, I found that if I could do this then I was more likely to receive an understanding and favourable response. So, by a process of negotiation, and as more counsellors joined, the service has developed and evolved into one where we initially offer a contract of six sessions which can be extended for up to 12 as agreed between the counsellor and the client.

Service and policy

Mental health services are subject to government policy and the drive for improved quality and efficiency in the NHS (Department of Health [DoH], 1997). We have had to cope with the *National Service Framework for Mental Health*, clinical governance, and the need to demonstrate performance by clinical audits and national benchmarks (DoH, 1999).

Alongside this there has been the drive for evidence-based practice and the National Institute for Clinical Excellence (NICE) guidelines (NICE, 2004a, 2004b). Although the person-centred approach has been throroughly researched, none of the research meets the strict criteria which must be met in order to be included in the guidelines. On the other hand, a great deal of the CBT research meets the criteria and, therefore, CBT is recommended as the most effective treatment for all primary care mental health conditions. This has become a very real threat to the continued funding of person-centred counselling in primary care and I was aware that if we did not engage with these NHS initiatives and perspectives, then, as a Service, we would not survive. So we used the CORE (Clinical Outcomes in Routine Evaluation) System (see, for instance, Mellor-Clarke, 2006) to collect quantitative information, such as the problems clients present with and their severity, the percentage of clients who drop out of therapy, and the percentage which shows an improvement after therapy. We also used an exit questionnaire to collect qualitative feedback about the client's experience of counselling. In this way we have been able to convince both managers and commissioners that we are effective, efficient and value for money.

In 2005, the Counselling Service was reorganised and, along with graduate primary care mental health workers, nurses and CBT therapists, became part of a Primary Care Mental Health Team. In the beginning it was unclear where the place of counselling was going to be and I was profoundly worried that we were going to find ourselves in competition with the graduate workers. If that had happened there is no doubt that the graduate workers would have replaced counsellors as they are cheaper, they carry caseloads of 50 to 60 patients and they work according to the CBT principles set out in the NICE guidelines. This did not happen as the clients with whom the counsellors work are now from the so-called moderate to severe end of the spectra of anxiety and depression, while the graduate workers continue to work with clients from the mild to moderate end. In effect the Counselling Service has become a specialist mental health service within primary care. It has been a challenge for us to continue working within the short term with such a complex client group and we are now faced with similar dilemmas when reaching session 11 or 12. It is possible to extend for longer than 12 sessions, but again, only when there are exceptional circumstances and only after discussion with management. The difference is that now I am the manager and counsellors have to discuss their clients with me. For a further description of the service see Gibbard (2007).

This approach may be regarded by many as colluding with a hierarchical management structure which exercises power, authority and control over the counsellors and the clients we are supposed to be helping. This conflicts with the person-centred approach which promotes respect and trust in both counsellors and clients. I certainly experience a great deal of tension. Whilst respect is integral to the person-centred approach, I often find that the focus of respect is the individual engaged in counselling. As a service manager I am responsible for the whole service which includes the management of the waiting list. Each week I receive telephone calls from distressed clients wanting to know how much longer they will have to wait; requests from GPs to expedite the appointment of one of their patients who is on the waiting list and who is deteriorating; and enquiries from referrers for someone who is desperate to be seen as soon as possible. The problem, when faced with the inevitably long waiting lists and waiting times created by limited resources, is that one client's choice to stay longer in therapy will limit another's choice to be seen sooner, if at all. Respect for the needs of an individual client needs to be balanced with the respect I have for all the other clients who are waiting for a service.

I have also discovered over the years that some counsellors are quite comfortable working in a short-term way and hardly ever approach me to negotiate an extension. Other counsellors seem to struggle to work in a short-term way, and see a greater proportion of their clients as needing more sessions or longer-term therapy, and it is these counsellors who often negotiate for more time or refer their clients for further counselling elsewhere. I have gradually concluded that, just as the ability to work in a person-centred way is due to the attitudes and beliefs held by the counsellor, so is the ability to work short-term.

Our attitudes and beliefs are communicated to clients in various and subtle ways. This may be out of our awareness. We may be fearful of the disturbing or painful parts of our client's world and our ability to deal with them in the time available, or anxious about the client's ability to live with them afterwards. We may inadvertently be giving the message that there is only time to talk about superficial and immediate problems while the deeper more painful experiences remain beneath the surface. In this case, the client is unlikely to show any improvement, and will be left feeling that they did not have the time to talk about what was really important. On the other hand, our attitudes may be well within our awareness. If we think that working within a time limit is compromising our person-centred principles, and are open with the client that we think they need longer-term work, and that we are unable to give it to him, then the client may end counselling feeling angry and resentful that he could not have what he needed. On the other hand, if we believe that lasting change does not require a sustained period of time but can happen quickly, we will communicate an attitude that the client has plenty of time to talk about and resolve deep-seated and painful issues. If we believe that we can facilitate relationships that clients can use to help themselves significantly within the time available, and we trust that clients have the necessary resources within themselves to continue the process when counselling finishes, then we will communicate this to the client and he is more likely to feel that the time he has had is sufficient.

The NHS is an uncomfortable place for a person-centred counsellor. We work within a different model to the dominant medical model; we have a different philosophy, different beliefs and speak a different language. The NHS is faced with large numbers of people who want fast, effective treatments, and government demands for evidence and cost-effectiveness. All practitioners experience pressure from long waiting lists, pressure to demonstrate activity and efficiency, outcomes and results; and competition from other professional groups and from other providers. Faced with all this, it is no wonder that many within the person-centred approach choose not to engage directly with the medical world. It is hard being part of the medical world and yet separate from it. However, as I have argued, I believe it is both possible and essential for person-centred practitioners to do so if the person-centred approach is to survive here.

References

Baker, N. (2004) 'Experiential person-centred therapy', in P. Sanders (ed.) *The Tribes of The Person-Centred Nation* (pp. 67–94). Ross-on-Wye: PCCS Books.

Baker, N. (2007) *The Experiential Counselling Primer*. Ross-on-Wye: PCCS Books.

Binder, U. (2007) [Review of *Person-Centred Psychopathology: A Positive Psychology of Mental Health*] *Person-Centred & Experiential Psychotherapies*, 5(4): 295.

Brodley, B. (2006) 'Non-directivity in client-centered therapy', *Person-Centred & Experiential Psychotherapies*, 5(1): 36–52.

Department of Health (1997) *The New NHS: Modern, Dependable*. London: HMSO.

Department of Health (1999) *The National Service Framework for Mental Health*. London: HMSO.

Freeth, R. (2007) *Humanising Psychiatry and Mental Health Care: The Challenge of the Person-Centred Approach*. Oxford: Radcliffe.

Gibbard, I. (2007) 'Person-centred stepped care in Chorley and South Ribble', *Healthcare Counselling and Psychotherapy Journal*, 7(3): 36.

Mearns, D. (1994) *Developing Person-Centred Counselling*. London: Sage.

Mearns, D. and Thorne, B. (2000) *Person-Centred Therapy Today*. London: Sage.

Mellor-Clark, J. (2006) 'Developing CORE performance indicators for benchmarks in primary care psychological therapy and counselling services: An editorial introduction', *Counselling and Psychotherapy Research*, 6: 1–2.

National Institute for Clinical Excellence (2004a) *Clinical Guidelines for the Management of Anxiety in Adults in Primary, Secondary and Community Care*. Document available online at: www.nice.org.uk/nicemedia/pdf/cg022fullguideline.pdf

National Institute for Clinical Excellence (2004b) *Depression: Management of Depression in Primary and Secondary Care*. Document available online at: http://www.nice.org.uk/nicemedia/pdf/cg023fullguideline.pdf

Rogers, C. (1957) 'The necessary and sufficient conditions for therapeutic personality change', *Journal of Consulting Psychology*, 21(2): 95–103.

Rogers, C., Gendlin, E., Kiesler, D. and Truax, C. (1967) *The Therapeutic Relationship and Its Impact: A Study of Psychotherapy with Schizophrenics*. Madison, WN: University of Wisconsin Press.

Wakefield, M. (2005, August) 'Person-centred practice in primary health care: Evidence that without time limits the majority of clients opt for short-term therapy', *Person-Centred Quarterly*: 1–5.

Worsley, R. (2004) 'Integrating with integrity', in P. Sanders (ed.) *The Tribes of The Person-Centred Nation* (pp. 125–47). Ross-on-Wye: PCCS Books.

Worsley, R. (2007) *The Integrative Counselling Primer*. Ross-on-Wye: PCCS Books.

8

Expert Systems versus Moments of Volatility: A Person-Centred Therapist's Perspective of Employee Assistance Programmes

Pam Winter

My practice

I have worked as an independent practitioner in private practice for many years. One of the main sources of consistent client referral has been via Employee Assistance Programmes (EAPs) which, as their name suggests, are programmes set up and paid for by an organisation to offer assistance by means of a range of services for its employees and in most cases their family members. A central component of these services is the provision of face-to-face short-term counselling, near to where the employee works or lives. As one of the few British Association for Counselling & Psychotherapy (BACP) accredited practitioners in my area, I have had regular referrals from EAPs. (EAPs usually require their affiliates to be registered or accredited.) These referrals have also steadily increased over the years. In addition to this work, for the past three years, I have also managed the counselling provision of a small staff support service for a local borough council; and I have done so using the same model of short-term counselling. So, the main bulk of my work has been with stressed/distressed employees who are increasingly turning to and using EAP services for their emotional and psychological distress, rather than waiting for a referral from an already overstretched GP service (Arthur, 2001). This reliable source of work has been a welcome one; it has also been a source of great challenge and some stress and soul-searching at times. For example, when I first began this work I felt that I was somehow guilty of 'limiting' the client to a set number of sessions and, thus, of both disrespecting and disempowering them. I felt very uncomfortable to put myself in some kind of gate-keeping role, alongside which I felt an increased responsibility for getting the client 'well' or 'fit for work' again. These feelings left me questioning my role and my practice, and wondering if I could offer short-term work and still be person-centred. This, in turn, also led me to question assumptions, specifically about time and about the nature of change, assumptions I had not even realised I was making.

With the rise in work-related stress, the demand for counsellors to undertake EAP work has increased. Over the years, I have found that the necessary attitudes, qualities and skills required to undertake and manage this work are complex. In this chapter, I articulate and consider some of the issues and challenges of this work from the therapist's perspective.

What being person-centred means to me?

My original training was in the person-centred approach. Since then I have also followed a number of interests, principally one in body psychotherapy. The central tenet of person-centred therapy is that of the actualising process and, thus, the valuing both of the client's personal authority and of his or her functioning as a whole organism, 'a pulsing biological entity', as Tudor and Worrall (2004, p. 45) put it. The actualising tendency is both individual and universal, and is a 'directional process' towards development and the realisation of potential. It is, according to Bozarth (1998, p. 29) 'the motivational force function[ing] throughout all systems of the person. It is expressed in a variable, dynamic and fluctuating manner through the subsystems of the whole person'. This variable, dynamic and fluctuating process is dependent on the environment and the conditions in which the person/organism lives. This description also suggests the 'volatility' of the organism/person in process. According to the *Oxford Paperback Dictionary* (1994), volatility, as related to a person, means 'lively, changing quickly or easily from one mood to another'. I think we fluctuate all the time: we fluctuate, for example, between our organismic valuing process, and who we think we 'should' be, our self-concept, and our 'subsystems'. For example, I want to leave my office job, which I find constrictive, and enrol on an art course. I also know I have to and want to provide for my family. Thus, according to Bozarth (1998, p. 29), the actualising tendency is the motivation for 'all activity of the person, under all circumstances, favourable and unfavourable to the person'. Sometimes the organismic valuing process is described as our 'authentic' or congruent self. The alienation and suffering that arises from being disconnected and estranged from our organismic experiencing and internal valuing process is often what leads people to seek counselling. Counselling offers the possibility of an authentic person-to-person relationship between therapist and client which is in itself healing (Jordan *et al.*, 1991; Mearns and Cooper, 2005). I value this relational approach and see it as central to my way of being and working with clients. The therapeutic conditions of that relationship as hypothesised by Rogers (1957, 1959) provide me with an invaluable guide to the relational conditions and process of effective therapy. I view Rogers' organismic perspective as representing a holistic view of the person. As mind and body are inseparable, we are, in effect, embodied beings processing our experience somatically; our thoughts and feelings are accompanied by ever-changing internal and kinaesthetic sensations. We also have a sense of being – or not being – in our bodies in a particular place and time, and relationship: our environment. In this sense, I agree with Fernald (2000) who argues that Rogers is a body-oriented therapist.

Employee Assistant Programmes: The growing UK provider of counselling

Like many facets of our cultural life in the UK, EAPs are an American import. They originated in the USA in the 1950s as services of care and welfare provided by employers, usually concerning alcohol and drug rehabilitation programmes (see Arthur, 2001). In the UK, between 1995 and 2000, EAPs started to be seen as an essential component of an organisation's integrated healthcare management. A number of factors have contributed to this:

1   The effects of stress in the workplace has been a growing financial concern for employers. In 2004, the Health and Safety Executive (HSE) Annual Report estimated that 13.4 million days had been lost due to stress. The continued increase in work-related stress led to the HSE launching its Management Standards to tackle stress at work (Palmer *et al.*, 2004). Also in 2004 the Trades Union Council estimated the cost to the UK economy of work-related stress, taking into account sick pay, lost production and NHS costs, as £7 billion (Palmer *et al.*, 2004). In recent years, the costs of stress estimated by other organisations exceed £5 billion p.a.
2   The economic cost of common mental health problems, such as depression and anxiety has been cited as being around £23 billion per year (Grove and Seymour, 2007, p. 4) Private medical insurance has become more costly, and employers have seen that they could make savings by focusing on employees' health (Grange, 2005).
3   Under UK law, employers have a legal duty of care to ensure their employees are not harmed by work-related stress (*Management of Health & Safety at Work Regulations*, 1999). This is a crucial incentive for offering counselling.

In response to these factors and costs, EAPs are reported to show a benefit to the company of between three and seven times the actual costs of the programme (Arthur, 2001). McLeod's (2001, p. 2) study reported that 'the provision of counselling can have a significant impact on mental health problems at work, and contribute to a reduction in sickness absence rates. The overall findings of the second edition are stated to be 'broadly similar'. This kind of reporting is also used by EAPs to make a business case for organisations saving money by offering counselling provision to employees.

There are now around 20 major EAP providers in the UK alone. They contract with the organisation to provide employees with free, confidential access to an affiliate network of qualified counsellors. EAPs rarely take on trainee counsellors. EAP services are usually provided via a 24/7 freephone number whereby the employee can discuss their difficulty and, if appropriate, are then referred to an affiliate, off-site counsellor for an assessment/consultation. If this assessment process, conducted by the counsellor, concludes that short-term work is appropriate, then the work goes ahead, usually for up to six sessions. In 2006, Right Corecare, one of the largest EAPs in the UK, carried out a survey of employers, asking them what their key reasons were for purchasing EAP services. The top three reasons were: (1) to provide additional support to employees; (2) to meet the employer's duty of care; and (3) to support employees through times of organisational change (Friery, 2006). Here, the focus appears to be on protecting the organisation. ICAS (Independent Counselling & Advisory Services Limited), which, according to its website (www.icasworld.com) is one of the biggest EAPs in the world, states that it works with organisations not only to enhance employee performance and well-being, but also to 'reduce the costs associated with human behavior'. This is a telling description, suggesting that in their complexity and messiness human beings pose a threat to organisational order and corporate aims. Elsewhere on the same website organisations are encouraged to 'protect themselves from the threat posed by potentially volatile workforces'. The other definition of volatile, again from the *Oxford Paperback Dictionary*, in relation to a political situation is: 'liable to erupt into violence'.

EAPs are big business now. This is the social, political and organisational context in which EAP therapists work, even as independent practitioners, and is the context in which I see some clients. This context makes it clear that the aims of the people who pay me, the aims of the client/s, and my aims as a therapist may well be very different.

Domains and dilemmas – a way of thinking about the complexity of EAP work

Working for an EAP is likely to raise concerns for the therapist which may be ethical, confidential, professional, organisational, social and political. Tudor and Worrall (2004, p. 83) view these as domains:

> Issues, questions and dilemmas arise in and belong to particular domains …
> We think it's important to identify which domain we're operating in on any one
> occasion, so that we can appeal for guidance to the most relevant and appropriate
> guidelines … we identify the following domains: clinical; professional; ethical;
> personal; legal; social and cultural.

I think of these like a Russian Doll: they nest inside one another. For me, the central, innermost domain is me as a person, including my own personal philosophy; clinical practice is the next layer; then comes the professional/ethical, which, in my view, includes legal issues; and then come the social/cultural/political domains. I have already articulated something of myself and my personal philosophy (above); in the rest of the chapter, I explore some of the dilemmas EAP work has raised for me, first, with regard to my clinical practice.

The clinical domain

This domain refers to my practice as a therapist, and the particular body of experience, theory and research from which I draw. From the outline above, it is clear that my idea of therapy is possibly quite different from that of EAPs. It seems, as Totton (2004, p. 5) puts it, that: 'two very different activities might be trading under the same name'. EAPs are concerned to support the organisation for which they are providing a service, and that means being cost effective in getting people back to work. Rowan (2004) describes this EAP treatment approach as fitting with the 'instrumental' self of both therapist and client, in that the therapist regards the client as someone with problems, which need to be 'put right' by the therapist using his or her technical expertise in a time-limited way. This represents what Totton (2004, p. 6) calls an 'expert systems therapy' which: 'has evolved to cope with an environment that demands expertise ... in which both clients and purchasers are demanding [the] maximum amelioration of distress in minimum time'.

The pressure to present as 'expert' both to clients and to EAPs themselves has been at times both distressing and deskilling for me. First, it's not how I define or locate myself as a therapist. As outlined above, my practice rests on the fundamental belief that the client is his or her own best 'expert', via the actualisation process which, therefore, I need to support, specifically by not taking power away from them by presenting as 'expert'. This has meant that, from the start, I have to be clear and explicit both with the referring EAP and with the client about how I will be working. With clients, I talk about the counselling process and what they can expect from me; what I will and won't do. I support clients to listen to and to understand themselves more fully. I don't and won't have an agenda about any outcome, although they might. Being explicit has proved to be helpful for clients and for me. Most employees who show up for a session feel backed against the wall: it's not something they ever thought they would be doing. They are not members of what Mindell calls 'the grower's club' (Totton, 2004). They have come as a last resort, and usually just want to get back on track as fast as they can. They also know that this is what their employer wants too; and most of the clients I see feel a huge amount of guilt that they are not 'functioning' like clockwork anymore. This can feel like an enormous pressure on me as the therapist, as around a third of the EAP clients I see might 'present' with 'appropriate' issues for time-limited work, but sometimes when we get two or three sessions in what emerges are underlying and deep-seated concerns which represent the kind of complex issues and needs to be designated as 'inappropriate' for this work. Many EAPs emphasise and even require that counsellors must assess clients' symptoms both for risk and for the efficacy of short-term work; and advise referral on in the case of drug/alcohol misuse, personality or character disorder, early childhood trauma, or a complex history of mental health. Some of the narratives that illustrate this point:

- 'We have one session left and you have taken an overdose' – The client had come with a 'relationship issue'.
- 'You have told me today, our third session, about the sustained childhood abuse you suffered, and this is the first time you have told anyone' – This person had come because she was feeling tearful and low at work, and unable to concentrate.
- 'You have been affected by a raid at your branch and this assault has triggered memories of an earlier trauma which you had forgotten until now'. – This person came because as a manager he wanted to support other staff 'more affected' by the raid but was struggling to do so.

I have spent many hours in supervision struggling with the conflict between my philosophical and theoretical stance and the pressure from cases (as above), a conflict which has left me feeling I should be working 'differently', i.e. more 'quickly', spotting underlying issues 'sooner', or doubting the efficacy of the person-centred approach in this context. Wakefield and Wakefield (2005) argue that person-centred therapists should not be doing time-limited work. In auditing one of their practices they found (p. 10) that: 'The average length of therapy has been between six and 10 sessions. This significant data shows that by trusting the client there is actually no need to time limit the service since it is self-regulating'. They also report that clients who needed longer-term work (p. 10): 'would never have begun to heal from their pain if their time had been restricted'. Whilst I agree with the argument that trusting the client is central to the therapy process, I disagree that clients are 'hurt' by an externally imposed time boundary. My experience is that when employees are given the option of short-term work not only do they often make full use of what they have, but that they also make a start. One client I worked with decided by session three that she had to leave her workplace and the overwork culture that was destroying her life. She also found a way to continue with her therapy. In those six sessions, we had made a start on a massive change process. My experience and thinking is that, for the clients who want it, some therapy is better than no therapy. Being upfront with the client, 'We have up to six sessions', sets a clear boundary. It is also a simple reflection of reality: life is time-limited, as is all therapy. I have found that clients have been far less bothered by this boundary than I have been. I used to find myself saying to my EAP clients: "We *only* have six sessions", which fed my guilty sense of being a gatekeeper of scarce resource and an underlying assumption that long-term therapy was somehow better.

My supervision group and debates with colleagues has proved crucial in enabling me to become clearer about some of the implicit assumptions I was making. This helped me continue to believe that I can do this work and retain my integrity as a person-centred practitioner. It's clear from the vignettes above that it is simply unrealistic, and possibly grandiose, to think that, as therapists, we can find out in the first assessment session exactly what the client is bringing, and then to formulate some 'outcome'. Yet this is what EAP referrers expect, locked as they are in the 'expert systems' model. What I know and use from my experience and theory is that, in terms of our own inner experience and meaning construction, human beings are complex, and that we are also orientated towards the full development of our own potentiality which, when blocked, causes dysfunction. For me, trusting in the client's ability to be at the centre of their own assessment process is of central importance. It might be the focus throughout all the sessions we have together, and thus, eases the pressure both with regard to the initial assessment and, more broadly, to a time-limited perspective. What this means in practice is that I find ways of working with each client so that he or she can begin to access and thus bring to awareness his or her own inner experience, and then to symbolise and express it. That capacity for self-reflective awareness is uniquely human. Once that process of change has begun, constructive personality change follows . From this perspective, the fact that the client and I may have 'only' six sessions is not the issue. O'Hara (1999, p. 65) clearly demonstrates that Rogers saw short-term help as 'offer[ing] a very definite kind of clarifying help'. She also demonstrates, however, that the paradigm in which this way of practice sits is clearly very different from the medical model/expert system paradigm. I agree with O'Hara when she says that person-centred practitioners are not there to solve the problem or heal the client but (p. 67) to 'build a space in which clients can heal themselves'. Trusting in the 'self healing properties of living systems' enables me to work with EAP clients just as I would with any clients.

Thus, the agenda for each session is mutually agreed and always determined by the client; any forms required (for the EAP) are completed together. I have learned, however, that just as I needed to unearth my own implicit assumptions about 'time-limited' work in supervision and then be explicit with the client about the time we have and what we might achieve together, I also needed to be explicit, assertive and confident with the EAP about who I am and what I can and cannot 'do'. This means taking into account the *context* of this work, that is, the value base of both the EAP and of the organisation/s for which it is providing the service. So, when an EAP referrer rings me to ask if I can take a client, and follows this up with questions about whether I do cognitive behavioural therapy, I respond by saying that I work holistically with clients, i.e. that I work with their somatic, emotional, cognitive and behavioural processes. Thus, I stay true to my experience and belief that the organism behaves as an organised whole, and that people process their experience in different and unique ways. I also hold to the principles of autonomy, equality and holism defined by Sanders (2000) as criteria by which to judge whether I am working in a person-centred way or not. So, if the referrer and/or client wants only to work cognitively or behaviourally, then I can't take the case. Usually, they do refer the client.

The professional/ethical domains

These domains represent professional issues with regard to my relationships with colleagues and relevant professional bodies, and the ethical issue about who the EAP service is really for, and whose ends are being served by the Programme.

My position as therapist is to hold the client and their agenda as central. The BACP's (2000) *Ethical Guidelines for Good Practice in Counselling and Psychotherapy* state that 'the protection of the client's interests and maintaining trust in the practitioner should be paramount' (p. 6, clause 55). Valuing client autonomy by respecting the client's right to be self-governing is a central principle of counselling. Therapeutic services should, therefore, be primarily for the client. In the context of an EAP, however, sessions are paid for by an employer, and provided through the EAP. This means that I have a contract not only with the client but also with the EAP. In fact, my contract with the client is determined by the EAP which, in turn, is contracted to provide services to the organisation. This suggests what Tudor (1997) has referred to as 'a complexity of contracts', in response to which I have found the concept of the three-cornered or three-handed contract useful. The agreement/contract I have with the EAP is one which sets out what is required from me as a competent professional practitioner and which is seen as standard for the profession, covering items such as qualifications, training, accreditation, premises, supervision, insurance and so on. I am also required to perform my professional responsibilities in particular ways. In an article in the journal of the Association for Counselling at Work Turner (2005) discusses the responsibilities, competencies and opportunities for an EAP counsellor. He states that the first and most necessary 'quality' of an EAP counsellor is 'speed', by which he means being able to 'move fast' and offer appointments quickly. I think that being efficient and businesslike is an important skill for any practitioner, but it's hardly a 'quality'. He also cites being 'flexible' and a 'team player'. In response to this kind of debate within the profession, it has been important for me to be clear about my philosophy and practice as a clinician, and to be business-like about the requirements the EAP has of my professional practice, without feeling pressured to behave in a way which might compromise my practice. Being clear and explicit with regard to the contracts I have both with the EAP and with clients is crucial. This is particularly the case regarding confidentiality. I have found EAPs to be very clear about their relationships with organisations, and about holding client confidentiality, as well as explicit as to the limits of that boundary in relation to the client. Arthur (2001, p. 9) is very clear about this:

> ... confidentiality, except in appropriate circumstances, cannot be breached, and this means attention must be paid to what information is passed from counsellors to the EAP provider, and subsequently to the employer ... (Counsellor's) codes of practice, guidelines and ethics must take precedence over any requirements of the EAP provider, or the sponsoring company'.

It continues to be the case, however, that because of the short-term nature of EAP work and the corporate culture in which it sits, the debate within the profession is couched in what I have referred to above as the 'expert systems' model implying as it does the therapist's 'technical' ability to work in a somewhat programmed way (Rowan, 2004). As this is the professional body (ACW) to which I have turned and subscribed for guidelines on good practice as an EAP counsellor, I have often felt in a lonely and isolated place.

What has sustained me has been belonging to a person-centred supervision group in which the concepts of being in relationship, and presence, were understood and, more importantly, embodied. I would arrive in a state of stress and incongruence, often paralleling my clients, and leave restored and resourced. It is presence rather than speed which is crucial in EAP work: being present in the moment with the client, and not letting the forms, or the pressure to come up with an 'outcome' or a magic wand get in the way, to the point of consciously slowing things down inside myself. This is what my supervision group has helped me with, and it is what I find most helpful when working with clients in this context. If I can be fully present, this is in and of itself very supportive to the therapeutic environment, and counters and resists the pressure to become the 'fast' 'expert'. By fully acknowledging the contextual 'limits' of EAP work, such as time, confidentiality, clear contracting with the client, it doesn't follow that I have to also buy into the 'expert systems' paradigm in order to be 'professional' such that my clients have to feel better or have all their problems solved or, indeed heal their childhood traumas. Both clients and organisations want a 'return to ordinary functioning' (Totton, 2004, p. 6), particularly if the 'volatility' of the workforce is seen as a potential threat to the smooth running of the organisation. From the point of view of the organisation, this is seen as the best outcome from the practice of psychological helping and, in my experience, is often conflated with short-term work. It does not have to be so. I am in the practice of therapy as what Totton (2004, p. 6) refers to as 'psychological truth telling' for the client, irrespective of the number of sessions or context. So, in some of the cases (above), people were referred on for longer-term work; in others, we managed to do what they needed in the time we had. The person who had named her abuse for the first time was immensely relieved; she knew that she would do more work, but 'not yet'. She had made a start. Moments of volatility and change were expressed and experienced in an environment of acceptance and understanding, rather than one in which the client was pathologised. As I hope I have made clear, my work is based on a client-centred perspective in which the client is the expert, rather than an 'expert systems' approach in which the counsellor or the Programme is the expert. In this EAP context then client-centred counselling is a beginning exploration of the client's understanding of symptoms, and questioning of what 'ordinary functioning' had covered over in their families, relationships, communities and, of course, through work and in organisations.

Organisational issues

In his critique of EAPs, Arthur (2001, p. 10) warns that counselling provision should not become 'psychological first aid' which simply puts the employee back into a dysfunctional organisation and leaves the counsellor colluding in that process. Organisations cause distress and he asserts 'the challenge for counsellors … is to bring to attention the organisational mechanisms that cause distress'. Offering counselling as an 'add-on' whilst the organisation continues to place its employees under stress and insecurity is not only untenable, it is unethical, yet it is often the case that an employee's distress is the result of an interaction between individual and organisational factors, such as bullying, poor management, poor systems, or overwork. EAPs do offer a mechanism for the counsellor to do what Arthur suggests by way of case closure/feedback forms. How much the EAP provider then takes this back to the organisation is not always clear. Orlans and Edwards (2004) argue that attending to the needs of the organisation might be an important concern for the workplace counsellor, and, as Claringbull (2006, p. 21) puts it: having a 'better understanding of organisations' and some 'sympathy to employers' needs' are appropriate developments for workplace counsellors. I have, where appropriate, given feedback to an EAP about stresses in the organisation. I have done this in a generalised way and one which protects the anonymity of the client. In my role of providing staff counselling, I have also reported on organisational issues and, in turn, have had to take into account the legitimate concerns of the organisation, for example, in relation to absence through sickness. As therapists working in the context of an EAP, we cannot discount or overlook organisational issues and, in general, need to think more broadly about the role we can play. For me this is not simply due to a personal interest in this work, but also because I view the person-centred approach, and the relational conditions Rogers identified as necessary for individual change, as having a much wider application than just within the therapy room. This view has been well-documented by Rogers himself (1969, 1978, 1980) and many others, including Barrett-Lennard (1998); Natiello (2001); Embleton Tudor *et al.*, (2004).

I have found Natiello's (2001) concept of collaborative power extremely helpful in resourcing my ability to work with organisational issues and to stay empathic, connected and hopeful. She defines collaborative power as having the following properties: openness, i.e. all information is fully shared; responsiveness, i.e. all needs and ideas are carefully heard; dignity, i.e. everyone is respected and considered; personal empowerment, alternating influence, i.e. different people have a say at different times depending on experience, need, self-awareness and wisdom and cooperation. This is echoed in some recent organisational thinking by Wheatley (2005) which I find heartening, and which explains the deep crisis in which many organisations appear to be mired, and the ensuing stress this causes employees (p. 19):

> The engineering image we carry of ourselves has led to organisational lives where we believe we can ignore the deep realities of human existence. We can ignore that people carry spiritual quests and questions into their work; we can ignore that people need love and acknowledgement; we can pretend that emotions are not part of our work lives; we can pretend we don't have families or health crisis, or deep worries. In essence we take the complexity of human life and organise it away ... People can be viewed as machines and controlled to perform with the same efficiency and predictability.

Of course human beings are not machines, but, as Wheatley and others are saying, there is a tension between different images of the person and of organisation. Thus, stress at work is on the increase and, partly because employers are scared of litigation, EAPs are on the increase. The urgent need to tackle stress at work has led to publications, notably the Health and Safety Executive's (2001) publication *Tackling Work Related Stress* which advocates taking work-related stress seriously and, significantly, is a guide for managers on how to work actively to improve the health and well-being of employees. This support is needed as, according to Bunting (2004, p. xxv), those who are in work are being made increasingly ill by the 'sheer invasive dominance of work in people's lives and the price it exacts on their health and happiness'.

As a therapist operating within an EAP, I believe that I need to think more broadly, *together with clients*, about the effect of the organisational culture on them; and what the promotion of concepts such as 'success', 'team spirit', and 'continual achievement' has on them as measures of their self-worth, especially when they are no longer able to 'keep going' or to 'cope', and may have become anxious or depressed. Sometimes I say to clients who have been overworking for months and, in some cases, years, 'But you're not a machine, you are a human being'. In response, clients sometimes look puzzled, and other times cry; in any case, they usually begin a process of increasing self-awareness about both their individual (intrapersonal) and their interpersonal experience of work. Again, I have come to term such therapeutic exchanges as *moments of volatility* as the client's organismic valuing process fluctuates and conflicts with their self-concept of what being a 'good employee' means. One client I worked with, as a result of such a process then got her whole team involved in monitoring overworking, looking out for one another, so that they could tell one another to leave at 5.30 pm. The actualising tendency in humans is towards constructive social behaviour (Bozarth, 1998 p. 31). It is crucial that the individual is not pathologised for the structural and cultural problems of the organisation, and that together we look at what the 'culture' deems as 'normal functioning', and that test against the experience of the client's organismic valuing process. This process is bound to create more moments of volatility for clients as they recover a sense of personal empowerment. It is easy to explore stress management strategies with clients so that they can 'cope' again. This, again, is the 'expert systems' paradigm at work. It is less easy to hold the complexity of the context or system, for example, institutional bullying, and to find a way both to explore this with the client and, crucially, to feed back to the organisation the structural causes of stress and distress.

The counsellor's role is social and political

The wider social and political issue of the overwork culture in our society is also part of the EAP counsellor's context and remit. The debate about what it means to be human, and our needs for rest, leisure, caring for dependants, the welfare of our children, and what it means to reach our full human potential, cannot be left to managers or politicians. As counsellors we must reclaim our legitimate role in that debate and encourage our clients to do the same, starting with how to re-humanise the workplace. Working as an EAP counsellor allows me to take on this challenge and presents me with the continuous challenge of balancing my person-centred theory and practice of working with collaborative power, as opposed to becoming an expert and taking 'power over'. What also helps me in this challenge is remembering that the very 'volatility' of the workforce is, in fact, a blessing, as it is the actualising tendency at work! As Wheatley (2005, p. 20) puts it: 'the mechanistic story has led us to believe that we, with our unpredictable behaviors, our passions, our independence, our creativity, our consciousness, that we are the problem rather than the blessing'.

Employee Assistance Programmes mean that far more people now have access to counselling than would have had previously. In this sense, as Arthur (2001) puts it, EAPs have become the 'new mental health services'. However, as Arthur also says, we should not let them be used as a psychological first aid, or to determine the process or content of therapy if, as person-centred therapists, we think that our aim is to promote the well-being, empowerment, and human potential of both our clients and our organisations.

References

Arthur, A. (2001) The EAP debate. *Counselling & Psychotherapy Journal*, 12(1): 7–10.
Barrett-Lennard, G. (1998) *Carl Rogers' Helping System*. London: Sage.
British Association for Counselling & Psychotherapy (2000) *Ethical Framework for Good Practice in Counselling and Psychotherapy*. Rugby: BACP.
Bozarth. J. (1998) *Person Centred Therapy: A Revolutionary Paradigm*. Ross-on-Wye: PCCS Books.
Bunting, M. (2004) *Willing Slaves: How the Overwork Culture is Ruling our Lives.* London: HarperCollins.
Claringbull, N. (2006) 'Workplace counselling: New models for new times', *Counselling at Work*, 54: 17–20.
Embleton Tudor, L., Keemar, K., Tudor, K., Valentine, J. and Worrall, M. (2004) *The Person-Centred Approach: A Contemporary Introduction*. Basingstoke: Palgrave.
Fernald, P.S. (2000) 'Carl Rogers: Body-centered counsellor', *Journal of Counselling & Development*, 78: 172–9.
Friery, K. (2006) 'Workplace counselling: Who is the consumer?' *Counselling at Work*, 54: 24–6.
Grange C. (2005) 'The development of EAPs in the UK', *Counselling at* Work, 49: 2–5.
Grove, B. and Seymour, L. (2007) 'Workplace interventions', *Counselling at Work*, 58: 4–5.
Health and Safety Executive (2001) *Tackling Work Related Stress: A Manager's Guide to Improving and Maintaining Employee Health and Well-Being*. Sudbury: HSE.
Health and Safety Executive (2004) *Annual Report*. Sudbury: HSE.
Jordan, J.V., Walker, M. and Hartling, L. (1991) *Women's Growth in Connection: Writings from the Stone Centre*. New York: Guilford Press.
McLeod, J. (2001) 'The BACP review of research into workplace counselling', *Counselling at Work*, 58: 2–3.
Mearns, D. and Cooper, M. (2005) *Working at Relational Depth in Counselling and Psychotherapy*. London: Sage.
Natiello, P. (2001) 'Collaborative power: Can it succeed in the world of work?' in *The Person-Centred Approach: A Passionate Presence* (pp. 62–85). Ross-on-Wye: PCCS Books.
O'Hara, M. (1999) 'Moments of eternity: Carl Rogers and the contemporary demand for brief therapy', in I. Fairhurst (ed.) *Women Writing in the Person Centred Approach* (pp.63–77). Ross-on-Wye: PCCS Books.

Orlans, V. and Edwards, D. (2004) 'Counselling the organisation', *Counselling at Work*, 11: 132.
Palmer, S., Cooper, C. and Thomas, K. (2004) 'A model of work stress', *Counselling at Work*, 47: 2–5.
Rogers, C.R. (1957) 'The necessary and sufficient conditions of therapeutic personality change', *Journal of Consulting Psychology*, 21: 95–103.
Rogers, C.R. (1959) 'A theory of therapy, personality and interpersonal relationships as developed in the client-centered framework', in S. Koch (ed.) *Psychology: A Study of Science* (pp. 184–256). New York: McGraw-Hill.
Rogers, C.R. (1969) *Freedom to Learn*. Columbus, OH: Charles E. Merrill.
Rogers, C R. (1978) *Carl Rogers on Personal Power*. London: Constable.
Rogers, C.R. (1980) *A Way of Being*. Boston, MA: Houghton Mifflin.
Rowan, J. (2004) 'Three levels of therapy', *Counselling & Psychotherapy Journal*, 15(7): 20–2.
Sanders, P. (2000) 'Mapping person-centred approaches to counselling and psychotherapy', *Person-Centred Practice*, 8 (2): 62–74.
Totton, N. (2004) 'Two ways of being helpful', *Counselling & Psychotherapy Journal*, 15: 5–8.
Tudor, K. (1997) 'A complexity of contracts', in C. Sills (ed.) *Contracts in Counselling* (pp. 157–72). London: Sage.
Tudor, K. and Worrall, M. (2004) 'Issues, questions, dilemmas and domains in supervision', in K. Tudor and M. Worrall (eds), *Freedom to Practise: Person-Centred Approaches to Supervision* (pp. 79–95). Ross-on-Wye: PCCS Books.
Turner A. (2005) 'EAPs: A beginner's guide', *Counselling at Work*, 49: 15–17.
Wakefield, M. and Wakefield, B. (2005, May) 'A response to time-limited person-centred counselling', *Person-Centred Quarterly*, 8–10.
Wheatley, M.J. (2005) *Finding Our Way. Leadership for an Uncertain Time*. San Francisco, CA: Berrett-Koehler.

9

Overcoming the Effects of an Aggravated Burglary: Traumatic Incident Reduction in Action

Henry J. Whitfield

In Chapter 4, we saw an overview of how traumatic incident reduction (TIR) and Applied Metapsychology techniques can be tailored to a range of situations in brief therapy practice. In that chapter we also saw a discussion of the factors that contribute to the briefness and efficiency of TIR. In this chapter, I examine the details of a case in which a range of techniques were applied over five meetings, reaching the client's goals in five hours and 25 minutes, including the assessment; following which I discuss why this case might have run the particular course that it did, and place it in a broader context of TIR practice.

Case study

Client background

The client, Lucy, is in her late 30s. She was the victim of an aggravated burglary. Whilst sleeping in the privacy of her own home, she was awoken by the sound of an intruder who, when she tried to call the Police, proceeded to attack her physically. Despite the physical nature of the attack, Lucy did not suffer lasting physical damage. However, lasting psychological symptoms disrupted her life greatly. She developed many of the typical symptoms of post-traumatic stress disorder (PTSD). Seven months after the attack, Lucy still complained of: flashbacks; tiredness; difficulty concentrating; and a pounding heart. She reported hypervigilence, particularly with sounds at night that would prevent her from sleeping; she was unable to settle down after she had been startled; she still felt that she was reliving the incident; and had a fear of the intruder returning to her flat. Her inability to sleep was Lucy's greatest concern. This greatly affected her ability to function in a very demanding job in the emergency services. When her symptoms had not changed for seven months, Lucy believed she would never recover from what had happened. She was taking diasapam occasionally in order to help her sleep. After receiving practical and emotional support from her local branch of Victim Support, Lucy was referred for trauma counselling.

First meeting: Assessment and an introductory exercise
around safety

Typically, TIR practitioners complete extensive assessments before TIR treatment plans are prepared. Questionnaires of 60–80 or more questions are often used. The average length of such an assessment is between 90 and 120 minutes. In this case, the assessment lasted less than an hour. This was apparently because this client had less to say than most other clients. In addition to the problems already mentioned, the assessment also brought to light the following:

- Previous traumas: a bereavement and a mugging.
- Tiredness: feeling too tired to be able to have a social life.
- Shame: feeling ashamed of how affected she was by the attack
- Anger: towards her attacker.
- Fantasies: of destroying her attacker.

Lucy also reported not feeling safe at night; feeling very let down by the lack of responsiveness of the Police; and feeling distressed: 'I cry a lot – at least once a week'.

The briefness of the assessment left us with time in the same initial meeting for an experiential exercise. As the client clearly had a problem feeling safe in her flat, I offered her the opportunity of doing an exercise that explored safety. This exercise lasted for approximately 10 minutes. I began by presenting the three instructions of the technique to the client, explained the purpose of repetitive questions (see description of Unlayering in Chapter 4, p. 71), and told her that we could do the exercise as long as she was interested or until she felt she had benefited from it in some way (see description of 'endpoints' in Chapter 4). The three instructions were:

1 'Tell me something it would be safe to be'.
2 'Tell me something it would be safe to do'.
3 'Tell me something it would be safe to have'.

These instructions were asked in a three-part loop, that is: 1, 2, 3, 1, 2, 3, 1, etc.

I chose to offer this in that moment for a number of reasons: (a) I usually start therapy with an exercise that does not require a lot of ego strength, so that I can observe how the client processes material, and engages with her mental environment before asking her to look at something more demanding; (b) To introduce the client to the use of repetition; and (c) Because this client felt she was struggling to feel safe. It was therefore likely that examination of her constructs relating to what actually could be safe would be useful to her. After doing this exercise, clients often report feeling safer right there and then.

In this case, the client found six examples of safety for each form of safety, thus finding 18 examples of potential safety in her world. My observation at the time was that the client had not engaged particularly well with the exercise, and that she had only found the instructions marginally useful. When a client engages well with this exercise, he or she tends to reach clear insights and experience feelings of safety. In this case there were only mild signs of this. For homework I gave the client some reading, that is, a written description of the Basic TIR procedure for addressing known traumatic incidents. The purpose of this was to demystify what the trauma counselling might involve.

Second meeting: Repetitive imaginal exposure to the trauma (Basic TIR technique)

When she returned for the second meeting, Lucy reported that she had only had five hours sleep during the previous night; nevertheless, she showed a willingness to look at traumatic incidents. It is never predictable how many hours sleep a client needs before she is able to process major traumatic incidents. TIR training recommends that clients are in optimum physical condition and aware that factors such as rest, nourishment and drowsiness-inducing drugs can inhibit this. TIR practitioners, therefore, ask their clients to be as well fed and rested as they can be, and to avoid as much as they can, any drugs which induce drowsiness. I told Lucy that we would go with her perceptions as to whether she was ready to look at the particular traumatic incident for which she was referred, using the Basic TIR procedure. I also said that we could start with a lesser traumatic incident if she preferred. Lucy chose to examine a road traffic accident that she had suffered several years previously.

Lucy, at her own pace, re-experienced the road traffic accident three times. At the end of the third description of the accident, she felt the emotional charge had dissipated and even seemed quite cheerful about how the exercise had gone. Lucy then expressed a desire to address the incident of the aggravated burglary, the incident that had caused her seven months of sleepless nights. Once a client has experienced the reduction of the emotional charge from a traumatic incident, then that client often demonstrates an increased willingness to re-experience traumatic incidents.

In Basic TIR, once the client has identified the time, location and duration of the incident, the rest of the session largely consists of the client redirecting her awareness through her memories of the incident in a repetitive manner. This begins with a silent re-experiencing followed by a description of that re-experiencing. The client then alternates between silent re-experiencings and verbal descriptions. Occasionally, other related incidents also need to be addressed before the client reaches a full endpoint, i.e. insights, extraversion and positive indicators (see p. 71). This repetitive exercise, which is presented to the client as a possibility to try out, continues as long as the client is interested, as long as new content is surfacing, and until some kind of endpoint is reached. 'New content' consists of either new factual details or changes in the client's affect. In response to a major traumatic incident, significant insights usually emerge as the client attains a fuller awareness and a broader perspective on what happened. In addition, the client will become able to see the incident from a more detached and more equanimous viewpoint: the client stops resisting her experience and allows it to become the past. In this case, the client chose to end the exercise after four re-experiencings and five descriptions of the incident:

1   During the first re-telling the client expressed the thought: 'Is this reality or am I dreaming?' This is a classic indicator of an unassimilated and unaccommodated traumatic experience, in other words: the experience seems unreal.

2   The second re-telling revealed many more details and themes. These included: 'Was he breaking in to kill me?'; 'I was embarrassed for being naked'; revulsion for his 'invading my body space'; 'I trembled so much, even after he'd gone'; '*He* was in control'.

3   The third re-telling (subsequent to the third re-experiencing), had a different focus. Whilst phoning 999, Lucy was 'stunned into silence' when all she got was an answerphone. She also recalled banging her head.

4   The fourth re-telling had yet another focus: 'Now it sticks out that I can't keep him [the intruder] in the bathroom'. Lucy also mentions 'flashbacks of feeling him in my back'. At the end of the fourth retelling, I asked Lucy how the incident seemed to her. This is an example of a common question in TIR, used to give the client the opportunity to re-appraise where she is in relation to processing a traumatic incident. It is also a slightly different angle from which to view the incident. At this stage, the client continued to express a huge anger towards the intruder. She placed emphasis on the point that she 'had no control', a point she had made during the second re-telling. However, she also mentions that she feels calmer and that: 'I feel he didn't want to hurt me'.

From my point of view I could see that Lucy had successfully processed *some* of the incident. In metapsychology theory, therapeutic processing is closely equated with a shift in the client's viewpoint and the dissipation of negative emotion. The clearest example of closure was the shift from 'Was he breaking in to kill me?' to 'I feel he didn't want to hurt me'. Note that the client made the second statement in the present tense, which suggests that it was a new feeling in that session. In this case, the client's viewpoint of the incident had evolved, but did not appear to have been fully resolved. There was still evidence of emotional charge in the form of anger and anxiety. The fact that there was still evidence of unresolved emotional charge suggests that it might have been worthwhile to continue with further repetitions. However, Lucy made it clear that she did not want to recount the incident again. I suggested that, before ending, if she was interested and felt the incident was still on her mind, we could do a grounding technique. Lucy thought it might be useful. The grounding procedure consisted of the client repetitively focusing her awareness on large, stable, physical objects in the room, and my pointing out such objects with repetition. This is similar to the word-for-word and situational contact reflections of pre-therapy.

Third meeting: An application of the unblocking procedure regarding 'noise'

When the client returned the next week, she mentioned that she had a week of feeling really good. She no longer had flashbacks, or felt she was reliving the incident, and could now sleep a little better. However, she felt she was still rather sensitive to noise. It seemed that much of the work was already completed at this point. Lucy had apparently processed the traumatic incident significantly in that many of the presenting symptoms had already gone or had reduced. The incident itself was no longer important to her. This was after just one hour of Basic TIR, following the initial meeting.

The PTSD symptom of hypervigilance is often one of the last symptoms to resolve during trauma counselling. This is probably because the action of vigilance, or awareness of one's environment, is actually useful to a client. It follows that a lack of vigilance could help allow a future similar trauma. However, too much vigilance can be very disruptive to sleep and therefore to life in general. In contrast, consistent nightmares, which are another common PTSD symptom, are not very useful and tend to resolve almost immediately after the incident has been processed.

After some exploration, Lucy decided that the word 'noise' was the most accurate label to describe her problem. In this approach, counsellors take a lot of care to find a label that fits most closely with the client's inner experience. This search is comparable to the step of 'finding a handle' in Gendlin's (1978) focusing. In response to this issue of noise, I presented the unblocking technique (see p. 74). I suggested unblocking because it is particularly well suited to reducing charge and expanding awareness of generic, abstract concepts such as noise, people and emotions.

During this process, Lucy identified many examples of mental blocks as presented in the unblocking list. Some examples of what Lucy discerned within the structure of unblocking were:

• that she tried to suppress her hypersensitivity to noise;
• that she felt her sense of perspective had been belittled;
• that she felt she was cautious but only at night time;

- that she had resisted feeling calm and
- that she judged people a lot more as possible muggers or rapists.

At the end of the exercise Lucy noted feeling 'less panicked', but also pointed out that she wanted to be awake if it happened again.

Fourth meeting: A fear of not sleeping, addressed
with Future TIR

At the fourth meeting, Lucy reported that she still had problems with sleeping, even though she felt much better. She would lie in bed at night, fearing how she would cope with her pressured job if she hadn't had enough sleep. Lucy was no longer focused on what had happened in the past and was now focused on what might happen in the future.

An exercise designed for fears of what might happen in the future, is 'Future TIR'. Incidents that have not yet happened in reality can already be very alive in the client's imagination. Such future projections can be examined in detail, in much the same way that past actual incidents are examined. A difference, however, is that it may be necessary to explore a number of versions that the client is imagining. Memories of actual incidents do not fluctuate as much as projected future incidents. In Future TIR, the practitioner asks the client to start with the worst case scenario, then, if necessary, asks the client to look at scenarios in which the client handles the feared situation better.

In this case, we first addressed incidents of not being able to sleep all night. Then we addressed versions including having a terrible time at work due to the lack of sleep. Finally, we addressed versions in which the client was really tearful due to several days of no sleep. Retrospectively, the client actually looked at worse and worse scenarios, even though the technique leans towards starting with the worst scenarios, and then addressing versions in which the client is less upset. The fact that this happened in reverse is an example of how clients can move freely in any direction they choose, even when there is a structure (see Coghlan and McIlduff, 1990). This client knew she could go wherever she wanted. The structure is more to support the client when he or she feels unable to find her own way.

The end point of this session was evidenced when Lucy, of her own accord, stated with confidence 'I can do this'. With Lucy's consent, we then ended the session.

Fifth and final session: Unlayering regarding 'Letting your
guard down'

At the beginning of the next session, in response to my asking how she had been since the last session, Lucy replied, 'Quite good. I still fear not getting enough sleep, but I have really improved. I do get good nights' sleep'.

Lucy identified that she still had the remaining goal of not being so jumpy and not freaking out if she hears something. In response to this I asked Lucy to define any triggers she was aware of. These included: noises, loud noises, and not knowing the source of noises. Lucy emphasised that: 'When you sleep, you let your guard down'. At this point it appeared to me that 'letting your guard down' was a central part of what was on Lucy's mind, whilst trying to sleep. After checking Lucy's interest in focusing on this area, I devised an unlayering technique (see p. 70) to structure a repetitive focusing in that area of concern. The questions were:

1 Where or when could you let your guard down?
2 Where or when would you rather not let your guard down?

When presented with these questions, Lucy showed a clear interest in trying them out. Lucy found 15 answers to the first question and 14 answers to the second question. The questions were designed to create the opportunity for an experiential exploration of what Lucy's 'guard' actually was, including when it was appropriate to have it up, and when it was appropriate to let it down. Also, the second question provides a form of repetitive imaginal exposure to that which disturbs Lucy, relating to letting her 'guard' down. Repetitive unlayering questions (or instructions) are a way to enable repetitive exposure to very specific and even very abstract private events. Such highly targeted repetitive focusing of awareness, when based on thorough assessments, appear to be an efficient way of accelerating therapeutic process. When Lucy ran out of answers to the above two questions, her attention shifted to an 'anxiety' and a discomfort with being alone at night. To examine this, we used the following two repetitive instructions:

1 When you are alone at night, tell me something you could face?
2 When you are alone at night, tell me something you would rather not face?

Lucy found seven answers to the first and 10 answers to the second question.

Sixth and final meeting: Rounding off

Lucy and I met one more time. Lucy reported that she was no longer anxious going to bed, and that she was no longer waking up in the middle of the night. In her own words: 'I think I heard something but I couldn't be bothered'. No formal exercises were done as Lucy didn't have an area of concern to focus on. Lucy decided she no longer was in need of therapy so we agreed to end. This meeting lasted 15 minutes.

Follow up

Just over 18 months later, Lucy and I spoke on the phone (when I contacted her to ask for her permission to write this chapter). I asked her how she was doing. She replied that she was still fine, was thankful, and added that if she ever had 'a wobbly moment' she got over it very quickly. The work we had done had had a clear lasting effect for Lucy.

Discussion

The following discussion offers some theories as to why this case went the way it did and places this case in a broader context of general TIR practice. However, it is important to be aware that, as human beings have so many variables and complexities, we do not have all the data we might like to have. For example, we do not know if there were other important issues on Lucy's mind at the time of therapy which she simply chose not to tell me about.

In my experience it is common to see such changes, as in this case, in three to four sessions. Also, in this case, the traumatic incident was largely processed after the first full session. However, the remaining hypervigilance had to be addressed with four additional techniques before it was resolved. These were: Unblocking, Future TIR, and two tailor-made sets of Unlayering.

Hypothetically, this client may have required fewer sessions on the hypervigilance if she had spent more time on the central incident itself. This statement is based on the hypothesis that resolving emotional charge – defined as repressed, unfulfilled intention (Gerbode, 1995), or 'stuck' latent emotion from the past – reduces or resolves most of the unwanted private events that relate to an issue. The job of the TIR practitioner is to provide opportunities for the client to access and release the emotional charge that relates to the problems that the client wants to resolve. In this case, Lucy had not resolved all the charge on the initial incident (in the second meeting). Had other techniques not been effective enough in addressing the hypervigilance, I would have checked the client's perceptions of that initial incident again, looking for evidence of further emotional charge. Finding more charge there would have suggested that more could be achieved by addressing that incident, either by revisiting it as before, or with a different technique. However, Lucy would only have revisited that incident if she herself felt it would be interesting to do so.

A variety of techniques are usually employed in TIR treatment plans in that the client may be more engaged in the process if he or she continually has fresh angles from which to view the issue. TIR and metapsychology theory hypothesises that a more engaged, focused client, leads to more productive therapy (Volkman, 2003).

According to the assessment, this client did not have any other issues that she felt she needed to address at the time. This factor may have made this case faster to resolve than average. A simpler case with fewer complications usually requires less time. For example, if most of the relevant emotional charge is in the same place, i.e. in one incident, then it can often be resolved in one session, if the client is willing to go there. This case seems to have been such a case, except that the client did not choose, or perhaps was not able, fully to resolve the trauma in the first full session. The client let go of the remainder of the emotional charge in the following three meetings, through four further exercises.

Comparable cases that take much longer might involve multiple child-hood traumas, which are re-triggered by the recent trauma. Unprocessed trauma that is outside the client's awareness can still be accessed in most cases through awareness expanding exercises, tracing current themes backwards into the client's past. However, this might take 20 to 30 hours, as distinct from five hours.

Another factor that contributed to the brevity of this case is that each session was shorter than average. Some clients process their material faster than others. Another client might have had an average session length of two hours. In this case, whilst the number of sessions (five) is fairly typical for such a presenting issue, each session was approximately 30 minutes shorter than the average within the context in which I work. Occasionally, some clients may need to review an incident repetitively for several hours. If time does not permit, this could be done in more than one sitting, though ideally it is better to finish what you have started in the same session.

In evaluating a client's ability to process and, therefore, to change, TIR and metapsychology place emphasis on 'ego strength' and/or free 'intention units'. Gerbode (1995, p. 194) defines 'personal power' as: 'The capacity to intend … At any particular time, a person has only a limited capacity to intend things, a limited number of "intention units" '. Based on the information presented above, one can argue that this particular client was very able to process. She appeared not to have created many 'hang-ups' or 'issues' in her life. The only issue she presented to counselling was that of the trauma of being attacked in her home. Contrarily, one could argue the possibility that this client simply did not want to look at any of her other issues, and therefore chose not to mention them. If this was the case, Lucy would still have needed substantial ego strength to hold off any other issues on her mind at the time. Either way, logically it follows that Lucy had above average ego strength. What is clear is that the aggravated burglary proved too much for her, leading to hypervigilance, which then caused sleep problems, which then caused chronic fatigue problems. Such fatigue is enough to reduce severely a person's 'capacity to intend' or ability to focus. Fortunately, this did not happen to the extent that the client could not process incidents: indeed, she was still able to process incidents quickly.

Clients that do not have sufficient ego strength to look at imagery, or to relive past traumatic experiences, can usually still make progress with techniques that don't require such an ability to focus, or as much willingness to face difficulty. Such less demanding techniques include Unblocking and other Unlayering techniques. As a client resolves more emotional charge, he or she regains the ability to process incidents. Such a change leads to an acceleration in the client's speed and ability to process.

In summary, other than the use of TIR, factors that arguably contributed to the brevity of this case were:

- a lack of other issues to cloud her awareness;
- an ability to process traumatic incidents that was faster than average, leading to shorter sessions;
- a willingness to look at the most significant trauma in the first session, after the assessment and
- a focus on just one issue.

Another client with the same problems might have taken nine to 10 hours to achieve the same result. A client with a great many other issues and other traumas, might require 20 to 30 hours of therapy, usually in 10 to 15 meetings, in order to clear the mental space necessary before the client is able to address the heavier, early traumata that are complicit with the client's presenting problems.

References

Coghlan, D. and McIlduff, E. (1990) 'Structuring and non-directiveness in group facilitation', *Person-Centered Review*, 5(1): 13–29.

Gendlin, E.T. (1978) *Focusing: How to Gain Direct Access to Your Body's Knowledge*. London: Rider Books.

Gerbode, F.A (1995) *Beyond Psychology: An Introduction to Metapsychology* (3rd edn). Menlo Park, CA: IRM Press.

Volkman, M.K. (2003) *Traumatic Incident Reduction – Expanded Applications Workshop Manual* (rev. edn). Kansas City, KS: AMI Press.

10

This Could be the Last Time: Person-Centred Counselling with Young Men in a Young Offenders' Institution

Barrie Hopwood

Well this could be the last time
This could be the last time
Maybe the last time
I don't know

(The Rolling Stones)

Today I was able to give Andy a 21st birthday card, the day before his birthday, and to look at the work we have been doing together over the last three months about his future hopes and fears. Now that he is 21 he may well be moved on to an adult prison before my next visit to the Young Offenders' Institution (YOI). Andy and I have always been aware of the possibility that we won't see each other from one week to the next, but I hope he has come to know that I am glad to have spent time with him; that I look forward to meeting him again, if there is a next time; that I hope that his week will go as well as he can reasonably expect it to; and that I will be praying for him each morning, knowing that we may never be able to say a proper goodbye. I was also able to see Brendan, who is waiting for his trial and who, because of his intense fear of being bullied by the other lads on the wing, only ventures from his cell once a week when I come to see him. His trial has been adjourned several times, and so each session we never know if we will meet again. We work in the moment and look at how he can manage the dread of each day in prison, while continuing to hold out hope for the future, following the outcome of his trial.

I mention Andy and Brendan because they illustrate both the uncertainty around almost every ending with our clients who are in prison, and the necessity of immediacy in the counselling. In our work with young offenders in prison, we have learned to adapt to what might appear to be a constraint on our work, and to work here-and-now to ensure that every session is whole and complete as it is 'all that we know we have'.

A week later, and the significance of treating each session as if it's our last is brought home to me when I phone to book to see these clients, only to be told that Andy was transferred to adult prison the previous day, and that Brendan went to court two days ago and was discharged. Both of them have the address and phone number of Hounslow Youth Counselling Service (HYCS). I shall write to Andy at his adult prison to wish him well, but it is very unlikely that I will hear from or about either of them again. I hope that the time I have spent with both of them has helped them to begin to feel that they are unique, valuable and gifted young men with a future, a contribution to make and a new sense of self that transcends the toxic effects of abuse, rejection and punishment which they have suffered in their attempts to survive in the cruel and unjust world into which they were born.

Moving forward another two months, and I am reflecting that, after five years as Project Manager for HYCS at the YOI, it has taken writing this chapter for me to realise fully how incredibly important and also how incredibly demanding it is 'to treat every session as though it is our last'. I write this as I begin the return to work after a personal burn-out which I believe was triggered by the 'permission' granted me by the coincidence, for the first time in those five years, of ending the work with all the clients I was seeing at the YOI on the same day. As I hold the view that every session with a client could be our last, the level of commitment to each client is great. This commitment had been so extensive that, apart from holiday breaks, I hadn't taken 'time out' from the prison because there was always at least one ongoing client whom I felt I couldn't 'let down' However, in doing this, I had neglected my own needs in terms of self-care, and hence my burn-out. I hope that my personal reflection on this experience and learning at the YOI will lead to a constructively critical perspective on the demands, as well as the benefits of this work in relation to both client and counsellor.

The YOI counselling service in context

In 1994, volunteer counsellors from the Hounslow Youth Counselling Service began to counsel young men at the YOI as part of the Service's objective of providing all young people in the Borough of Hounslow with a free, confidential and independent person-centred counselling service. HYCS aims to serve young people by offering them a reflective space which can help them to attend to their problems and issues in the context of a relationship in which they can feel safe, accepted, understood and valued.

From 2002, we have had up to 10 volunteer counsellors working in the prison alongside the Project Manager and myself; both of us are paid for one day a week. Each counsellor sees between two and four clients per week. We choose counsellors not only because they have expressed an interest in working in a prison, but also because they possess qualities such as robustness and flexibility which will enable them to flourish in the complex, demanding and unpredictable world of a YOI. All of our counsellors go through a very intensive and thorough recruitment into the Service as a whole before undertaking a separate process with myself and the prison authorities which prepares them for the specific world of prison counselling.

From the first day of training for prison counselling each of the HYCS counsellors is made aware of the importance of treating each session with a client as though it may be the last. This principle or attitude arises from the often painful reality that, whilst we may expect to see our clients, we may be told that they are in court; having legal or social visits; at classes, the mosque, the library, or the gym; or they have been 'shipped out' or released; or that there is a 'lock down', i.e. that no visitors are allowed on the units. For his part, the client may not want to see us because he has been misinformed about who we are, for example, the lad who shouted through the flap in his cell door: 'Why the fuck should I want to see a Housing Service when I've just been given life'; he might be resentful of an officer who shouts across the wing: 'Your counsellor's here to see you' when he is engrossed in a game of pool with the other lads. Recently a client who desperately wanted counselling, and with whom I had built up a very strong bond, chose to end our work because he knew I could not guarantee total confidentiality in relation to his suicidal intention, and because his lawyers had 'gagged' him from talking to me about anything to do with the circumstances of the crime with which he had been charged.

So the nature of a remand YOI means that once we receive a referral we don't even know that there will be a first session, never mind a last one! The client may no longer be at the prison or, often, even if he is still there, we may not be able to see him on the day. So, although the Service offers open-ended counselling for an hour a week for as long as the client is at the prison, the reality is that the inevitable uncertainty around the next session and endings imposes its own dynamic on our work which, in turn, leads to a philosophy of 'make the most of every moment'.

Our counselling project, at what is the largest YOI in Western Europe, serves one of the most marginalised groups in contemporary society and it is my belief that for many of these young men the counselling intervention provides a new form of relationship. This results in them making changes in their self-perception and in their understanding of relationships with others and society. Counselling offers an opportunity for them to address their offending behaviour with a view to 'making it' in the outside world, rather than repeating the behaviour on release, and re-entering the prison system. As well as understanding the past and preparing for the future, many clients find that weekly counselling enables them to cope with the present reality of being in prison, especially in managing their anger and offloading painful and powerful thoughts and feelings. These young men are 'locked in' psychologically as well as physically and, if we are to help them free themselves from some of the emotional and mental sentences they have been serving for most of their lives, I believe we are contributing to their better futures and to wider societal well-being.

Although England and Wales have the highest rate of imprisonment in Western Europe, it is likely that most of the readers of this book have never been or will never be detained 'At Her Majesty's Pleasure'. It is one of the few client environments which is totally alien to the life experiences of most counsellors. Essentially, YOIs are prisons for 15 to 21 year olds who have either been convicted and sentenced to a custodial term, or who are remanded in custody prior to trial or sentence. Young Offenders predominantly come from tough environments where survival of the fittest or the 'law of the jungle' prevails, and come to an even tougher one in prison where to be 'a pussy' or to be unable to respond to the taunt of 'suck your mum' is to invite humiliation and relentless bullying. In the context of this alien world, I invite you to imagine preparing to see a client for the first time!

The first time

Some clients immediately decide that they do not want to see a counsellor while others think we can 'do something' for them which we are unable to promise and choose not to carry on with the session. Most, however, will either launch into their stories or be passive. Clients in the latter category will avert their eyes with nervousness, uncertainty and mistrust hanging in the air. I used to be surprised that usually such clients actually do want us to stay with them for the session and to return the next week and I now know how important it is not to assume that passivity or a 'whatever' attitude means that they don't want to see me. These early stages are crucial in building up trust and encouraging psychological contact in a way which will invite some receptivity to our genuine interest, warmth and attunement to the client.

A common experience among our counsellors is that their initial handshake with the client can be an organismic shock! When we meet clients we often experience their hands as sticky or wet, even though that might be because they have washed them before greeting us or just because they are nervous. Our reaction may be compounded subsequently by seeing the client's hands moving around inside the back and or front of his trousers, or his fingers up his nose or picking at scabs on his body. However we react, we cannot underestimate the importance of this very first connection with the client, and that shaking hands at the beginning and end of the session helps to establish contact and sets the session within a boundary: by shaking his hand we are showing him that we do not experience him as untouchable. The humanity of the handshake is a vital non-verbal communication, especially in a context in which many of the other professionals with whom he is in contact do not shake his hand. I believe we are conveying that the work we do is different; it is for him, with him at the centre of it.

My core belief about the clients I work with at the YOI can be summed up in the phrase: 'There but for the Grace of God, go I'. Both in psychological and spiritual terms, I recognise that when my client was born he was a perfect gift to the world, and that he is a physical, psychological and spiritual being. I know right from the start that I can only expect to earn his trust by showing respect, genuine interest and empathy, attitudes so rare that they are like gold dust to the clients I meet. Once the process of building trust is flowing, I'm not surprised at the positive response of most of our clients which is to welcome the undivided attention of another and to look forward to the weekly meeting for an hour or so. Often it will only be with the counsellor that they have the privacy to be free to be themselves, and with whom they have any trust to open up, to share their week and to voice their frustrations. I believe that the therapeutic potential of our work hinges on me as a counsellor trusting myself, my client and the relationship and, on the client's process of becoming more trusting of himself, of me and of the relationship.

The intensity and complexity of the prison context is hard to describe and, here, I invite you to enter into the spirit of our work by imagining that I am addressing you as if you have just been remanded to the YOI for the first time, and I am introducing the counselling service available to you and your peers.

You've recently arrived at a YOI for the first time. Often lads tell us that the first few days can be hell and that they feel frightened, angry, lonely, confused, despairing or even suicidal. I don't suppose anything could have prepared you for the shock of being deprived of your liberty, and yet you daren't show any vulnerability in front of the other lads who are already flexing their muscles and trying to find chinks in your emotional armour. I hope you will find that the prison officers treat you well and that you are able to phone your family and friends. I also hope that you are able to get out of your cell as much as you need to for work, education, gym, library, association, chapel or mosque, and legal and social visits. I realise, however, that for much of the time you will be alone in a small room with just your TV and your thoughts and feelings for companionship, and that you may find that the past, present and future all seem confusing and overwhelming right now. I don't care what you have been charged with or convicted of, but I do care about how all of this is impacting on your health, happiness and human dignity. I wonder if you are wondering who the hell I am and why I am reaching out to you, and asking why you should believe in me any more than in all the adults who may have abused, rejected, punished or bullshitted you in the past.

You may not need to know all or any of what I'm saying to you but I hope that if you should be asked if you want to see a counsellor, or feel one day that the pain is too much too bear on your own you will know a little bit more about what you are 'letting yourself in for' and what you could expect to gain from asking to see a HYCS counsellor. When I see you for the first time I will probably know nothing about you other than a word or phrase such as 'bereavement' or 'childhood issues' given to me by the referring department. We will often not know the offence for which you have been convicted or with which you are charged, and often we may never find out. We work with the person not the crime and we do our utmost not to be contaminated by staff perceptions and judgements of our clients.

We believe our contract guidelines help us ensure that we fulfil the ethical obligation to you of informed client consent. Nothing is set in stone but the following might encapsulate what I feel you are entitled to know about this new relationship and which I might introduce at the beginning of or, if inappropriate then, at some time during our first session.

'I'm Barrie from Youth Counselling and I've been told by X from Outreach that you thought it might be helpful for us to meet up … (pause) … if you would like me to stay I can be here for as long as you want for up to an hour … if at the end of the session you want me to come back next week then I'll be happy to do so … I am committed to be here for you but I also recognise that circumstances may mean that you might not be here or for some we reason we may not be able to meet so this and every session could be the first and last time we meet … this time and space is for you to use as you wish … I need to let you know now that I won't be able to write any letters in relation to your criminal case on your behalf … I also want you to know that I'm not part of the Prison Service and I will respect the confidentiality of what you say to me. I do however have an obligation to discuss with you and possibly with the Head of Safeguards what to do with what you tell me if it raises a significant risk of serious harm to yourself or another person … Is there anything would like to ask me?'

The last time

I hope some of my significant learning around therapeutic, ethical, practical, philosophical and contextual issues will encourage more practitioners and organisations to expand into this territory knowing that 'the facts are friendly!' and think constructively about the challenges of work where we need to hold in mind that each session may be our last.

Make the most of every session

I must never underestimate the fact that one session can be hugely important to help a client share something that they may really need to and it may be all they need. I recognise that sometimes clients can engage more quickly and deeply because they know each session may be their last and they need to get something off their chest; it certainly makes us work harder! I try not to underestimate the importance of 'Working in the Here and Now' (or, as I think of it, 'the sacrament of the present moment') because it's the only thing we know we've got! This type of potentially brief work helps focus and clarity to emerge much more quickly than in most of my work with private and University clients! It may not, however, be 'counselling as we thought we knew it'!

I work towards an ending being built-in to every session and remember that is often appropriate to thank the client for what he has shared with me and to reflect the richness of the session back to him; he may well take away that reflection as a gift of great value to him. It sometimes pays to think 'have I left anything unsaid which if he isn't there next week would lead me to inwardly exclaim "Oh God, I wish I'd said … to him!"' I often feel 'gutted' at my own loss when a client leaves and I only make it worse for the client and myself by leaving a session with unfinished business.

Containment

I am aware that nothing prepares me for the shock of ringing in to see my client only to be told 'he was shipped out yesterday'. This leads to me never taking anything for granted in terms of the raw emotional power of the work on the client and on myself. Often the longer I am working with a client – as is the case with all 'lifers' who will spend at least six months in the prison before they move on – the greater the 'shock' of sudden departure is on me; so how painful might it be for the client who has grown to trust an adult for the first time in his life?

I am often aware that I feel left alone with a lot of 'heavy stuff' and maybe even feelings of panic about the overwhelming nature of the material after a session with a lad in prison. However, I'm soon back into a world outside and I have my own life, complete with home and family to return to, supervisor to offload to and process with, and colleagues who can give support and encouragement. But what has my client been left with until we meet next week (if indeed we do meet)? He may feel alone, with his only refuge—a prison cell—which entombs him and a mask to put on to cope with the rigours of prison life.

I also need to bear in mind that many of the clients referred to us are on ACCT documents (following suicidal or self-harm risk assessment) and to be aware of the potential for a one-off session to open up more than can be adequately dealt with by the client's fragile process. Using Pia Melody's definition of abuse as 'Anything less than nurturing' I am mindful of the possible 'abuse' inherent in my work if I forget the importance of containment and establishing 'holding' boundaries. My responsibility will sometimes extend to talking with the client about my concerns for him and I may encourage him to talk to his Personal Officer, Outreach, the Chaplaincy or the Prison Samaritans. In extreme cases of bullying, self-harm or illness I may ask his consent to talk to one of the Outreach Workers about my concerns and my experience is that on nearly every occasion the client has welcomed this concern and the subsequent interventions made. My rule of thumb about the boundaries in prison work is that my boundaries expand as my sense of security in myself, the client and our work expands and conversely my boundaries become more rigid as I feel less secure about myself, the work in the prison and my relationship with a particular client.

Go the extra mile but don't let the client down by promising too much

Most of my YOI clients expect to be let down by adults because for them there has been a common experience of rejection and abandonment. That is why it is so important to 'go the extra mile' to ensure that we overcome the chaotic nature of the prison regime. The number of times I have gone in at additional times in order to ensure I meet with a client whom I have not been able to see at our regular time is a reflection of my absolute commitment to him.

I need to be very open and honest with my clients and not promise, either explicitly or by my silence, something that I cannot commit to, and remember that this may be the first time that the client may have experienced such honesty from a professional – or from any adult – in their lives before. It is so important not to underestimate the importance of the visit or to be thwarted by obstructive staff or poor channels of communication.

Hold the tension between collusion and 'splitting'

It is important for me neither to collude with the client nor to act out their feelings in my dealings with the system of authority. Equally, I seek not to collude with the officers and staff by a passive acceptance of what they tell me about my clients. I need to manage my feelings of anger towards some of the officers' behaviours as described to us by our clients and the prison system in general in order to be still and focused with my clients, and in order not to feel too frustrated with a chaotic and often inadequate system. Treating each session as our last helps me to treat each additional session as a gift rather than rant and rage with frustration when our work is prematurely ended.

'Letting go'

Patience is a virtue in prison work and if my client's interest is in rugby and he chooses to play for the YO's prison team on the day I am coming to see him, I rejoice in his choice (and if he's there next week I'll ask him how he played)! Client autonomy must come first even where we may have little time to work with our clients. Obviously each counselling relationship has to come to an end whether it is today, next week or any week within the next year or two or three, but what is pertinent to the prison work is that it is very rarely brought to an end by mutual agreement. On a very few occasions a release date is set but more usually we don't know that any session will necessarily be the last. Sometimes we think it is our last session and we will have said our goodbyes but back he comes following adjournment, or he is back pending further charges or is later transferred back from another prison asking to see his previous counsellor. So, we learn to be prepared to 'let go lightly' as 'no shows', endings, false endings and temporary endings are all part of the territory. It is constrained by circumstances beyond our control such as the demands of the daily prison population quotas and the transient nature of remand prisoners.

Sometimes through evaluation forms or letters sent to HYCS I will hear from prison clients who have left, but generally if a client has been released I will probably never hear from him again. If the client is transferred to another prison before I have had a chance to say goodbye, I will usually write a letter on HYCS headed paper to honour the time we have spent together and to wish him well. Some of my colleagues mention this in their original contract with the client as an expression of their commitment towards the work with him. The following shows how we tailor each letter to each client to reflect the uniqueness of the relationship:

Dear L

You can imagine that I had a shock this morning when I rang to arrange to see you and was told you are going to —— today. I will miss our Thursday sessions. It has been a privilege to know you and hear about your life. I hope that it is good for you to know what strength of character, goodness and potential I see in you.

I hope you will be able to ask for counselling at —— as you have made very good use of our sessions and it may help you to prepare for release in the summer.

I will never forget you and wish you all good things for the future.

God Bless You
Barrie

Hope

There is more significant learning on which I could expand but the greatest is that this work gives young men hope by seeing in themselves what I so often see: a special, worthwhile and talented individual who has much to give to and receive from life. In each session, I feel privileged that it is my role to help clients wrestle with, repair and begin to rebuild shattered lives. My life is enhanced by being in this work which continues to demonstrate the belief that led me into counselling which is in the essential worth of every human being and in their capacity for growth and healing no matter what has previously occurred in their lives. However brief the companionship is, I believe a seed of hope may have been sown which will remain and grow. I can only wonder and hope because I will never know.

11

Brief Encounters: Time-Conscious Person-Centred Therapy with Couples

Keith Tudor

When two individuals get together and become a couple, in a sense 'two become one'. However, as the individuals involved also remain as individuals, it perhaps makes more sense to say that 'one and one equals three', where the relationship is the third entity. Moreover, when a couple comes to therapy, more often than not they are presenting and wanting to get help with their relationship, and hence the term 'relationship therapy'.

In this chapter I present an argument in favour of couples or relationship therapy being brief, based on my experience working with couples. The argument is based on three premises:

1 That the couple create a unique relationship and, in this, they become a system.
2 That the couples' therapist is primarily working with this relationship or system.
3 That for the duration of the work, the therapist becomes a part of this system, and that, therefore, it is better for this involvement to be brief.

The couple as system

It is sometimes said that in a marriage, civil partnership or committed relationship, there are metaphorically six in the bed: the couple and two sets of parents! If the relationship has any chance of surviving, the couple needs to keep their parents out of the bed – and preferably out of the bedroom. Nevertheless, there is a third party or entity in the life of the couple and that is the relationship itself, which is unique to them, and which they create and co-create as long as they are together. Thus, when we consider a couple from a person-centred perspective, it may be more accurate to think and talk about a 'relationship-centred approach'. In theory and in effect this represents a systems approach to 'the couple' and their relationship. Within the person-centred approach a number of authors have explored this transition from person to system (Barrett-Lennard, 1984; Levant, 1984; Natiello, 1999/2001; O'Leary, 1999; Embleton Tudor *et al.*, 2004). Interestingly, there are many more articles on the application of the approach to families, family systems, and family therapy than there are to couples therapy.

A systems approach to the couple and, for that matter, to larger systems, is entirely compatible with person-centred thinking, since the human organism is itself a complex system (see Tudor and Worrall, 2006). In his book on a person-centred approach to counselling which encompasses both couples and families (but which is more about families), O'Leary (1999) identifies a number of ideas about systems thinking, some of which I think are also useful for the relational or systems therapist or facilitator:

- *The whole is greater than the sum of its parts.* This idea or concept is certainly consistent with an holistic view of the human organism. When one partner talks, albeit often jokingly, about 'my better half' he (for instance) is, in effect, saying that he feels himself to be one (rather than two) and that his 'other half' completes him in some way. In this sense individuals may both complement and supplement each other. What I take from this concept as a practitioner is that it helps me to hold the whole of the particular relationhip to which I am a witness as greater than the sum of the two individuals, and that the language of *wholes* may be more accurate and supportive of the relationship and system than the language of *parts*: 'So you have ambitions for your relationship'. 'When you argue or row, you seem to create a certain passion between you'. 'You speak as one'. If the couple or the therapist do think and talk in terms of parts, this concept helps the therapist to look with the clients at *all* parts of the system that is the couple's relationship, not just at the 'presenting problem', or even the 'presenting person', for instance, when one individual is identified as 'the problem' (see below).
- *Any change in one part of a system affects the whole system.* As one person changes, so the relationship changes; as the relationship changes, so both individuals change. Such changes and their affect or effect, of course, includes the broader family, social and cultural systems in which the couple is enmeshed. Thus, a bereavement on one side of the family is likely to affect individuals on the other side. Equally, a change, such as seeking help for a relationship through therapy, is likely to affect the whole system. Indeed, this is the basis of the argument in favour of 'filial therapy' (see, for instance Guerney, 1964, 1984) or relationship consultation (see Boukydis, 1990) whereby parents or carers seek help for their parenting rather than sending their child/ren to therapy. When a couple seeks the help of a therapist, they are, of course, inviting another person into their relational system, a person who they hope will help them and effect change in their relationship. It is precisely because of the therapist's inevitable and necessary influence

on the couple that I think couples therapy is most appropriately a brief therapy. The longer the couples therapy continues, the more the therapist becomes part of the system, and the less autonomous the couple is.

- *Causality is circular, not linear.* This idea helps us move away from linear causal thinking and blaming: 'I did z because you said y'. 'Well I said y because you'd done x'. One individual may, in effect, carry the 'sick role' in the relationship: 'You're the problem'. 'I know I'm the problem' (see the first point above). This perspective and position, literally, 'com-part-mentalises' the problem and the person so that, despite only being a 'part', the individual rather than the relationship becomes 'the problem' and, therefore, the focus of the therapy. If the couples' therapist does therapy with one of the individuals in front of the other, this can confirm the sense of blaming – and linear causality – and, moreover, can be shaming. The circular view of causality, on the other hand, helps the therapist to take the role and attitude of a facilitator rather than an arbitrator or a referee. It follows that the therapist will seek to help the individuals to understand each other and their causal processes, rather than to find fault with or to blame each other.

- *Individual reality and patterns of behaviour and perceptions are co-created.* From this perspective there is no 'sick role' or sick individual, only a relational system which is in some way incongruent, and whose vulnerability or anxiety is being expressed by a person or a pattern of behaviour in the system. This concept supports, as O'Leary (1999, p. 27) puts it: 'the consistent belief in human flexibility and resiliency, and [the] avoidance of pathologizing, which makes relational counselling compatible with the person-centred approach'. Just as a couple co-creates patterns of relating which may be helpful, such as certain rituals about caring for each other, or unhelpful, such as familiar ways of putting each other down, so they have the potential to co-create new relational possibilities (see Summers and Tudor, 2000). On this basis, when faced with a disagreement, dispute or row, rather taking sides or even trying to 'sort it out', the couples' therapist – or, at least, the person-centred couples therapist – attempts to understand both parties and, perhaps most importantly, to see how they *both* create, co-create and recreate this particular pattern and way of relating, and to reflect this back to the couple. Some couples (and family) therapists describe themselves in their approach to this work as 'neutral'; the family therapists Boszormenyi-Nagy and Ulrich (1981) talk about having 'multi-directional partiality' whereby the therapist is experienced as being on more than one side at once. This contributes to the practice of possibilities.

Having described some ideas about systems and their implications for the practice of couples therapy, I now turn to the implications of the person-centred approach for a relationship therapy which works with the system of relationships.

Relationship therapy: Working with the system

Some view person-centred therapy as individualistic in that it views the individual as at the centre of his or her perceptual field (see, for example, Vitz, 1997; Bowden, 2002) and that it supports the individual's 'self-worship' principally through the concept of *self*-actualisation (see Buber, 1957/1990; Vitz, 1997). Person-centred psychology, theory and practice is, however, more complex and subtle than this. In 1942 Rogers referred to his then 'newer psychotherapy' as 'relationship therapy' (– and, personally, I wish he'd kept this term –) by which he emphasises the importance of the therapeutic relationship, a concept for which research over the past 20 years shows to be a more significant factor on the outcome of therapy than, for instance, the theoretical orientation of the therapist. Nevertheless, and despite his emphasis on the therapeutic relationship, the relational implications of Rogers' work have not been sufficiently or explicitly explored or elaborated until recently, and from different perspectives within the person-centred and experiential approach (see Mearns and Cooper, 2005; and Tudor and Worrall, 2006). I think that it is possible – and desirable – to articulate an organismic/relational perspective to couples or relationship therapy, based on certain principles, originally identified by Sanders (2000) and refined by Tudor and Worrall (2006), which define the person-centred approach:

Principle 1: That the human organism, as other organisms, tends to actualise – to maintain, enhance and reproduce the experiencing organism.

This principle, applied to couples, asserts, first, a view of the couple as an entity, relationship, system or organism, as well as the fact that the couple comprises two individuals; and, second, that, as an organism, the relationship itself tends to actualise. In his early papers Rogers (1963) elaborates this in terms of maintaining, enhancing and reproducing the experiencing organism. This makes sense in two ways: firstly, that every relationship is unique and has particular qualities which people may describe: 'good', 'supportive', 'edgy', etc.; and secondly, that it accounts for the unconscious processes in a relationship whereby a couple works together, for example, taking a similar line with children without necessarily talking to each other about a particular decision, and plays together, for instance, when making love, which is a good example of an activity which maintains and enhances a relationship – and which may lead to reproduction! If the couples' therapist adopts this first principle – and some don't ('though it's hard to see how a person-centred therapist wouldn't') – and thinks that it's useful, it supports a therapeutic perspective which, in turn, supports a holistic, experiential relationship. It also places couples therapy in the context of a wealth of literature on the organism, its nature and qualities (for a summary of which see Tudor and Worrall, 2006), and its tendency to actualise. One example of this is the perspective that, in and through their relationship, the couple seeks both homonomy and autonomy (see Angyal, 1941), both integration and differentiation, a tension which is often a key dynamic in a couple's relationship, and a perspective, which, incidentally, is not unique to the person-centred approach (see Bader and Pearson, 1988). With regard to human systems O'Leary (1999) thinks in terms of the formative rather than the actualising tendency. Writing about family therapy, he gives an example of this (p. 17) which illustrates:

> the way family counselling can turn from an awkward conversation to the formation of a self-directing process in which the whole family offers more meaningful and durable healing than any one member could achieve or than the counsellor could predict.

Principle 2: That, therefore, in order to be facilitative of another, others or a relationship, the therapist adopts a non-directive attitude to her client's or clients' experience.

This principle represents the non-directive attitude of the person-centred therapist, certainly as far as the content of the presented material is concerned (see, for instance, O'Leary, 1999; Levitt, 2005). In my experience, a common presentation of couples who seek therapy is that one wants outside help, the other doesn't; that one says there's a problem, the other says there isn't; even that one wants to separate, the other doesn't. In these situations, rather than getting into whose experience or perception is 'right', it is more effective and relevant for the therapist to reflect back to the couple that there is or appears to be a difference between them. The ensuing discussion often helps them to focus on how they feel about, understand and negotiate difference, and on their conceived values; on how contactful they are with each other, or not; on how accepting of each other they are, or not; on how they understand or misunderstand each other; and whether they experience each other's love and understanding, or not.

Principle 3: That, together, the therapist and client/s create, and continually co-create, certain facilitative conditions.

Person-centred therapy is, in effect, an environmental therapy in that it proposes that the presence of certain (six) 'necessary and sufficient' therapeutic conditions facilitates change (see Rogers, 1957, 1959). Whether these conditions are necessary and sufficient is a matter of great debate, both within and outside the person-centred approach; nevertheless, they are widely recognised as describing essential attitudes of both therapist and client/s. As part of the reclamation and development of an organismic perspective on person-centred therapy and, partly to counter the rather crude view that some therapists have of 'providing' or 'offering' the conditions, Tudor and Worrall (2006) present Rogers' therapeutic conditions as describing certain attitudes and qualities of a co-created relationship. In the major exposition of his theory, Rogers (1959, p. 240) offers what he refers to as 'a tentative law of interpersonal relationships' and, in doing so, captures a sense of mutual facilitation in a relationship:

> Assuming a minimal mutual willingness to be in *contact* and to receive communications, we may say that the greater the communicated *congruence* of *experience*, *awareness* and behavior on the part of one individual, the more the ensuing relationship will involve a tendency toward reciprocal communication with the same qualities, mutually accurate understanding of the communications, improved *psychological adjustment* and functioning in both parties, and mutual satisfaction in the relationship.

Thus, a couple's relationship may be facilitated with reference to these conditions by the couple themselves (see Rogers, 1959, 1973), as a result of individual therapy (Rogers, 1954/67), or through couples therapy (see Snyder, 1989; Mearns, 1994; O'Leary, 1999; Embleton Tudor *et al.*, 2004).
Rogers (1959, p. 240) continues:

> Conversely, the greater the communicated *incongruence* of *experience*, *awareness* and behavior, the more the ensuing relationship further communication with the same quality, disintegration of accurate understanding, lessened *psychological adjustment* in both parties, and mutual disatisfaction in the relationship.

It is often at this point that the couple seek help.

Brief encounter

In this final part I outline and comment on two arguments as to why it is both possible and desirable to work briefly: (1) That the couples' therapist is more separate from the client couple than the therapist working with an individual; and (2) that the person-centred couples' therapist supports the couple development towards interdependence, and eschews the development of dependence.

Being separate

In a paper published in 1958 Rogers (1958/1990) reflects on a number of questions raised by his research on the characteristics of a helping relationship. He poses one of these in the following terms (p. 121): 'Can I be strong enough as a person to be separate from the other?' He follows this with a related question: 'Am I secure enough within myself to permit him his separateness?' He asks these questions in the context of therapeutic work with individuals in which the primary relationship is the therapeutic relationship (Figure 11.1).

In couples therapy this is different (see Figure 11.2): the primary relationship is the couple's and the therapist is, *de facto*, separate, which makes the therapist's task of holding the client, in this case, a couple, separate that much easier. This, in turn, makes it more possible for the therapist to work with the material present, as it were, in front of him or her precisely because it is in front. The therapist is, in effect, experiencing and encountering the relationship and, because of his or her position *vis-à-vis* the relationship can see it more clearly and work with it more quickly.

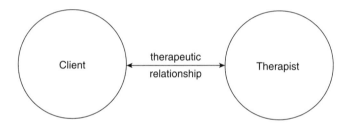

Figure 11.1   *The therapeutic relationship in individual therapy*

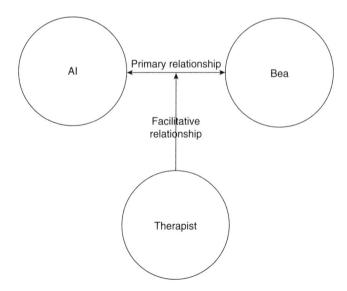

Figure 11.2   *Relationships in couples therapy*

When a couple seeks help, the therapist will listen to their stories – and, in my experience, there are more often than not two or more stories or narratives about whatever the couple is presenting – and, generally, act as the facilitator of communication between the couple, helping each to listen to the other. Sometimes a couple will argue:

Al 1:   I didn't say that.
Bea 1:   Yes you did.
Al 2:   No, I didn't.
Bea 2:   But I *thought* you did.
Al 3:   No, I didn't.

Here, when Al makes his third, repeated assertion, he misses an opportunity to improve the relationship. Bea says that she *thought* Al had said such and such when, according to Al, he hadn't. Assuming that Al continues in his defensive behaviour, and that Bea doesn't break the pattern either, the conversation can continue *ad infinitum* and even escalate. This dialogue is an example of what Berne (1966, p. 225) refers to as the first rule of communication by which he suggests that, if the parties to a conversation maintain a parallel series of transactions, 'communication can proceed indefinitely'. If, however, Al responds by saying something like: 'Oh ... so you thought I said that. Well I can imagine if you thought I said that, you would be upset' then he would have acknowledged Bea's experience/perception, without giving up his own experience of what he'd said. In effect, Al would cross the series of miscommunications, by giving up his 'position' and expressing some empathy for Bea's *perception* of what he'd said. Any couples' therapist is likely to make some comment on this series of transactions. A person-centred couples therapist is most likely to help the couple focus on their willingness to be in *contact* with each other, to make and receive transactions which communicate each other's *congruence* of *experience*, awareness and behaviour and, on this basis, to be more *acceptant* and *understanding* of each other's frame of reference, however much it may be based on some denied awareness and/or distorted perceptions (see Figure 11.3).

When the couples therapist facilitates the communication in a relationship, however, either client or both clients may experience the therapist as more acceptant and understanding than their partner, in which case the therapist can be drawn into, in effect, relating to each client individually with the result that the communication between them may break down (see Figure 11.4). This can happen in the course of a single exchange, or conversation, or over time.

As the point of couples therapy, at least from a Rogerian perspective, is to facilitate an improving relationship with a tendency toward reciprocal communication and so on, the point is for the therapist to help the couple to understand each other, not for the individuals to feel understood by

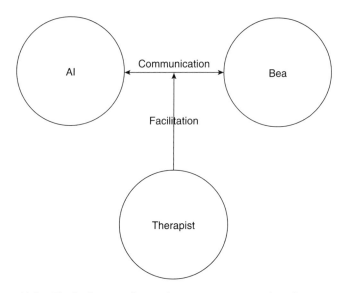

Figure 11.3   *The facilitation of a couple, communication with each other*

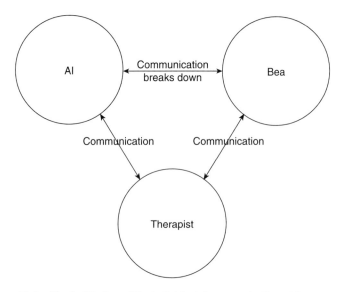

Figure 11.4   *The facilitation of the individuals' communication with the therapist*

the therapist. Of course, it is likely that, if the couple better understand each other, they will feel understood by the therapist *as a couple*; but it doesn't follow that if, as individuals they each feel understood by the therapist, then they as a couple will understand each other. In fact, the therapist's understanding of one party can exacerbate the other party's feeling of isolation. So, a person-centred couples therapist who is working from a systems perspective and, therefore, holding the relationship in mind, will tend to facilitate the communication between the couple and, thus, their relationship; and will tend not to be drawn into facilitating the two individuals separately. If this does occur and continues on a regular and sustained basis, the therapist may consider this an indication of the need for the individual/s concerned to have individual therapy. The reader will note that this elaboration is based on an exchange of some five sentences. This reflects my experience that couples therapists who are separate can work quickly, effectively and, therefore, briefly.

Being independent and interdependent

The second argument in favour of working briefly, and one which follows from the first, concerns the therapist's support for the couple's development as a couple. When a couple get together they often become enmeshed, sometimes literally so! Based on the hypothesis of a necessary process of separation-individuation in normal human development, based on the work of Mahler *et al.* (1975), Bader and Pearson (1988) describe this as the symbiotic phase. They describe different phases of development, through differentiation, practising and rapprochement, to mutual interdependence. They identify and describe various combinations of these processes, when partners may be in the same or different phases: symbiotic-symbiotic, characterised by the sense that 'We are one', symbiotic-differentiating 'Don't betray me', or differentiating-differentiating 'I'll change if you change'. When a couple go to therapy, another person, the therapist, becomes party to this relationship/system – which is why it's so important for the therapist to be separate. However, even the most separate and systemic couple-centred therapist can get drawn into the client/couple system, and this is not necessarily a bad thing. For instance, when a therapist is helpful in facilitating the communication between a couple, they may well be grateful and may internalise the therapist: 'We thought of you during the week, and what you might say'. When discussing a particular problem or issue, they may turn to the therapist and say: 'What do you think?' – and it may be appropriate to answer this and withholding not to answer. What I find useful about the Bader and Pearson process model is that it provides me with some framework for understanding when, for instance, it may be helpful to answer a question rather than simply encouraging a couple to be independent from me as a therapist and interdependence between themselves. The point is that the greater the separateness, the more brief the therapy can be. This perspective and attitude is in the context that person-centred therapy generally eschews the development of any dependence on the part of the client on the therapist. In his critique of the 'involved and persistent dependent transference relationship', Rogers (1951, p. 201) comments that 'The possibility of effective brief psychotherapy seems to hinge on the possibility of therapy without the transference relationship'. Whilst he acknowledges the existence of transference 'attitudes', Rogers is clear that the therapist's response to the client's transference is the same as his or her response to anything else: that he or she endeavours to accept and understand it. Thus, it is clear that, if the couples' therapist is separate and not encouraging transference or a transferential relationship, then he or she can-and perhaps-should work briefly.

References

Angyal, A. (1941) *Foundations for a Science of Personality*. New York: Commonwealth Fund.

Bader, E. and Pearson, P.T. (1988) *In Quest of the Mythical Mate: A Developmental Approach to Diagnosis and Treatment in Couples Therapy*. New York: Brunner/Mazel.

Barrett-Lennard, G.T. (1984) 'The world of family relationships: A person-centred systems view', in R. Levant and J. Shlien (eds), *Client-Centered Therapy and the Person-Centered Approach: New Directions in Theory, Research and Practice* (pp. 222–42). New York: Praeger.

Berne, E. (1966) *Principles of Group Treatment*. New York: Grove Press.

Boszormenyi-Nagy, I. and Ulrich, D. (1981) 'Contextual family therapy', in A.S Gurman and D.P. Kniskern (eds), *Handbook of Family Therapy* (pp. 159–86). New York: Brunner/Mazel.

Boukydis, C.F.Z. (1990) 'Client-centered/experiential practice with parents and infants', in G. Lietaer, J. Rombauts and R. Van Balen (eds), *Client-Centered and Experiential Psychotherapy in the Nineties* (pp. 797–811). Leuven: Leuven University Press.

Bowden, A.R. (2002) *Is There a Fundamental Psychotherapy for the World? – Theory and Method 'On Hold'*. Keynote address. World Congress for Psychotherapy, Vienna.

Buber, M. (1990) 'Martin Buber', in H. Kirscenbaum and V.L. Henderson (eds), *Carl Rogers Dialogues* (pp. 41–78). London: Constable. (Original work published 1957.)

Embleton Tudor, L., Keemar, K., Tudor, K., Valentine, J. and Worrall, M. (2004) *The Person-Centred Approach: A Contemporary Introduction*. Basingstoke: Palgrave.

Guerney, B.G., Jr. (1964) 'Filial therapy: Description and rationale', *Journal of Consulting Psychology*, 28(4), 303–10.

Guerney, B.G., Jr. (1984) 'Contributions of client-centered therapy to filial, marital, and family relationship enhancement therapies', in R. Levant and J. Shlien (eds), *Client-Centered Therapy and the Person-Centered Approach: New Directions in Theory, Research and Practice* (pp. 261–277). New York: Praeger.

Levant, R. (1984) 'From person to system: Two perspectives', in R. Levant and J. Shlien (1984) (eds), *Client-Centered Therapy and the Person-Centered Approach: New Directions in Theory, Research and Practice* (pp. 243–60). New York: Praeger.

Levitt, B. (ed.) (2005) *Embracing Non-Directivity: Reassessing Person-Centered Theory and Practice in the 21st Century*. Ros-on-Wye: PCCS Books.

Mahler, M., Pine, F., and Bergman, A. (1975) *The Psychological Birth of the Human Infant: Symbiosis and Individuation*. New York: Basic Books.

Mearns, D. (1994) 'How to work with a couple', in *Developing Person-Centred Counselling* (pp. 56–60). London: Sage.

Mearns, D. and Cooper, M. (2005) *Working at Relational Depth in Counselling and Psychotherapy*. London: Sage.

Natiello, P. (2001) 'From group to community', in *The Person-Centred Approach: A Passionate Presence* (pp. 121–40). Ross-on-Wye: PCCS Books. (Original work published 1991.)

O'Leary, C. (1999) *Couple and Family Counselling: A Person-Centred Approach*. London: Sage.

Rogers, C.R. (1942) *Counseling and Psychotherapy: Newer Concepts in Practice*. Boston: Houghton Mifflin.

Rogers, C.R. (1951) *Client-Centered Therapy*. Constable: London.

Rogers, C.R. (1957) 'The necessary and sufficient conditions of therapeutic personality change', *Journal of Consulting Psychology*, 21, 95–103.

Rogers, C.R. (1959) 'A theory of therapy, personality and interpersonal relationships, as developed in the client-centred framework', in S. Koch (ed.) *Psychology: A Study of Science. Vol. 3: Formulation of the Person and the Social Context* (pp. 184–256). New York: McGraw-Hill.

Rogers C.R. (1963) 'The actualizing tendency in relation to "motive" and to consciousness', in M Jones (ed.) *Nebraska Symposium on Motivation 1963* (pp. 1–24). Lincoln, NE: University of Nebraska Press.

Rogers, C.R. (1967) 'The characteristics of a helping relationship', in *On Becoming a Person* (pp. 39–58). London: Constable. (Original work published 1954.)

Rogers, C.R. (1973) *Becoming Partners: Marriage and its Alternatives*. London: Constable.

Sanders, P. (2000) 'Mapping person-centred approaches to counselling and psychotherapy', *Person-Centred Practice*, 8(2), 62–74.

Snyder, M. (1989) 'The relationship enhancement model of couple therapy: An integration of Rogers and Bateson', *Person-Centered Review*, 4(3), 358–84.

Summers, G. and Tudor, K. (2000) 'Cocreative transactional analysis', *Transactional Analysis Journal*, 30(1), 23–40.

Tudor, K. and Worrall, M. (2006) *Person-Centred Therapy: A Clinical Philosophy*. London: Routledge.

Vitz, P. (1997) *Psychology as Religion: The Cult of Self-Worship*. Grand Rapids, MI: William B. Eerdmans.

12

A Process of Transformation: Time-Limited Group Counselling with Women Survivors of Childhood Sexual Abuse

Très Roche

This chapter explores the modality of time-limited group counselling as an effective therapeutic intervention for women survivors of childhood sexual abuse. Drawing on current understanding with regard to the long-term psychological impact of early sexual trauma, the author discusses the use of brief group counselling as a potent client experience, which enables the core dynamics of childhood sexual abuse to be contained, examined and utilised as a framework for inter- and intra-personal transformation.

The look of shock on her face was evident. Tears began to flow from her eyes as she leant forward and cradled her head in her hands. The conversation in the group was gaining pace as women began to share the ways in which they felt they had been affected by the sexual abuse they had suffered as children. Moments of recognition as one woman described her failed marriages, as another spoke of the fear that torments her in any relationship she attempts to form, as another spoke of alcohol being the only thing that enables her to quell the omnipotence of the memories: 'I can't believe that you're actually describing how I feel. I didn't think anyone could ever really know'.

These are the first moments of the first meeting of a 10-week therapy group for women survivors of childhood sexual abuse. These moments of sitting in a circle with a small group of women, where the only known factor is that everyone present has experienced some form of sexual abuse in childhood, are incredibly powerful. It is within these first moments that women experience the rare and often unique occurrence of commonality with others, where connection to others is felt through similarity rather than difference. It is within these first moments that the journey of transformation begins.

From childhood experience to adult symptomology

The link between childhood sexual abuse and the onset of mental health problems in adulthood is now well established (see Browne and Finklehor,

1986; Bryer *et al.*, 1987; Department of Health [DoH], 1999). Whilst sexual abuse experienced in childhood has not been identified as an independent causal factor of mental health problems in adulthood, there is clear evidence describing a large prevalence rate of sexual abuse within the population of clients seeking help from statutory services for a wide range of mental health problems (Finklehor, 1988; Morgan and Cummings, 1999; Roberts *et al.*, 2004).

The long-term health implications of childhood sexual abuse have been well documented (Lewis Herman, 1998; Finklehor, 1996; Hall and Lloyd, 1997; Hooper and Koprowska, 2000). Issues such as low self-esteem, problems with sexuality, vulnerability to domestic abuse in adulthood, problems forming and sustaining close relationships, together with higher rates of alcohol and substance abuse, eating disorders and depressive disorders have all been evidentially linked, as possible outcomes, to the traumatic experience of being sexually abused as a child.

The understanding that childhood sexual abuse is a contributing factor to the formation of adult pathology is not a new hypothesis. However, the acceptance of the idea that childhood sexual abuse has lasting psychological consequences has a history which is marked by what Lewis Herman (1998, p. 7) describes as 'episodic amnesia'.

The first and clearest description of women's experiences of sexual violence, abuse and exploitation linked to lasting psychological conse-quences in adulthood, can be found in Freud's (1896/1962) *Aetiology of Hysteria*. This revolutionary text provided the framework within which women's traumatic presentations could be seen as symptomatic of sexually abusive experiences in childhood. However, within the political, social and intellectual climate of the time, the incendiary consequences of accepting such ideas, forced Freud personally to repudiate his own theory detailing the external origins of neurosis, and led him instead to advance a theory in which he posited an internal etiology. As Bolen (2001, p. 14): describes it: 'the young child, needing to release sexual tensions, wished for the sexual attention from her father. He believed that these tensions were universal and unfolded in developmental stages'. Subsequently, exploration of the sexually traumatic origins of adult symptomology disappeared from view, as did any description of women's experiences of childhood sexual abuse. This amnesia continued though the first half of the 20th century. Even the Kinsey report, *Sexual Behaviour in the Human Female* (Kinsey *et al.*, 1966), which detailed several studies related to the sexual development of pre-adolescent girls, noted the existence of 'emotional upset' (p. 121) as a result of premature sexual contact with adults, yet still concluded that such 'upset' was more likely to be a result of adverse cultural conditioning rather than of any psychological impact of the experience of being sexually abused as a child: 'It is difficult to see why a child, except for cultural conditioning, should be disturbed at having its genitalia touched' (p. 121).

Nowadays, it is difficult to accept such a view as a serious commentary on the experience of sexual abuse.

However, even within a cultural climate which minimised women's experiences of abuse and oppression, there was some acknowledgement that the act of touching a child's genitalia did happen and that this act causes some disturbance. The established view at this time however, fell short of making sense of why.

Models of understanding

In thinking beyond symptomology and to the delivery of group therapy services for those survivors seeking help, it is vitally important to understand what links the occurrence of the long-term effects of childhood sexual abuse, with an explanation as to why these effects might occur in the first place. Two models that clearly position childhood sexual abuse within a trauma-focused framework are the post-traumatic stress disorder (PTSD) model, defined by the American Psychiatric Association (1980), in the third edition of its *Diagnostic and Statistical Manual of Mental Disorders* (*DSM-III*), and the traumagenic dynamics model of child sexual abuse (CSA) developed by Browne and Finklehor (1985).

The PTSD model had begun to include childhood sexual abuse within its framework in the mid-1980s. However, as a model of understanding the link between sexual abuse in childhood and adult mental ill health, PTSD did not in any way explain how the specific acts of sexual abuse engender the reported long-term effects. The traumagenic dynamics model was developed as an additional formulation to PTSD. The inclusion, within an established model, of an understanding of traumatic responses, finally enabled the cluster of emotional and physiological responses many survivors had been reporting over time to be organised and, as Finklehor (1988, p. 63) put it: 'looked at in a structured way. What may be involved is a syndrome with core aetiology rather than just a catalogue of symptoms.' Adding the effects of childhood sexual abuse to the accepted concept of PTSD has proved important on a number of levels:

- It concretises the descriptions of the long-term effects of sexual abuse within a medical establishment that had, historically, denied its existence.
- It provides a framework within which the reported effects of CSA could be systematically studied.
- It moves some way to recognise that the cluster of survivor responses to the trauma of sexual abuse was due to the traumatic event, rather than due to the 'hysterical' personality of the individual survivor themselves.

Finklehor and Browne's traumagenics dynamics model focuses directly on offering an explanation as to why and how sexual abuse can lead to such damaging long-term effects. The model cites four trauma causing factors which account for the impact of sexual abuse:

1 Traumatic sexualisation – whereby a child experiences sexual contact which regulates or influences normal sexual development.
2 Stigmatisation – whereby a child ingests the negative dynamics held in the act of abuse: shame, vileness, worthlessness and, in so doing, distorts their own sense of worth.
3 Powerlessness – whereby a child's own sense of efficacy in the world is constantly thwarted, either through constant frustration, or through the threat of annihilation, thus fracturing the belief that they can control their own life.
4 Betrayal – whereby a child discovers that someone to whom they are dependent causes them harm, thus distorting the child's sense of feeling able to rely on self or others.

Each traumagenic dynamic is an experience 'that alters a child's cognitive or emotional orientation to the world and causes trauma by distorting the child's self concept, world view or affective capacities' (Finklehor, 1988, p. 68) The idea that sexual abuse actually ruptures the healthy development of the child, and distorts the emotional and psychological landscape that the child occupies both internally and externally, begins to lay the foundations for understanding the devastation that being sexually abused can cause.

For Ruth, the effects of persistent sexual abuse, emotional and physical abuse, and grinding neglect in childhood, were devastating. She inhabited a very lonely world where she had learnt very early to distrust people and keep herself as far away from others as was possible without drawing too much attention to herself. Here she remained hyper alert to the possibility of being hurt again. She existed with clear 'facts' about herself and her childhood history that seemed to provide her with an impenetrable shell: she thought of herself as mad, that what she had experienced wasn't sexual abuse, but had instead been a relationship and therefore, there were no good reasons why she was as messed up as she was, anyone else would have coped OK. Ruth despised herself for the ways in which she behaved: self-harming, pushing her partner away, being so different from everyone else. She thought of herself as a destructive force and that if others got too close she would undoubtedly damage them, so she needed to keep herself away from people. This rigid understanding of herself made intimate relationships virtually impossible; she could list the relationships that had failed, and the partners that she felt she had hurt or destroyed. This distorted sense of responsibility and accountability and self-blame surrounded her like a choking fog, and was exacerbated by the contact she continued to have with her family. Though she was beginning to accept that the trauma and degradation she suffered as a child was real, what she then faced was a constant battle with a family that continued to deny and distort her history. This battle between what she knew and what she was repeatedly told left her feeling confused, blamed and, ultimately, hating herself more. It was a further recapitulation of the traumatic dynamics she lived through as a child. 'Whenever I try and talk to my mum about what happened and why she didn't do anything to protect me, she refers to it/him as "That boyfriend I used to have". It's unbelievable. I was 11 years old, he was in his sixties, but she just says that if it was abuse then why didn't I do anything to stop it. I can't answer. What kind of a person does that make me?'

The traumagenics dynamics model suggests that having to cope with and negotiate the world through these kinds of rigid, traumatically-based distortions about self and others, gives rise to associated behavioural characteristics such as self-harming behaviours, suicide ideation, drug and alcohol misuse, continued flashbacks, depression, difficulties in significant relationships. In other words, it makes sense that someone who survives this level of trauma behaves in these kinds of ways.

At the Sexual Abuse Project (SAP) in Nottingham, it is precisely this understanding of sexual abuse and its effects that underpins the group therapy services devised and delivered to women survivors. SAP is a specialist counselling service set up to provide short-term group therapy to women survivors of childhood sexual abuse. Started in 1997, the project has to date run over 30 short-term groups, working on a cycle of three groups each year, with each group convening for two hours per week for 10 weeks.

Why group therapy?

There is a wealth of documentation exploring the links between the early experiences of sexual abuse and lasting psychological impacts into adulthood, though there are still relatively few research studies on the use of group therapy as an effective treatment option for the deleterious effects of childhood sexual abuse. Those studies that have been published have shown positive results: Westbury and Tutty (1999); Morgan and Cummings (1999); Higgins Kessler *et al.* (2003); and Ryan *et al.* (2005). As a model for working with survivors, group work holds a different potential for exploring and ameliorating the lasting effects of childhood sexual abuse than individual, one-to-one psychotherapy. Group therapy offers the space for the client to experience reconnection to others and empowerment, thus redressing the core dynamics of stigmatisation and powerlessness alongside others and within the here and now of the group, rather than solely through the psychotherapeutic concept of mutuality with the therapist. As Lewis Herman (1998, p. 133) puts it: 'The core experiences of psychological trauma are disempowerment and disconnection from others. Recovery, therefore, is based upon the empowerment of the survivor and the creation of new connections'. The potency for change within a group is offered through experiencing oneself as part of the group experience; reactions, responses and behaviours, what Yalom and Leszcz (2005, p. 1) refer to as: 'the intricate interplay of human experiences'.

At SAP, we have taken as our base the psychological understanding provided by the Finklehor and Browne model, and have constructed a way of working in which the group services we provide speak directly to the redressing of each of the traumagenic dynamics. With regard to group therapy and, specifically, to understanding groups as the principal vehicle for therapeutic change, we have drawn on Yalom's research on the therapeutic or 'curative' factors of groups (see Yalom and Leszcz, 2005). Table 12.1 correlates these two models and shows our thinking about the relationship between the psychological understanding about why sexual abuse has specific long-term deleterious effects (Browne and Finkelhor, 1985), and how group therapy is a particularly potent medium for survivors of sexual abuse in redressing the traumagenic dynamics of sexual abuse.

Why short-term?

It is through my experience of facilitating brief, homogeneous psychotherapy groups, where sessions are unstructured, though clearly and tightly boundaried, that I have developed a view that time-limited group interventions can be powerful in providing the fertile ground for this interplay of human experience. For many clients, particularly where there has been no previous experience of therapy, a short-term group offers an introductory space in which important work can be undertaken. The possibility of thinking about, connecting to and talking about experiences of the abuse feels, for many clients, is dangerously overwhelming. However, the clear boundaries of a short-term contract, offer group members a containing framework in which the effects of sexual abuse can be experienced and managed. The limited number of sessions acts as a motivating factor – if there's only a specific amount of time, we need to make the most of every moment – and enables rapid cohesion between group members. Whilst the experience of being in the group is intense and often distressing, group members have the reassurance from the start that the process is brief and will end.

Table 12.1   *The relationship between psychological understanding about the effects of sexual abuse and therapeutic factors of groups.*

Therapeutic/ curative factors of groups (Yalom & Leszcz, 2005)	Traumagenic dynamics (Browne & Finkelhor, 1985)	How group therapy for adult survivors of childhood sexual abuse responds to the traumagenic dynamics
Universality	Stigmatisation	It offers immediate relief to the aloneness and isolation.
Installation of hope	Traumatic sexualisation Betrayal	Where survivors have lost the belief that life can change or that distortions can shift, it offers a process which engenders hope and engages with positive outcomes.
Imparting information	Stigmatisation	Through giving information about why and how CSA affects the survivor in the way that it does, it normalises feelings and emotions.
Altruism	Powerlessness	It offers the opportunity for clients to be of help to others.
Corrective recapitulation of the primary family group	Betrayal Powerlessness Stigmatisation Traumatic sexualisation	It offers a space in which the authority figures do not do harm, and where there are 'many mirrors' and many potential repetitions of family dynamics that can offer opportunities of reparation and learning about healthier ways of relating. This is linked to feelings of personal effectiveness, to being able to articulate one's own needs and to allow others to effectively respond to them.
Development of socialising techniques	Stigmatisation Powerlessness	It offers a space where accurate interpersonal feedback can occur, where members can receive and give feedback about how they impact on others and the world around them.
Imitative behaviour	Stigmatisation	It encourages reconnections with others, thus, lessening the experience of isolation.
Interpersonal learning	Stigmatisation Powerlessness	It redresses the universal misconceptions and misunderstandings that inhibit interpersonal relationships. Through a positive 'here and now' experience that allows for new and different experiences of self, a more accurate and accepting sense of self can emerge.
Group cohesiveness	Stigmatisation Powerlessness	It offers a space where the sharing and ensuing acceptance of one's inner world increases a sense of belonging. Power and responsibility are addressed through a felt experience of impacting and affecting others as well as the group as a whole organism.
Catharsis	Powerlessness	It invites group members to express strong affect, and to bear witness to what often

(Continued)

Table 12.1   *cont'd*

Therapeutic/ curative factors of groups (Yalom & Leszcz, 2005)	Traumagenic dynamics (Browne & Finkelhor, 1985)	How group therapy for adult survivors of childhood sexual abuse responds to the traumagenic dynamics
		feels like an unspeakable truth. Where there is an experience that the individual and the group can survive extreme, destructive feelings and where powerful feelings can be accepted and managed, the group can provide a reparative experience.
Existential factors	Betrayal Powerlessness	It encourages self responsibility; that a survivor's healing journey is not dependent upon any future actions of the perpetrator. It redresses the ultimate betrayal of the perpetrator through reparative connection with others whilst still acknowledging the essential aloneness of existence.

The SAP brief therapy group

Given the evident usefulness of groups to address the specific and fundamental dynamics of childhood sexual abuse, the SAP offers a brief therapy group at the core of its services. Access to the 10-week group process is via self-referral and the waiting list time, from the point of referral to engagement in services, is, on average, between two and six months. The project does not offer any crisis services, and has no 'out of hours' contact with clients. In order to join one of our time-limited groups, women must complete a short, written, questionnaire form, and attend a formal, individual assessment meeting with the two therapists who facilitate the groups. Once accepted into the group, women commit themselves to attending all 10 sessions. On completion of the 10-week group, women are invited to an individual review meeting, which is usually six to eight weeks after the group has ended, where further options of support are discussed, including a longer-term therapy group.

The SAP time-limited groups fall within a matrix of conventional brief, group treatment models, integrating concepts from the psycho-educational group, the interpersonal dynamic group, and the affect management group. We endeavour to provide a group space where there is an involved curiosity shared by all group members – including the facilitators – where we can all bear witness to the atrocities committed against the women as children; where we can hold the possibility that thinking about the experience is survivable; and where it is possible to think and speak about feelings without needing to act impulsively upon them.

The 10-week groups are all facilitated in an open, unstructured way, which allows the issues and themes that are explored in the group to emerge organically. This method speaks directly to the dynamic of powerlessness; by being open to the process and not driven by a particular agenda, we support women to prioritise their need to talk about what they consider to be of importance. What remains consistent in every group that we have run over the past 10 years is that members talk about their anger towards their abuser, and their anger with their mothers; they also talk about their intimate relationships, and how these have been impacted and affected by their childhood sexual abuse. They talk about their support networks, coping strategies, management of their responses to the trauma of abuse, and they talk about their hopes for themselves. It is through the process of these major themes emerging, rather than being imposed as weekly topics, that the time-limited unstructured group transpires to be a rich and diverse arena for a wealth of content and relational dynamics to co-exist in the immediacy of the 'here and now'. It is a vital and potent process.

For Ruth, being part of the group presented her with a major challenge to the rigidity of her thinking, both about herself and about the external environment. Each week she would arrive, just in time for the beginning of each session and for the first 15 minutes would sit, wrapped tightly in her coat, at the back of her seat, muscles tight, in readiness to move. Each session, she arrived with the expectation that 'Today I will be rejected, today I will be asked to leave'. It was the expectation through which she lived her life, an expectation that belied her desperate hope to connect and to belong. Ruth would often talk about the pain of feeling so alone, and the anguish that consumed her when she thought about the futility and hopelessness that she felt about anything changing in her life. With each thought she shared with the group, she risked, in her understanding and experience of the world, ridicule and rejection. For so many years Ruth had completely disconnected from her childhood abuse and neglect. She talked in the group about how she had invented a childhood that was happy, one where she was loved and supported. If anyone had asked her, it was the invented story of her life that she gave to people and wanted so desperately to believe herself. What this left Ruth with was an intolerable polarity of experiences: on the one hand, her life was littered with failed relationships, she raged at herself and partners, she was often in fights, and cut herself when she felt overwhelmed; on the other hand, through ongoing contact with her mother, she believed and was supported to believe that the abusive history she knew and lived through hadn't happened. The dilemma she was caught in was immense, and left her questioning her sanity. If there were no reasons that could substantiate the extreme and sometimes

*savage ways in which she behaved to herself and others, she believed
she must be mad. As Ruth began to recount the truth of her history,
it was the group's capacity to bear witness to her story that enabled
her to begin to connect with what she had survived as a child. The
group seemed to understand why Ruth had re-invented her childhood:
some members spoke of the amazing creativity that Ruth had possessed
to create something beautiful amongst the sordid reality; others were
envious of her 'escape'. In the conversations that ensued, Ruth began to
think about and understand her disconnection from her past as a strategy
for survival rather than a symbol of madness. Other women shared their
experiences of remembering and forgetting their traumatic experiences
and, rather than receiving the expected rejection, Ruth allowed herself
to be seen, and experienced being heard. No longer was she different
and mad; she could now see herself as part of a group of women joined
in their task to understand the impact of their past on their present lives.*

In the seminal text *Trauma and Recovery: From Domestic Abuse
to Political Terror*, Lewis Herman (1998) conceptualises a three-stage
model of recovery from trauma. The stages are: safety, remembrance
and mourning, and reconnection. Lewis Herman argues that, over time
and by focusing on these stages, people can recover and heal from the
complexities of trauma syndromes. The model poses a series of tasks that
enables victims of trauma to integrate their history; to make sense of their
traumatic experiences and to engage with the complexities of ordinary life
whereby the impact of the trauma is contained and manageable. At the
SAP, we find this model useful in framing our recovery work. The focus
on the three stages of safety, remembrance and mourning, and reconnection
provides the framework for the therapeutic tasks of recovery and healing.
Moreover, the major themes that Lewis Herman links to each recovery task
can be identified as emerging through the life of our short-term groups.
Over a period of 18 months we recorded and collated the descriptions
of all the major themes that occurred in each week of each group, in an
attempt to capture and to begin to articulate the process of transformation
that was clearly evident. Table 12.2 represents the stages of recovery, and
the major themes identified, together with the common tasks as identified
by the model. The weekly log comprising the distillation of the emergent
themes forms Appendix 2.

Lewis Herman's model clearly describes a process of transformation:
from trauma to recovery. She does, however, emphasise the need for
considerable time in therapy in order to address each stage. In the case
of brief group therapy for survivors of sexual abuse, time in therapy is
obviously limited. However, where the time limit is a known factor from
the start and where the group is homogeneous, it is my view that brief
group therapy offers an alternative base from which to address the tasks

Table 12.2 *Stages, major themes and tasks in recovery from trauma.*

Stages of recovery	Major themes	Recovery tasks
Safety	Naming the problem	Diagnosis.
	Restoring control	Gaining mastery over the trauma.
		Beginning to mobilise support networks.
		Paying attention to basic health needs and general functioning needs.
		Self care.
	Establishing safe environment	Developing trust in interpersonal relationships.
		Beginning to trust the therapeutic relationship.
Remembrance and mourning	Reconstructing the story	Telling the story of trauma.
	Transforming the traumatic memory	Integrating the abusive experiences, rather than exorcising them.
		Mourning the traumatic loss (usually there is some resistance to mourning and the elaboration of 'magical' resolutions through revenge, forgiveness, and/or compensation).
		Confronting existential despair, including the impossibility of getting even.
Reconnection	Learning to fight	Discovering personal aspirations and agenda.
	Reconciling oneself	No longer being possessed by the traumatic past, the woman is in possession of herself.
		Understanding that she was a victim, and the effects of victimisation.
		Repudiating those aspects of herself that were imposed by the trauma.
		Becoming more forgiving of herself.
	Reconnecting with others	Speaking out to family members.
		Risking deepening connections with others and revealing self.
	Survivor mission	To engage with the wider social and political aspects of the personal trauma. Participating at an organised level with others holds the potential of deep connection with others.
	Resolving the trauma	Recognising the importance of holding the perpetrator as responsible for the crime and, at the same time, transcending the personal grievance against the perpetrator.
		Renewed attention away from the tasks of recovery and towards the tasks of ordinary life.

of recovery. The short-term homogeneous group offers an immediate de-stigmatising experience of being in a group of other women survivors. The perceived experience is of similarity rather than difference; women who have attended the SAP groups have spoken about the initial meetings as being the first time that they had ever felt safe, understood and accepted. This experience of feeling the 'same as' rather than 'different from' engenders a very powerful and intense attachment to the group. The short-term group may not explore many of the inter-relational complexities that can be contained within a long-group context, for instance how group members may be involved in stigmatising each other, or the assumption that no men in the group equates to there being no abusers in the group. However, this positive attachment generates feelings and experiences of the group as being immediately trustworthy, safe and accepting, which are not only reparative experiences in themselves, but provide a strong and immediate base from which women feel able to address tasks Lewis Herman describes.

The emergent themes that women in each group struggle with in engaging with their traumatic histories, including languaging: their experiences, understanding their behaviours and, in general, linking the past to the present, all evidences the process described by Lewis Herman (see Table 12.2). The unstructured nature of the brief therapy group may sit uneasily with a stage theory of recovery, but the distillation of the 10-week group therapy process (see Table 12.2 and Appendix 2) clearly indicates that the tasks of healing from trauma as described by Lewis Herman, do indeed occur within a short period of time. Transformation is without doubt a process that requires considerate attention, focus and motivation, but perhaps it does not require a set structure or necessarily unlimited time. Ultimately, the most important factor is the survivor herself: 'While the therapist's technical expertise, judgement, and moral support are vital to the enterprise, in the end it is the survivor who determines her recovery through her own actions' (Lewis Herman, 1998, p. 174).

For Ruth, the transformation was symbolised by a movement from fear, to a freedom to think and feel. No longer was her perceived experience of herself solely based on inaccurate, rigid distortions shaped by the dynamics inherent in the acts of sexual abuse. The 10-week group gave her the opportunity to experience herself differently; and to begin to understand some of the difficulties she experienced within the context of understanding the diverse impact that surviving sexual abuse has on women's lives. From the position of believing that connecting with others was dangerous and therefore to be avoided, Ruth began to recognise her need for support and connection.

In working with a present-day focus in the group, women are encouraged to link present-day difficulties with childhood experiences. Whilst we do not refer to it directly in the groups, the Finklehor and Browne model provides us, as therapists, with a framework through which we can view, process and understand the major themes of power, interpersonal relationships, adult behaviours and shame, thus helping women move from the place of feeling like a refugee in a foreign land to a sense of belonging in their own life. 'Abuse is not destiny. It is damaging and that damage, if not always reparable, is open to amelioration and limitation' (Mullen and Fleming, 1998). The journey for Ruth, as with the other women, will continue, as she embarks on further therapy, but for now, those experiences of change and transformation have helped her to mobilise a different, more compassionate way of relating with herself and, though the resolution of the trauma is not complete, her transformation of some key intra-relational dynamics has enabled her to limit the impact and effects of the early damage.

References

American Psychiatric Association (1980) *Diagnostic and Statistical Manual of Mental Disorders* (3rd edn). Washington, DC: American Psychiatric Association.

Bolen, R.M. (2001) *Child Sexual Abuse: Its Scope and our Failure.* New York: Kluwer Accademic/Plenum Publishers.

Browne, A. and Finklehor, D. (1985) 'The traumatic impact of child sexual abuse: A conceptualisation', *American Journal of Orthopsychiatry*, 55(4): 530–41.

Browne, A. and Finklehor, D. (1986) 'Impact of child sexual abuse: A review of the research', *Psychological Bulletin*, 99(1): 67–77.

Bryer, J.B., Nelson, B.A., Miller, J.B. and Kroll, P.A. (1987) 'Childhood sexual and physical abuse as factors in adult psychiatric illness', *American Journal of Psychiatry*, 144(11): 1426–30.

Department of Health (1999) *National Service Framework for Mental Health: Modern Standards and Service Models.* London: Crown Copyright.

Finklehor, D. (1988) 'The trauma of child sexual abuse: Two models', in G.E. Wyatt and G.J. Powell (eds), *Lasting Effects of Sexual Abuse* (pp. 61–82). London: Sage.

Finklehor, D. (1996, August) *Long-Term Effects of Sexual Abuse.* Paper presented at Child Abuse and Neglect Conference. Dublin.

Freud, S. (1962) 'The aetiology of hysteria', in *The Standard Edition of the Collected Works of Sigmund Freud. Vol. 3* (J. Strachey, trans). London: Hogarth Press. (Original work published 1896.)

Hall, L. and Lloyd, S. (1997) *Surviving Child Sexual Abuse: A Handbook for Helping Women Challenge their Past.* London: The Falmer Press.

Higgins Kessler, M.R., White, M.B. and Nelson, B.S. (2003) 'Group treatments for women sexually abused as children: A review of the literature and recommendations for future outcome research', *Child Abuse and Neglect*, 27(9): 1045–61.

Hooper, C.A. and Koprowska, J. (2000) 'Reparative experience or repeated trauma', in U. McCluskey and C.A. Hooper (eds), *Psychodynamic Perspectives on Abuse: The Cost of Fear* (pp. 275–90). London: Jessica Kingsley.

Kinsey, A.C., Pomeroy, W.B., Martin, C.E. and Gebhard, P.H. (1966) S*exual Behaviour in the Human Female.* New York: Pocket Books Inc.

Lewis Herman, J. (1998) *Trauma and Recovery: From Domestic Abuse to Political Terror*. London: Pandora.

Morgan, T. and Cummings, A.L. (1999) 'Change experienced during group therapy by female survivors of childhood sexual abuse', *Journal of Consulting and Clinical Psychiatry*, 67(1): 28–36.

Mullen, P.E. and Fleming, J. (1998) 'Long-term effects of child sexual abuse', *Issues in Child Abuse Prevention*, 9: 1–18.

Roberts, R., O'Connor, T., Dunn, J. and Golding, J. (2004) 'The effects of child sexual abuse in later family life: Mental health, parenting and adjustment of offspring', *Child Abuse and Neglect*, 28(5): 525–45.

Ryan, M., Nitsun, M., Gilbert, L. and Mason, H. (2005) 'A prospective study of the effectiveness of group and individual psychotherapy for women CSA survivors', *Psychology and Psychotherapy: Theory, Research and Practice*, 78: 465–79.

Westbury, E. and Tutty, L.M. (1999) 'The efficacy of group treatment for survivors of childhood sexual abuse', *Child Abuse and Neglect*, 23(1): 31–44.

Yalom, I. and Leszcz, M. (2005) *The Theory and Practice of Group Psychotherapy* (5th edn). New York: Basic Books.

Epilogue
Keith Tudor

I hope that by now, the reader who reads in a linear fashion will have enjoyed this book. If, by chance, you've skipped pages or are reading this first, I hope you go on to enjoy it!

My aim in editing and structuring the book in the way I have has been to provide a good account of the field of brief person-centred therapies and, as the plural indicates, of a number of tribes or approaches within the person-centred and experiential 'nation'. Now, having completed my task and having re-read the book, a number of things strike me, which form these closing reflections.

The first is on the range of applications of person-centred and experiential therapy. Although the contributors espouse a range of theories and demonstrate clearly diverse practice, each draws on the fundamental principles of the person-centred approach: the client's tendency to actualise, the therapist's non-directive attitude, and the framing of the therapeutic relationship in terms of certain conditions. Just how much the therapists trust in the client's tendency to actualise, how non-directive the therapist is, and whether the therapist regards Rogers' therapeutic conditions as necessary and sufficient varies. For some readers the variation represented may be too great, and put some contributors outside the person-centred nation; for others there may not be enough diversity of theory or practice.

This leads me to a second reflection on the richness of the dialogue between person-centred and experiential therapies, represented here in the three chapters in Part I. Those familiar with the different traditions encompassed by the person-centred approach will not be surprised by the strong presence of theorists and practitioners who draw on the experiential tradition. Its origins in focusing (Gendlin, 1981) and its emphasis on experiential work arguably lends itself to time-limited, brief work; and it is interesting that none of these authors have the same qualms about time-limited work as others represented in the discussion in Chapters 1 and 6. For those interested in reading more about this tradition, I recommend Rennie's (1998) book on an experiential approach to person-centred counselling, and Levin's (1997) excellent volume of reflections on Gendlin's philosophy.

My third reflection is about research. I am pleased to have been able to include in this volume an original paper (Chapter 5) which was part of a research project on time-limited work. I am also interested to note the number of references in other chapters to research and that practitioners such as Gibbard (Chapter 7) are conducting their own research and service audits. It is deeply ironic that, despite the fact that Rogers himself was a pioneer in psychotherapy research, and the fact that the person-centred approach has, over 65 years, been well researched and has, in turn, generated a lot of research, notably about the therapeutic relationship and its conditions, the person-centred approach still has a reputation of being not proven. This continues despite recent studies which demonstrate therapeutic equivalence (Friedli *et al.*, 1997; Stiles *et al.*, 2006; Stiles *et al.*, in press, 2008). For those interested, there are a number of papers on research in Cain's (2000) collection of articles from the now defunct *Person-Centered Review*; the international journal *Person-Centered & Experiential Psychotherapies* (www.pce-world/pcep.htm) also carries articles on research; there is at least one book on person-centred research currently being written; and more person-centred practitioners are having their work published in the generic psychotherapeutic press.

Obviously there are gaps in any book, of some of which I am aware; there are others, no doubt, of which I am unaware. Two that I know of are concern training and supervision – and they are deliberate. If one takes the view that short-term or brief therapy is a form of therapy in its own right, then, logically, it makes sense to argue that practitioners should undergo specialist training. If, on the other hand, one takes the view as I do (see Chapter 1) that, as practitioners, we need to be conscious of time, limits and limitations, then, it follows that we need to pay attention to these issues in our training, and continuing professional development, whether through further training, study, supervision and/or personal therapy. This represents an ongoing commitment to self-reflection, as distinct from a one-off training course. So, it is with supervision. Some, such as Feltham (1997), complain that there is a lack of experience amongst supervisors of short-term work. I have responded to this argument elsewhere (Tudor, 2007, p. 201), commenting that:

> Ultimately, this is a hierarchical model of supervision, based on the view that the supervisor has to have more and relevant experience of what the supervisee/therapist is working with than the supervisee him or herself does. This approach to supervision both mistrusts the therapist and misunderstands the facilitative, reflective and meta-role of the supervisor.

The chapter from which this is taken appears in the second of two books on person-centred approaches to supervision titled *Freedom to Practise* (Tudor and Worrall, 2004, 2007). It seems to me that, whatever differences there are between people who associate themselves with person-centred and experiential approaches, such freedom underpins or should underpin our common understanding, values, attitudes and practice.

References

Cain, D. (ed.) (2000) *Classics in the Person-Centered Approach*. Ross-on-Wye: PCCS Books.

Feltham, C. (1997) *Time-Limited Counselling*. London: Sage.

Friedli, K., King, M., Lloyd, M. and Horder, J. (1997) 'Randomised controlled assessment of non-directive psychotherapy versus routine general practitioner care', *Lancet*, 350: 1662–5.

Gendlin, E.T. (1981) *Focusing* (rev. edn). New York: Bantam.

Levin, D.M. (ed.) (1997) *Lanaguage Beyond Postmodernism: Saying and Thinking in Gendlin's Philosophy*. Evanston, IL: Northwestern University Press.

Rennie, D.L. (1998) *Person-Centred Counselling: An Experiential Approach*. London: Sage.

Stiles, W.B., Barkham, M., Twigg, E., Mellor-Clark, J. and Cooper, M. (2006) 'Effectiveness of cognitive-behavioural, person-centred, and psychodynamic therapies as practised in UK National Health Service settings', *Psychological Medicine*, 36: 555–66.

Stiles, W.B., Barkham, M., Mellor-Clark, J. and Connell, J. (in press, 2008). 'Effectiveness of cognitive-behavioural, person-centred, and psychodynamic therapies in UK primary care routine practice: Replication in a larger sample', *Psychological Medicine*.

Tudor, K. and Worrall, M. (eds) (2004) *Freedom to Practise: Person-Centred Approaches to Supervision*. Llangarron: PCCS Books.

Tudor, K. and Worrall, M. (eds) (2007) *Freedom to Practise II: Developing Person-Centred Approaches to Supervision*. Ross-on-Wye: PCCS Books.

Tudor, K. (2007) 'Supervision of short-term therapy', in K. Tudor and M. Worrall (eds), *Freedom to Practise II: Developing Person-Centred Approaches to Supervision* (pp. 195–204). Ross-on-Wye: PCCS Books.

Appendix 1

An Illustration of the Eight Communication Exercises in TIR Training in terms of Rogers' Six Conditions

Henry J. Whitfield

While Rogers is hailed for his groundbreaking and highly influential work on the qualities required for effective therapy, one might still ask how these qualities might be successfully acquired. Below is a description of how these qualities may be acquired and/or operationalised in current TIR training.

Presence – A foundation for communication

Rogers (1986/1990), particularly later on in life, put emphasis on his 'presence':

> When perhaps I am in a slightly altered state of consciousness in the relationship, then whatever I seem to do seems full of healing. Then simply my presence is releasing and helpful. There is nothing I can do to force this experience. (p. 199)

Like Rogers, TIR training puts a great deal of emphasis on presence. It employs three structured exercises for strengthening this ability. Meditational practices for practising the ability to be present have existed for millennia. Mindfulness meditation in particular, which has recently gained significant empirical validation as a therapeutic intervention, (Baer, 2003) focuses particularly on practising the ability to be present to both inner and external phenomena. TIR practitioner training makes extensive use of such meditational exercises. Out of the eight 'communication exercises' (CEs) in TIR training, the first three are applications of mindfulness meditation for developing one's presence:

CE1 – Being present (without a particular focus)
CE2 – Confronting (remaining comfortably present to a human being)
CE3 – Maintaining confront (or the ability to remain present during more challenging circumstances)

The remaining five communication exercises are:

CE4 – Delivery (of communication)
CE5 – Full acknowledgements (Receiving communication)
CE6 – Encouraging communication
CE7 – Getting questions answered
CE8 – Handling concerns (of the client)

The first two of these exercises (CE1 and CE2) are forms of mindfulness meditation. Dimidjian and Linehan (2003) describe mindfulness as:

> awareness of what is, at the level of direct and immediate experience ... the act of repetitively directing your attention to only one thing ... [and] the practice of willingness to be alive to the moment and radical acceptance of the entirety of the moment.

CE1 – Being present

In CE1 counselling, trainees are asked to sit comfortably on a chair with a hand on each knee, their feet flat on the floor, with their eyes closed. In yoga, this is known as the Egyptian position. The TIR training manual states:

> you should be comfortable just being present and being purely receptive, purely aware. Do not try to resist thoughts or feelings but rather simply remain aware of them without trying to change or affect them in any way. The point is for you to remain present and not to get lost in thought or preoccupied. Avoid using any system of being present [i.e. avoid *doing* anything]. Just remain aware of present time and location. (Gerbode and French, 1992/2007, p. 41)

Here the use of a system is advised against whilst practising the ability to be present. This appears to be a harmony of the preference for not using systems or techniques in person-centred therapy (PCT). In this exercise, trainee therapists are practising the ability to stop doing and just be.

Simply being aware or 'observing' is arguably the action that contains the least action. It still contains *some* active intention or doing, the fulfilling of the intention to be present. This 'minimal doing' of presence can still be perceived in the bodily and facial language of the person who is actively being present. Perhaps the only way to truly cease all doing is to be brain-dead. This form of meditation, done with eyes closed, is very similar to a form of mindfulness meditation known as 'choiceless awareness'. Choiceless awareness meditation is taught to clients in Kabat-Zinn's Mindfulness-based Stress Reduction, which has gained empirical validation in recent years (for more on which see Kabat-Zinn, 1990). Trainees are encouraged to do this exercise for extensive periods of time, although the time restraints of modern life and work can make this difficult in practice. This ability or quality of genuine presence is seen as the most fundamental element of TIR counselling training. This is because one's ability to remain present affects everything. Every quality that the therapist either exhibits or manifests in an action, touches the counselling relationship. This ability to be present can be significantly developed over time. It has a lot to do with being able to remain non-judgemental or the ability to stop doing the many automatic things that people tend to do (whether thoughts or involuntary physical movements). The non-judgemental present quality of this exercise aligns very well with Rogers' fourth condition that the therapist experiences 'unconditional positive regard'.

The remaining seven communication exercises consist of a gradient of abilities, each of which is added to the previous. Each subsequent exercise or ability is directly enhanced by the previous ones. Hence they are practised in sequence from CE1 to CE8.

CE2 – Confronting

CE2 is the second form of mindfulness meditation in TIR training. It is much the same as CE1 but with the added layer of eye contact. Trainees sit opposite each other and practise the ability to remain present for extended periods of time, whilst maintaining eye contact with a partner. This brings about a feeling of empathic attunement between the two engaged in the activity, once the two minds have quietened and come to meet in the present moment through visual contact alone. The time it takes to reach such an attunement decreases with practice. It is not uncommon for a new trainee to feel uncomfortable at first and to manifest such reactions as excessive blinking or fidgiting. Continuing CE2 provides the opportunity for trainees to (1) experience their own inner 'organismic' reactions as they wax, wane, and change in quality, just as the inner experience of emotions shifts when a client examines them in detail; (2) increase their ability to maintain empathic attunement; (3) resolve any inner reactions and judgements of their own that may surface during the exercise; and (4) to increase their ability to genuinely accept their own reactions as they arise moment to moment. The practice of these exercises helps foster at least three of Rogers' conditions. These are (1) that the therapist experiences unconditional positive regard towards the client (condition four); (2) that the therapist is experiencing an empathic understanding of the client's internal frame reference (condition five); and (3) that client perceives, at least to a minimal degree, the unconditional positive regard and the empathic understanding of the therapist (condition six; Rogers (1957)).

CE3 – Maintaining confront

CE3 adds the layer of facing a client who exhibits challenging behaviour or communication. It is harder to be unconditionally acceptant and empathic when a client projects his anger on to you or tells you they have done something you consider morally wrong. Whilst Rogers' six conditions may exist with *some* clients *some* of the time, how might this be increased to *most* clients *most* of the time? One approach is that of structured practice. PCT therapists are taught not to moralise to their clients. However, clients can easily perceive automatic, inner moralising in a therapist's face or physical attitude. These inner, automatic reactions can be overcome with systematic practice. Such practice (in CE3) is achieved through the searching and finding of such reactive 'buttons' followed by repeated exposure to each 'button' until it no longer produces a reaction. In TIR terminology this is referred to as 'flattening a button'. CE3 therefore provides practice in holding conditions 4–6 under more challenging circumstances.

The removal of all unnecessary actions in a session and the focused application of only what is necessary make TIR and related techniques highly efficient. The TIR style of working has a certain 'shortest distance between two points' philosophy to it. TIR's tenth rule of facilitation states 'Do not do anything in a session that is not directly conducive to the counselling process' (Bisbey and Bisbey, 1998, p. 15). This principle harmonises with Rogers' preference of 'being' over 'doing', if one argues that the less one is engaged in doing, the more one is able to simply be.

CE4 – Delivery

CE4 addresses the delivery of communication from the therapist to the client. In this exercise, trainees practise the ability to remain present, empathic, and in control of their non-verbal communications while speaking to the client. It is surprisingly easy to find oneself unconsciously adding to one's various utterances on a non-verbal level. As with the earlier communication exercises, CE4 trains therapists to do *less* than they would otherwise be doing. According to Applied Metapsychology theory, the presence of unnecessary actions (e.g. involuntary bodily movements) may interrupt the client's therapeutic process.

CE5 and CE6 – Acknowledgements

CE5 and CE6 (Acknowledgements) comprise structured exercises for making your client feel heard. As with all TIR-related methods, they are, again, done in a minimalist way. Great emphasis is placed on communicating that you are congruently with the client, and on doing nothing else. This is typically done with one or two words such as 'okay' or 'thank you'. In acknowledging well, you are neither verbally nor non-verbally evaluating, or assuming you have similar experience, or making comments or interpretations. You are simply communicating that you are humanly and congruently 'getting' the clients internal frame of reference, nothing more. CE5 provides practice in the 'full acknowledgment' or acknowledgments that have an air of finality about them. The therapist uses these when it is clear a client has completed describing a particular thing, or fulfilled a particular intention. CE6, encouraging communication, may also be achieved with a single word. This difference is in the tone of voice which communicates 'I'm with you and am interested to hear more about that'. This type of acknowledgment is largely used in situations where the client has stopped speaking, but clearly has more to say.

CEs 5–6 most closely align with Rogers' third and sixth conditions. These are respectively, the therapist's ability to maintain congruence and integration in the relationship, and for the client to perceive the therapist's unconditional positive regard for him and the therapist's empathic understanding (communicated to the client with congruent acknowledgements). CEs 1–3 (for strengthening presence and empathic attunement) enable therapists to experience psychological contact, unconditional positive regard and empathy to ever higher levels, and thus align most closely with conditions one, four and five (see Table 1 below). The degree to which a trainee therapist can be congruent is dependent on how present the therapist is. Hence CEs 1–3 are practised before CEs 4–6.

CE7 – Getting questions answered

CE7 and CE8, known respectively as 'Getting questions answered' and 'Handling concerns', both take the form of mock therapy sessions. During CE7, trainees experience and practise applying CE1–6 whilst asking repetitive questions. CE7 is called 'Getting questions answered' because trainees are tested in their ability to spot when a client (acted by a peer trainee) does not answer a question. This is test of the trainee's ability to be on the ball whilst continuing to apply CEs 1–6.

CE8 – Handling concerns

The final exercise focuses on responding to client concerns and momentary needs. This is structured practice in the ability to depart from a structure in order to go with the client's unique process, and then to return to the structure, if appropriate. Common examples of such a concern are: the client has questions he or she wants to ask, the client has distracting physical sensations or pains that arise during the session, or a client becomes aware of another issue during the session and seems more interested in that issue.

In the description of CEs 1–8 above, we saw how conditions 1, 3–6 are operationalised in TIR training. Rogers' second condition – 'That the first

Table A1   *A summary of the presence of Rogers' conditions in TIR practice.*

Roger's therapeutic conditions (1957/1990)	How they are operationalised in applied metapsychology/TIR practice
1. That two persons are in psychological contact	Eight 'communication exercises' or 'CEs' are used to train a therapist to maintain such contact consistently, moment to moment. Particularly CEs 1–3 develop the ability to make and maintain empathic attunement with a client, and therefore be in psychological contact.
2. That the client is in a state of incongruence, being vulnerable or anxious	1. CEs 1–8 + 13 rules of facilitation teach the therapist how to maintain an environment from the beginning to the end of a therapeutic relationship, that is safe enough for negative affect to surface. 2. Assessments are used to identify areas of incongruence, vulnerability, and negative problematic affect. 3. Structured exercises provide the opportunity for clients to hold their awareness in such assessed areas.
3. That the therapist is congruent in the relationship	CEs 1–3, enhance the therapist's ability to be present to the client. An enhanced reception of a client's communication, in turn, enhances the ability of the therapist to remain congruent. More attunement is more opportunity for congruence. The CEs 5–6 actively practise communicating where the therapist is in relation to the client (acknowledgements of client's responses).
4. That the therapist is experiencing unconditional positive regard towards the client	TIR therapists tell their clients that there is nothing they can do wrong. Great care is taken to ensure that nothing the therapist does could be perceived as an evaluation or even an interpretation (rules 1–2 of the 13 rules of facilitation). The trainee therapist is taught to accept unconditionally anything the client says. This is actively practice and tested in CEs 1–3, though all eight CEs contain this element.
5. That the therapist is experiencing an empathic understanding of the client's internal frame of reference	CEs 1–3 also provide active practice at maintaining empathy in order to be aware of how the client is doing.
6. That the client perceives at least to a minimal degree the unconditional positive regard for him and the empathic understanding of the therapist.	5th rule of facilitation: 'The counsellor makes sure he comprehends what the client is saying ... A client knows right away when she is not being comprehended. When this happens she feels alone and unsupported ... [the counsellor] must seek clarification by admitting her lack of comprehension'. Gerbode and French (1992/2007, p. 26) CEs 4–6 bring about a clear experience of unconditional positive regard and empathic understanding for the client. CE 8 focuses on maintaining this condition when it is more tricky to do so, e.g. when something is going on that the client is not telling the therapist, or the client has a concern that is interrupting the therapeutic process.

person, whom we shall term the client, is in a state of incongruence, being vulnerable or anxious' (Rogers, 1957/1990, p. 221) – is brought about by three principle factors:

1   The safety of the space held by the therapist and of the application of the 13 Rules of Facilitation (Bisbey and Bisbey, 1998). These rules may be summarised as a description of how to create an environment that is safe, distraction-free, and conducive to maximising the client's inner focus of awareness, without fear of consequence.
2   Extensive assessments are used to identify specific areas of emotional charge that the client is interested in addressing and that provoke anxiety other unwanted emotional reactions.
3   The use of structured repetitive exercises that systematically invite (if the client is willing and interested) the client to hold her awareness in an area he or she wishes to address. Such areas often contain incongruent material and negative affect.

The eight communication exercises and the 13 Rules of Facilitation all largely align with the principle that the client's degree of inward focus, or awareness of unprocessed material, is proportional to the degree of therapeutic process. Therefore, anything else that occupies the client's mind while he focuses may slow down that process. TIR and metapsychology techniques owe much of their briefness to the application of this minimalist principle.

Summary

I have illustrated how TIR training employs structured methodologies, not necessarily to contain the client, but to teach, develop, and operationalise in therapists, the six conditions advocated by Rogers. In line with Rogers' preference for principles or qualities over techniques or instruments, CEs actually enable therapists to do less of what is unnecessary to the therapeutic process, and to exhibit more the qualities that are necessary, according to Rogers, for therapeutic process or change.

References

Baer, R.A. (2003) 'Mindfulness training as a clinical intervention: A conceptual and empirical review', *Clinical Psychology: Science and Practice*, 10: 125–43.
Bisbey, S. and Bisbey, L.B. (1998) *Brief Therapy for PTSD: Traumatic Incident Reduction and Related Techniques*. Chichester: John Wiley & Sons.
Dimidjian, S. and Linehan, M.M. (2003) 'Defining an agenda for future research on the clinical application of mindfulness practice', *Clinical Psychology: Science and Practice*, 10: 166–71.
Gerbode, F.A. and French, G.D. (1992) *Traumatic Incident Reduction Workshop Manual*. Menlo Park, CA: IRM Press.

Kabat-Zinn, J. (1990) *Full Catastrophe Living: The Program of the Stress Reduction Clinic at the University of Massachusetts Medical Center.* New York: Delta.

Rogers, C.R. (1990) 'The necessary and sufficient conditions for therapeutic personality change', in H. Kirschenbaum and V.L. Henderson (eds), *The Carl Rogers Reader* (pp. 219–235). London: Constable. (Original work published 1957).

Rogers. C.R. (1986) 'A client-centered/person-centred approach to therapy', in H. Kirschenbaum and V.L. Henderson (eds), *The Carl Rogers Reader* (pp. 135–52). London: Constable.

Appendix 2

Time-Limited Group Counselling with Women Survivors of Childhood Sexual Abuse: Weekly Log of Themes

Très Roche

Week 1

Safety: Relief in joining the group, and in the similarities of group members. Relief at meeting other survivors. Need for the group to be 'good'. How feeling understood creates connection with others. Difference between group environment and 'real life'.

Naming the impact of childhood sexual abuse.

Trust: Difficulties in trusting others, yet an immediate sense of trusting the group – exploring connection between the dynamics of abuse and the development of trust.

Issues of control and choice and consent.

Survival strategies: Naming and understanding self-harming behaviours.

Week 2

Fear of engaging with the enormity of the impact of the abuse. Fear of connecting with histories of abuse and fear of overwhelm: Can feelings be contained and survived?

Fear of the judgement of others: 'If people really knew what happened to me they would despise me'.

The need to be understood, yet the utter terror of risking connecting to others.

Self-harm as a coping strategy.

Protection of others: Protecting family members as children and how that continues in ongoing family relationships.

Guilt/shame about the sexual abuse suffered.

Responsibility – exploring ways in which the context surrounding the abuse conspires to engender responsibility in the survivor.

Week 3

Some disclosure of abuse histories.

The huge complexity of feelings about the abuse. Naming the complexity of feelings towards the perpetrators of the abuse.

Terror of connecting with the feelings about the abuse, recognising that previous coping strategies have been about blocking the experience through fear of overwhelm. How can feelings be named, contained and survived?

Guilt and responsibility linked to feelings of self-blame and self-hatred.

Coping strategies as children and as adults: What is/was necessary to survive?

The difficulty in prioritising own needs above the needs of others.

Hope: The desire for aspects of life to be different alongside the fear that hope risks disappointment – how this connects to childhood experiences.

Trust and discernment.

Week 4

Some disclosure.

Languaging memories, flashbacks and nightmares.

Disappointment: A desire for a 'cure', and the acknowledgement that the pain isn't disappearing.

The absolute grief for the loss of childhood.

Powerlessness: Linking childhood experiences of power with assumptions about power as an adult.

The need for understanding and to make sense of the past.

What can and can't be spoken about. Speaking the unspeakable.

Naming of personal goals.

Sharing resources for surviving.

Week 5

Some disclosure.

Emerging anger towards mothers (or the non-protective parent).

Revenge fantasies.

Fear of madness.

Flashbacks: Understanding the need for memories and feelings to receive attention.

Distress triggers: Exploring and understanding what triggers distress and why.

Self-sabotaging survival strategies – other options?

Desire for and fear of change.

Belonging: Need to belong, fear of rejection.
Sense of self as contaminating and destructive.

Week 6

Some disclosure.
Rage: Acknowledgment and fear of rage.
Memories of childhood before the abuse.
Terror of connecting to and integrating abuse histories.
The effects of change perceived through the group process on partners and
    families.
A desire for a cure.
Power: Powerlessness being the familiar position.
Lack of self-esteem.

Week 7

Some disclosure.
The need for resolution – the anxiety of the unresolved.
Staying silent or speaking out as an adult. How this links with distorted
    thinking around protection of others – fear of rejection.
The personal cost of adaption.
Similarities and differences between the powerlessness of a child and the
    choices available to an adult.
Compassion for other group members, compassion for self.
Questioning impulsive behaviours – what is the underlying need?
Awareness of own vulnerability and vulnerability of others.
Responsibility, exploring more accurate descriptions of responsibility in
    childhood.
Endings.

Week 8

Hope for the future: Choice, power and autonomy.
Fear of ending linking to abandonment.
Some disclosure.
Choice and taking power.
Responsibility and self blame.
Fear of own needs.
Desire for and fear of more intimate relating with others.
Importance of self-expression and being heard as a basis for connecting
    with others.

Week 9

Endings linking to abandonment and betrayal.
Fear of causing damage to others: If members allow more intimate relating
   with others, others will be damaged by them.
Endings: Grief and loss.
Hope – imagining the future.
Recognising the difference between past and present.
Support needs for after the group.
The familiarity of rigid expectations for self, other, the environment.

Week 10

Achievements and disappointments within the group.
Next steps.
Realistic expectations of self and others.

Notes on Editor and Contributors

Keith Tudor has worked for 30 years in the helping professions in a number of settings. He is a qualified and registered psychotherapist, and has a private/independent practice in Sheffield offering therapy, supervision and consultancy. He is a Director of Temenos and its course in Person-Centred Psychotherapy and Counselling, the first of its kind in the UK, and is an Honorary Fellow in the School of Health, Liverpool John Moores University. He is a widely published author in the field of psychotherapy and counselling, and mental health with over 50 professional papers and 10 books to his name, of which five define, develop and advance the person-centred approach, its psychology, therapy and supervision. He is the series editor of 'Advancing Theory in Therapy' (published by Routledge), and is on the editorial advisory board of three international journals.

Robert Elliott, Ph.D., is Professor of Counselling in the Counselling Unit at the University of Strathclyde, and Professor Emeritus of Psychology at the University of Toledo, Ohio. He is co-author of *Facilitating Emotional Change* (Guilford, 1993), *Research Methods in Clinical Psychology* (Wiley, 2002), and *Learning Process-Experiential Psychotherapy* (APA, 2004), as well as more than 90 journal articles or book chapters. He is a Fellow of the APA in both Divisions of Psychotherapy and of Humanistic Psychology, and is the 2008 recipient of the Carl Rogers' Award from the APA's Division of Humanistic Psychology. He is Editor Emeritus of *Person-Centered Counseling and Psychotherapies*.

Isabel Gibbard originally completed a degree in Biology at London University in the early 1970s, but decided that she was not an academic and didn't want to spend the rest of her life in a lab. She then spent several years as a full-time mother bringing up children. She went into counselling through working as a volunteer in a prison, and qualified in 1995. She began work in the NHS in 1998, first as a staff counsellor for a hospital trust, and then as a primary care counsellor. She now manages the primary care service which operates in the community and in two prisons.

Barrie Hopwood is a counsellor, supervisor and trainer in private practice in Middlesex. He is also Project Manager for Hounslow Youth Counselling Service at Feltham Young Offender Institution and Student Counsellor at Cranfield University. Before training as a counsellor Barrie studied Law and Criminology, and taught in Further Education in Harrow. Barrie's particular areas of interest are exploring the potential of the spiritual dimension in the counselling relationship, developing ways of working with the 'Inner Child' in supervision, and raising awareness around the theme of men and masculinity in the world of counselling.

Bala Jaison, Ph.D., the author of *Integrating Experiential and Brief Therapy: How to do Deep Therapy – Briefly and How to do Brief Therapy – Deeply* (Focusing for Creative Living, 2003), is an internationally recognized lecturer, trainer and workshop leader. She is a psychotherapist in private practice for individuals, couples and families; Director of Focusing for Creative Living in Toronto, a government recognized training institution for mental health professionals; and a Certifying Coordinator for the International Focusing Institute, offering a focusing-oriented certification programme for therapists. Dr Jaison is also the co-editor of the *Folio*, the academic journal for the International Focusing Institute, and has written extensively on how to integrate focusing and brief therapy. She can be reached at balaj@sympatico.ca.

Mia Leijssen is Professor at the University of Leuven, Belgium. She teaches client-centred psychotherapy, counselling skills and professional ethics in the Psychology Department. She has been practising client-centred/experiential/existential psychotherapy since 1973.

Madge Lewis[1] was an instructor and then a counsellor in public schools in California in the 1940s. At the time of writing her contribution to the original chapter, she was a staff research counsellor at the University of Chicago, where she obtained her doctorate in 1959.

Paul McGahey has been a practising person-centred counsellor since 1993. He is a senior accredited counsellor with the BACP. Since 2003 he has worked as a full-time student and staff counsellor, supervisor and trainer at Loughborough University in the East Midlands. In 2002 he helped to establish a person-centred group in Brighton, a group which has been a continuing source of support and professional development for counsellors and therapists in the East Sussex area, and which is affiliated to BAPCA. Paul has been actively and passionately involved in promoting the person-centred approach through the group's activities, to which his

---

[1] Although Madge Lewis's work does not appear in Chapter 5, I include her biographical details here as she contributed her work and reflections to the original chapter with Carl Rogers and John Shlien.

main contribution continues to be organising the successful programme of workshops with nationally and internationally recognised person-centred facilitators/speakers. His current interests include the politics of therapy, and the imminent statutory regulation of counsellors and psychotherapists in the United Kingdom.

Carl Rogers was, at the time of writing his contribution to the original chapter, the Director of the Counseling Center at the University of Chicago.

John Shlien was, at the time of writing his contribution to the original chapter, the Service co-ordinator and a counsellor at the Counselling Center at the Institute for Communication on Human Development, and Research Associate and Assistant Professor at the University of Chicago.

Très Roche is a BACP accredited counsellor who has been practising for 15 years. Since 1997 she has been the co-ordinator and group therapist at the Sexual Abuse Project, a specialist group therapy service for adult women survivors of childhood sexual abuse. She is co-author, with Annabell Bell-Boulé of a chapter on 'Legal issues in therapeutic work with adult survivors of sexual abuse', published in a book on *Legal Issues in Counselling and Psychotherapy* (Sage, 2002). Très is also founder and principal consultant of Psych solutions, a training and organisational development consultancy, based in the East Midlands in the UK, which works with organisations to develop solution-focused strategies to help navigate through complexity.

Henry J. Whitfield, has run and supervised a Brief therapy for Post Traumatic Stress Disorder project for Victim Support Lambeth since 2005, and has regularly worked as a trauma counsellor for victims of crime since 2003. Henry regularly teaches and lectures at conferences and for training organisations, including the British Association of Anger Management (BAAM), and in doing so has trained the majority of the TIR practitioners in the UK. Being a qualified cognitive behavioural therapist, has contributed to his research interests in the theoretical and practical integration of mindfulness with cognitive behavioural theory, and in case-formulated applications of mindfulness, (the first field in which he published). Henry is also director of Mindfulness Training Ltd, based in Covent Garden, London, an organisation training practitioners in Traumatic Incident Reduction (TIR) and related techniques, Mindfulness-based Cognitive Therapy (MBCT), and Acceptance and Commitment Therapy (ACT) (see www.presentmind.org for more).

Pam Winter has an independent practice as a counsellor, supervisor and trainer based in Greater Manchester, at the Relationship Centre

202 NOTES ON EDITOR AND CONTRIBUTORS

(www.therelationshipcentre.co.uk), and is a Senior Registered Practitioner with the BACP. She has 20 years experience in working with people individually and with couples, groups, teams, and organisations. She founded the Relationship Centre with her husband in 2005, with the aim of developing person-centred work in both domestic and working relationships. She has a long-standing commitment to the person-centred approach and has also trained in body psychotherapy. She has had two previous articles published one on supervision (in the *British Journal of Guidance & Counselling*, 1994) and one on person-centred therapy and the bodymind connection (*Person-Centred Practice*, 2002).

Abbreviations

APA – American Psychological Association
BACP – British Association for Counselling & Psychotherapy
BAPCA – British Association for the Person-Centred Approach
MBACP – Member of the British Association for Counselling & Psychotherapy
NHS – The National Health Service
REBT – Rational Emotive Behavior Therapy
TIR – Traumatic Incident Reduction
TIRA – Traumatic Incident Reduction Association (accrediting body for TIR practitioners)

Author Index

Subject Index